T0284681

Pollinators of the American West

Pollinators of the American West

A Field Guide to Over 300 Invertebrate Pollinators

DENVER BOTANIC GARDENS
AND BUTTERFLY PAVILION

FALCON GUIDES

ESSEX, CONNECTICUT

FALCONGUIDES®

An imprint of The Globe Pequot Publishing Group, Inc.
64 South Main Street
Essex, CT 06426
www.globepequot.com

Falcon and Falcon Guides are registered trademarks and Make Adventure Your Story is a trademark of The Globe Pequot Publishing Group, Inc.

Distributed by NATIONAL BOOK NETWORK

British Library Cataloguing in Publication Information available

Library of Congress Cataloging-in-Publication Data

Names: Denver Botanic Gardens, author. | Butterfly Pavilion (Organization), author.
Title: Pollinators of the American West : a field guide to over 300 invertebrate pollinators / Denver Botanic Gardens and Butterfly Pavilion.
Other titles: Field guide to over 300 invertebrate pollinators | Falcon guide.
Description: Essex, Connecticut : Falcon Guides, [2024] | Series: Falcon guide | Includes bibliographical references and index.
Identifiers: LCCN 2024008017 (print) | LCCN 2024008018 (ebook) | ISBN 9781493066902 (paperback) | ISBN 9781493066919 (epub)
Subjects: LCSH: Pollinators—West (U.S.)—Identification. | Pollinators—Canada, Western—Identification. | Insect pollinators—West (U.S.)—Identification. | Insect pollinators—Canada, Western—Identification. | Field guides.
Classification: LCC QL551.W3 D46 2024 (print) | LCC QL551.W3 (ebook) | DDC 591.50978—dc23/eng/20240507
LC record available at https://lccn.loc.gov/2024008017
LC ebook record available at https://lccn.loc.gov/2024008018

∞™ The paper used in this publication meets the minimum requirements of American National Standard for Information Sciences—Permanence of Paper for Printed Library Materials, ANSI/NISO Z39.48-1992.

CONTENTS

ACKNOWLEDGMENTS

This guide would not have been possible without the contributions of many committed pollinator enthusiasts and experts. Much gratitude goes to Mary Ann Colley, Sarah Triplett, and Sarada Krishnan for their assistance and support with the initial planning for this guide. We also thank Hannah Brown and Jessica Goldstrohm for their contributions to the pollinator profiles. We want to especially recognize Brionna McCumber for not only spending hours assisting with the organization of photographs but also for contributing her own stunning photos to the guide. Finally, many thanks to all of the colleagues and volunteers from Butterfly Pavilion and Denver Botanic Gardens who shared their pollinator photos, as well as the community scientists from around the country who contributed their own images.

INTRODUCTION

Sarada Krishnan, director of programs for the Crop Trust

As a plant and nature lover, I have always been fascinated by pollinators, the act of pollination, and the relationship between plants and pollinators. Plants and pollinators exist in a mutualistic relationship. The life cycle of flowering plants depends on pollination. Plants are able to reproduce and create offspring due to the pollination services provided by pollinators. The mere act of transferring pollen from the male flower part (the stamen) to the female flower part (the stigma) leads to the development of fruits and seeds. And some of these fruits and seeds become food for animals, including humans.

Pollinators come in different shapes and forms such as honey bees and native bees, wasps, butterflies and moths, beetles, flies, birds, bats, and other animals. Many plants have special symbiotic relationships with a specific pollinator. Many orchids have specialist pollinators without whom their survival is doomed. In 1862, one of the many species of orchids from Madagascar that were sent to Charles Darwin was the beautiful star-shaped orchid with an exceptionally long spur (*Angraecum sesquipedale*). On examining the orchid flower, Darwin hypothesized that there must be a pollinator moth with an extremely long proboscis that could reach the nectar at the end of the long spur, suggesting coevolution of the plant and its pollinator. In 1907, twenty years after Darwin's death, a moth with a long proboscis (*Xanthopan morganii praedicta*) was discovered in Madagascar, though evidence of it feeding on nectar from *Angraecum sesquipedale* was not documented. It was not until 1992, 130 years after Darwin's coevolution hypothesis, that observations of the moth feeding on this orchid's nectar and transferring pollen from one plant to another were made. This is just one of the fascinating stories about the coevolution of plants and their pollinators. There are many more such coevolutionary stories.

Pollinators provide valuable ecosystem services and play an important role in human well-being. Through pollination services, benefits to humankind include provision of food, fiber, medicines, building materials, and other products. Additionally, the honey bee directly contributes by providing honey and other hive products. Seventy-five percent of our global crops are pollinator-dependent, with a value estimated at $351 billion/year.* This contributes to agricultural production that feeds millions of people globally, resulting in food and nutrition security.

---

* IPBES (2016). The assessment report of the Intergovernmental Science-Policy Platform on Biodiversity and Ecosystem Services on pollinators, pollination and food production. S. G. Potts, V. L. Imperatriz-Fonseca, and H. T. Ngo (eds.). Secretariat of the Intergovernmental Science-Policy Platform on Biodiversity and Ecosystem Services, Bonn, Germany. 552 pages. https://files.ipbes.net/ipbes-web-prod-public-files/downloads/pdf/individual_chapters_pollination_20170305.pdf.

Pollinators are in decline globally, one of the main causes being loss and degradation of habitats. Other drivers of decline include high use of agrochemicals, introduction of pathogens, and climate change. Key to combating pollinator decline is education and advocacy. When people are armed with information about a specific plant, animal, or insect, they are likely to pay more acute attention to that specific life-form and become champions in protecting it. Hence, field guides like this play a critical role in educating people about their local pollinators, their habitats, and plants critical for their survival. Creating a guide like this is a huge undertaking, and I commend and congratulate the authors from Denver Botanic Gardens and Butterfly Pavilion for creating this valuable publication that will serve as an educational and recreational tool for many people in the western United States and Canada.

One of my favorite plant-pollinator symbiosis stories from this region is that of the yucca plant (*Yucca* spp.) and the yucca moth (*Tegeticula* spp.). They have an extraordinary partnership in that one cannot survive without the other. The male and female yucca moths emerge from their pupae in the spring when the yucca flowers are starting to bloom. They mate in the yucca blossom; the female gathers pollen from the flower and visits another yucca flower on a different plant, lays eggs in the ovary of that flower, and deposits the pollen on the stigma of the flower, thus pollinating the flower. She ensures that she has laid only a few eggs so that the emerging larvae have enough to feed on while some of the seeds are retained in the developing fruit to perpetuate the plant and complete its life cycle.

Nature is fascinating and mesmerizing. We are all interconnected, and the loss of one species can have cascading effects on the balance of natural processes and survival of other species. It bodes well to ensure that we take care of this planet not just for ourselves but also for all the creatures we share this planet with and for future generations.

The Scope of This Guide

The goal of this field guide is to introduce you to some of western North America's most fascinating and beneficial wildlife species, the pollinators. By learning to identify these species and becoming more familiar with their habitats and life cycles, we hope you will come to appreciate not only all the benefits these animals bring to food production, our ecosystems, and our well-being but also how interesting and beautiful these animals are.

This book's scope covers pollinators found in the region bounded by the provinces of Alberta and British Columbia in Canada to the US border with Mexico. The entries focus on common species you are likely to see whether you are visiting a natural area or tending a garden. We have also included some of the less common but most iconic pollinator species of the region when they have important scientific, ecological, or cultural connections.

Each entry includes a physical description of the animal, when and where you can find it, its floral preferences, and information about its life cycle and behavior. This book focuses on our invertebrate pollinators—bees, wasps, flies, beetles, butterflies, and moths. The book also contains information about a few common flower visitors—invertebrates that can be found on flowers but aren't specifically adapted to carry out pollination.

Each entry also refers to the conservation status of the species, referring to the current ranking according to the International Union for Conservation of Nature and the United States Fish and Wildlife Service. These rankings may change over time as conditions change or as programs seek to conserve at-risk pollinators. In many cases, there is not sufficient population data to determine the ranking; this makes a strong case for more research about these important animals.

Pollinators are found in almost every terrestrial ecosystem, and they impact all our lives through their interactions with plants. The good news is that all of us can positively impact pollinators through our actions. We hope this book is a useful guide on your pollinator awareness journey.

Introduction to Pollinators

Pollination is the transfer of pollen (male cells) from the male part of the flower (the anther) to the female part of the flower (the stigma), allowing for fertilization and the production of seeds to spread plant genetics. While flowering plants have developed multiple ways to spread their pollen through wind, water, and other means, the most common method flowering plants utilize to spread pollen is through animal pollination, known as zoophily. The animals that perform zoophily are referred to as pollinators, and they play a key role in the health of our ecosystems. Many types of animals can be pollinators, such as mammals, birds, and even reptiles; however, this guide focuses mostly on insects due to the proportionately large role they play in pollination.

Between 75 and 90 percent of flowering plants are estimated to rely on animals for pollination; about one-third of our crop species also benefit from animal pollinators. Since at least the Cretaceous period, 145 to 66 million years ago, plants and their pollinators have been coevolving, with plants developing characteristics to entice animals to them, such as sweet nectar or even mimicking the appearance of females to attract males, and animals developing traits that increase their pollen-spreading success, such as branched hairs and pollen-carrying structures on their bodies.

The symbiosis between plants and their pollinators allows plants to spread their genes much farther than they could normally move on their own to reproduce, allowing for more robust and diverse genetics, resistance to pests and disease, and overall healthier plant populations. By enhancing and protecting the genetics of plants, pollinators are also protecting food and nesting resources, habitat, and entire ecosystem structures, not only for themselves but also for other wildlife and even for us humans.

Call to Action

Bees, wasps, beetles, flies, butterflies, and moths—the survival of these pollinators is threatened, as well as the survival of the world's flora, which depends on them to reproduce and survive. Conserving these pollinators contributes to the beauty, health, and biodiversity of our environment. It contributes to strong global economies by enhancing the yield and quality of crops. It helps conserve medicinal plant species which can benefit human health. And it directly and indirectly benefits our own health through our connection with nature.

Want to help? Learning about pollinators is a great step. Do you know that, in addition to honey bees, there are over 20,000 distinct types of native bees in the world, with about 4,000 alone in the United States? And, yes, beetles, wasps, and moths also pollinate. There is an entire tiny but mighty, fascinating pollinator world to dive into, starting with tools like this field guide. But do not stop there. Share what you learn. Educate friends and family about pollinators. Help cultivate awareness about these complex ecosystems.

Prefer to get your hands dirty? Create a pollinator-friendly garden. Provide food with flowering plants all season long and for all stages of pollinators' life cycles. Leave areas undisturbed for nesting opportunities and materials. Provide water, even if only a small dish in a sunny location. Replace turf with plant species that offer vital ecoservices. And after creating this inviting space, keep it free from harmful chemicals and garden maintenance practices.

Don't have a garden? Not into gardening? Become a steward of nature. Volunteer for conservation projects in your community. Join a Community Science project to contribute to the data needed to better understand pollinators, how they are doing. and what they need. With steps like these you can contribute to the health and resilience of pollinators, and your own as well. Spending time in nature, deepening your appreciation for the natural world, has been linked to improved mental and emotional well-being. This goes beyond environmental responsibility. It is investing in our own well-being and that of future generations.

Scientific Nomenclature

The tree of life we are all a part of is magnificent and diverse, but often convoluted and confusing. Taxonomy and nomenclature are valiant attempts to organize the many leaves and branches of this tree and create a standardized naming system for living things. This naming system lets us quickly understand the relationship between two or more organisms and gives species names that can be understood across languages. Scientific names are written in Latin and italicized. This naming system, while generally well-accepted in academic circles, is not without dispute. As we continue to expand our knowledge of the natural world around us, relationships as we understand them evolve, and names change to best reflect new discoveries. The taxonomic names in this book are the most current at the time this guide was written.

Taxonomy is hierarchical, with large groupings that can be subdivided into categories until a species is reached in a ladderlike fashion. Pollinators and their fellow animals all belong to the Animalia kingdom. Within animals, we find the phylum Arthropoda, to which insects, arachnids, and crustaceans belong. Within arthropods, we center this guide on the class Insecta. Different categories of insects fit under specific "order" labels. For example, all dragonflies and damselflies belong to the order Odonata. Butterflies and moths make up the order Lepidoptera. Within each order, we can further group animals by families that share common traits and evolutionary histories. Closely related individuals within a family will share a generic name, or genus. Occasionally in this book you will encounter pollinators described only up to this level, because narrowing any further would be prohibitive in the field. In this case, they will be designated under the format "*Genus* spp." Each member of a genus will have a unique "last name," known as its specific epithet, that separates it from others in its group. The combination of the generic name and specific epithet builds a name exclusive to each species. This two-part scientific name identifies each member in our tree of life.

Insect Morphology

We vertebrates wear our structure on the inside. Our internal skeleton gives us the ability to stand and move. Invertebrates are structured differently. Insects lack an internal skeleton entirely. Instead, they derive their structure, size, and appearance from an external chitin-based structure called the exoskeleton. While insects vary greatly in form and function, there are certain morphological traits that insects share with all fellow arthropods. Together these animals build the largest and most diverse phylum in the animal kingdom.

Arthropods share the following traits:

- A chitinous exoskeleton
- A segmented and bilaterally symmetric body plan
- Jointed appendages
- An open circulatory system

Within arthropods, insects reign as the largest class. Their incredible diversity of adaptations has allowed them to be a highly successful group; today they exist in almost all habitats our lands have to offer. Despite their incredible diversity, there are certain physical characteristics that are definitive of insects. For example, insects may also be referred to as hexapods, since all species within the group are six-legged. Other shared aspects include:

- A body composed of three segments (head, thorax, and abdomen)
- Six legs that originate from the thorax (the middle segment)
- Antennae originating from the head (the top segment)
- Two compound eyes, often accompanied by simpler eyes called ocelli

By taking a quick tour through general insect morphology, you'll be able to orient yourself along the insect body plan and identify pollinators efficiently.

Head

Insect heads make up the topmost section of their three-segment bodies. All insects have a pair of antennae that helps them sense their environment and move safely. The shape or number of antennae segments can often help differentiate groups of insects. Different groups of insects have different mouthparts that reflect their habits and diets. Beetles have chewing mouthparts with mandibles that allow them to grasp and grind their food. Hymenopterans, like wasps and bees, have chewing mouthparts too, with the modification of a long tongue that allows lapping. Lepidopterans, like moths and butterflies, often use a straw-like appendage on the underside of their head that looks like a coiled or extended tube called the proboscis to sip on nectar or sap; some moths lack mouthparts entirely. Dipterans, or flies, have stocky, spongy tubes as mouthparts that allow them to absorb liquids or pierce their food of choice.

Thorax and Abdomen

The thorax is the origin for the appendages of locomotion, including legs and wings and movement-associated muscles. The abdomen houses and protects most of the insect's soft organs and reproductive organs. Insect identification to species can be challenging, and taxonomists often must confirm a species through the examination of insect genitalia under a microscope.

Wings

While not all insects are winged, most pollinating insects have two to four wings that allow them to easily transit from flower to flower to perform pollination. While insect wings allow them to fly, they can also aid in thermal regulation, predator avoidance, courtship, and, of course, their identification. Wing colors and patterns are often (but not always) diagnostic traits. Insect wings are supported by a system of veins that are often one of the most important distinguishing attributes of this body part. There are terms that help us best describe and navigate wing sections. For insects with two sets of wings, the topmost set is referred to as the **forewing** and the bottom set as the **hindwing**. The area of the wing closest to the body is the **proximal area**; the section farthest from the body is the **distal area**. The top half of each wing is the **anterior section**; the bottom half is the **posterior section**. The **dorsal side** of the wing is the topside, seen when insects hold their wings spread open. The **ventral side** of the wing is the underside, often seen when wings are closed and held together. These terms can be applied generally to many morphological descriptions, but in this book you will see them most often used to describe insect wings.

Description of Orders and Dichotomous Key

Within the class Insecta, pollinators fall into four main orders: Diptera, Coleoptera, Hymenoptera, and Lepidoptera.

Diptera: Flies

Flies are often overlooked yet very important pollinators. Pollinating flies have one pair of membranous wings (two wings total), a major characteristic that differentiates them from the bees and wasps, which some fly species mimic very well. Flies are often covered in hairs, which are useful for holding on to pollen grains as they move from flower to flower. Their hairs are also useful tools for microscopic identification to the family level. Many plants that are pollinated by flies develop flowers with strong odors, similar to rotting meat, to attract these special pollinators.

Coleoptera: Beetles

In most beetles, the front pair of wings are developed into a hardened pair of structures called elytra that protect the second pair of soft wings, which fold under the elytra. Not all beetles are pollinators; however, many species are significant pollinators for specific plants. Flowers that attract beetles are often musky or spicy, with large and exposed sexual organs or tight clusters of small flowers.

Hymenoptera: Bees, Wasps, Sawflies, and Ants

This order includes bees, ants, wasps, and sawflies; however, in this guide we cover the most relevant pollinators, bees and wasps. Bees and wasps have two pairs of wings (four wings total). The wings are membranous, and the pattern of the wing veins is useful for identification. The front and hindwings are connected by hooks called hamuli, which allow for better flight. Hymenopterons have chewing mouthparts. Many carry pollen on their hairs and even on special structures on their legs. In general, bees tend to be hairier than wasps, though some bees and wasps are very difficult to tell apart. To differentiate between bees and wasps, it is sometimes necessary to microscopically examine specimens to see that bees have branched hairs whereas wasps have non-branched hairs.

Lepidoptera: Butterflies, Moths, and Skippers

This order includes butterflies, moths, and skippers. Insects in this order have two pairs of wings that are usually covered in scales. These scales are pigmented to give butterflies their brown and black colors; however, the microstructure of the scales scatters light and gives lepidopterans their beautiful iridescent blue, green, and red colors. These insects usually have siphoning mouthparts, though some have underdeveloped mouthparts if they do not feed as adults. Plants that are pollinated by butterflies and moths tend to have long tubular flowers that match the long, thin mouthparts of their lepidopteran pollinators.

Key to Pollinating Insect Orders

The dichotomous key below can be used to identify the order of an insect pollinator. To use the key, compare options A and B for each number while viewing your specimen. Choose the option that most closely fits your specimen and either continue to the next number indicated or find the appropriate order at the end of the option.

1A.	Wings scaly; often with coiled tongue	Lepidoptera
1B.	Wings not scaly; tongue is linear, or mouthparts may be chewing	Continue to 2
2A.	Forewings hardened into elytra	Coleoptera
2B.	All wings thin and membranous	Continue to 3
3A.	With one pair of wings, usually only sparsely covered with hairs, body usually not constricted between thorax and abdomen	Diptera
3B.	With two pairs of wings, body may be covered in dense hair or may have sparse hair, body often constricted between thorax and abdomen	Hymenoptera

The Landscapes of Western North America

In western North America, the guiding forces of geology, water, and fire are visible on the surface of the land. The region's diverse geology and hydrology regimes result in dramatic variation in ecosystems, including high peaks and low basins, lush forests and arid plains, each unique and distinctive in its beauty. North America's largest mountain chain, the Rockies, stretches from British Columbia in Canada to New Mexico. These geologically young, jagged mountains influence the weather and support high biodiversity. The presence and absence of water is dramatic in western North America, creating sharp distinctions in plant communities. Fire is a naturally occurring process in many ecosystems in western North America, and suppression of fire has limited the survival and reproduction of many fire-adapted species. Finally, the rapid population growth over the last one hundred years has impacted existing habitats and created novel ecosystems with introduced species in western North America.

Ecosystems found in this region include:

AMY YARGER

Alpine—Upland slopes above tree line; characterized by high winds, cold temperatures, heavy snow and ice, harsh sunlight, and a short bloom season.

AMY YARGER

Montane—Upland slopes below timberline; usually dominated by evergreen, cone-bearing trees and with a variable climate dependent on elevation.

AMY YARGER

Foothills—Transitional ecosystem characterized by mixed terrain, including canyons, forests, shrublands, grasslands, and river valleys; a moister and cooler climate compared to lower elevations.

AMY YARGER

Deserts—Ecosystem with less than 10 inches/year of precipitation, sparse vegetation, and low humidity. Plants and animals are adapted to withstand extreme temperatures and limited water.

AMY YARGER

Prairies and plains—Temperate lowlands dominated by grasses, often with little variation in topography. Prairies experience extreme weather events, and prairie plants are well adapted to hold on to soil and find water.

AMY YARGER

Riparian zones—Transitional environments between land and water, with soils and vegetation shaped by proximity to water. Riparian zones may border lakes, rivers, streams, and even man-made reservoirs and support high biodiversity, especially where water is otherwise scarce.

AMY YARGER

Urban/suburban—Landscapes dominated by human habitation and processes. These areas are characterized by fragmentation, disturbance, and changes to fire regimes. Landscapes are often dominated by non-native plants.

Some of the fastest growing cities in North America are in the western part of the continent, and yet many of us still think of these iconic landscapes as vast and wild. With the increasing pressures of climate change and habitat degradation, we have a responsibility to conserve these landscapes and the pollinators that support them.

Family Anthomyiidae

Root-maggot Flies

Members of the Anthomyiidae are small to medium flies, similar to house flies in shape and coloration, but more slender and with more prominent bristles on their body and legs. Adults feed on both nectar and pollen. Larvae feed on plant roots, including agricultural crops such as onions and rutabagas.

BOB KRUGMIRE

CABBAGE MAGGOT
Delia radicum

Size: 5–7 mm

Description: Small grayish fly, resembling a smaller, humpbacked house fly. It has dark bristles on its legs, thorax, and abdomen and a stout proboscis.

Habitat: Agricultural areas; developed landscapes in urban and suburban areas

Range: Northern North America from southern Canada south to Colorado

Active season: Late spring to early fall

Conservation status: None

Plant interactions: Adults visit plants with small, clustered flowers, such as members of the sunflower (Asteraceae) and carrot (Apiaceae) families to drink nectar.

Interesting facts: Likely introduced from Europe in the 1800s as a pest of crops in the mustard family (Brassicaceae). Larvae bore into stem bases and eat. This species cannot tolerate the warmer climate of southern North America, but in the north may have up to three generations per year.

Family Bombyliidae

Bee Flies

Bombyliids are fuzzy flies with stocky bodies, sometimes with dark markings on their wings, which are held out to the sides when at rest. Bee flies are named for their ability to mimic bees, even "buzzing" when flying. Bee flies prefer open, sunny environments and are key pollinators in deserts. Adult bee flies have long straight proboscises that don't retract. Larvae are often external parasitoids of beetles, bees, caterpillars, and other flies, but a few eat grasshopper eggs or are kleptoparasites. Adults feed on nectar and pollen from flowers.

LISA HILL

Anthrax georgicus

BLACK BEE FLY
Anthrax georgicus

Size: 4–9 mm

Description: Mostly black bee fly, with solid black pigmentation covering over half the wing. Last three abdominal segments white to silver-gray.

Habitat: Adaptable in most habitats, including wetlands, grasslands, and forest openings and edges

Range: Widespread throughout western North America

Active season: Summer to mid-fall

Conservation status: None

Plant interactions: Adults eat pollen and drink nectar from a wide variety of flowering plants.

Interesting fact: These bee flies are parasitoids of tiger beetles.

BEE FLY

Exoprosopa dodrina

Size: 13–14 mm

Description: Fly with mostly black body with yellow hairs. The abdomen is striped black and yellow with one thicker yellow stripe on the abdomen close to the thorax. The wings are clear, with anterior cells being darker/brown.

Habitat: Unknown

Range: Southwestern United States

Active season: Unknown

Conservation status: None

Plant interactions: These flies are generalist pollen and nectar feeders.

ERIC R. EATON

Exoprosopa dodrina

BEE FLY

Exoprosopa dorcadion

Size: 10–15 mm

Description: Hairy gray fly with rusty and black striped abdomen. Wings have well-defined dark patches from front edge, extending to trailing edge of wing; some variation among locations.

Habitat: High-altitude and coastal areas, including meadows, shrublands, developed landscapes

Range: Widespread throughout western North America

RON WOLF

Active season: Summer to mid-fall

Conservation status: None

Plant interactions: Adults feed on pollen and nectar, especially on members of the sunflower family (Asteraceae) such as gayfeather (*Liatris* spp.) and black-eyed Susan (*Rudbeckia* spp.).

Interesting facts: Since these bee flies are often found in cooler areas, they can often be observed basking on stones in the sun.

BOB KRUGMIRE

GRASSHOPPER BEE FLY

Systoechus vulgaris

Size: 5–10 mm

Description: Roundish fly with fuzzy thorax and body, reddish-brown scutellum, transparent wings, yellow or white halteres, and long proboscis.

Habitat: Found from montane to prairie elevations and in developed and disturbed landscapes; herbaceous meadows, shrublands, forest edges and openings, wetlands, and urban and suburban gardens, as well as roadsides

Range: Western North America

Active season: Midsummer to mid-fall

Conservation status: None

Plant interactions: These flies are nectar feeders, especially on plants in the sunflower (Asteraceae) family.

Interesting facts: Females sometimes hover over ovipositing grasshoppers so they can lay eggs on or near grasshopper eggs, which the larvae use for shelter and food.

Family Conopidae

Thick-headed Flies

Thick-headed flies are medium-sized flies, often mimicking thread-waisted wasps with yellow or white markings on a dark background, their long abdomens on a narrow "stem." Adults feed on flower nectar; larvae are endoparasites on many kinds of insects, including wasps, bees, crickets, cockroaches, and other flies. In some species, the female can lay her eggs on a host (often a foraging bee or other insect) in mid-flight, prying apart the host's exoskeleton to do so. The eggs of these species may be barbed to attach to the host more easily.

LISA HILL

THICK-HEADED FLY

Physocephala texana

Size: 9–13 mm

Description: Brick-red fly with yellow or white face, long and narrow waist. Front edge of wings is brown.

Habitat: Open, sunny areas, including meadows and savanna in the foothills and shortgrass and mixed-grass prairies

Range: Widespread throughout western North America

Active season: Summer

Conservation status: None

Plant interactions: Adults drink nectar and are often found foraging on members of the sunflower family (Asteraceae).

Interesting facts: A threadlike waist makes this fly look very much like a wasp. This fly is also a parasite of wasps and bees. Female flies pounce on host insects, then pry open the abdominal segments of the host to get their eggs inside the body.

Family Empididae

Dance Flies

Dance flies, also known as balloon flies or dagger flies, are found more often in forested environments, but sometimes also in agricultural areas, wetlands, and coastal environments. Dance flies are small, often dark in color, and humpbacked. They also have a small round head that appears to be on a "neck" and big eyes. Like flies in the family Hybotidae, some species in this family also gather in mating swarms. Many species in this family still haven't been described by science.

HEIDE KEEBLE

DANCE FLIES
Empis clausa

Size: 4 mm

Description: Small flies with feathery legs; rounded heads have long proboscises.

Habitat: Shortgrass prairies

Range: Texas

Active season: Spring to summer

Conservation status: None

Plant interactions: Feeds on nectar from plants in the sunflower family (Asteraceae), onion family (Amaryllidaceae), and carrot family (Apiaceae).

Interesting facts: This is a Great Plains species that occasionally extends into western Texas. Dance flies often gather in groups for mating and offer food gifts to entice females.

Similar species: These dance flies can be distinguished from the other dance flies by the size and orientation of their proboscis. *E. clausa* tends to have a thick, downward-pointing beak.

Family Mydidae

Mydas Flies

Mydas flies are known for their large size—the largest fly species in the world belong to this family. Many species appear to mimic wasps as a defense against predators. The larvae of some species hunt and eat beetle grubs and act as biological controls; adults are common flower visitors and pollinators.

RICHARD READING

MYDAS FLY

Mydas luteipennis

Size: 30 mm

Description: The body of this fly is all black with a dark blue, metallic sheen. Wings are bright orange; antennae are long and clubbed.

Habitat: Arid to semiarid regions

Range: Texas, New Mexico, Arizona, and western Colorado

Active season: Late spring to summer

Conservation status: None

Plant interactions: The larvae of flies in the *Mydas* genus feed on beetle grubs; as adults they feed on nectar. The food preferences of this species are unknown; however, other flies in the genus have been seen on milkweeds (*Asclepias* spp.), bee balms (*Monarda* spp.), and verbena (*Verbena* spp.).

Interesting facts: These flies mimic tarantula hawk wasps, which have one of the most painful stings in the invertebrate world. However, these flies are harmless to humans.

Similar species: This species is differentiated from tarantula hawk wasps by the large bulging eyes, which are typical of flies. They also have a stronger curve to their body and a more segmented thorax that isn't as sleek as a wasp thorax. Another fly species, *M. xanthopterus*, looks similar; however, *M. xanthopterus* has smoky coloration on the edges of the wings. *Wyliea mydas* is a robber fly that mimics tarantula hawk wasps and has similar coloration to *M. luteipennis*, but *W. mydas* has short antennae.

Family Stratiomyidae

Soldier Flies

Soldier flies often have bold markings, resembling those of wasps. They are notable for folding their wings scissorlike across the abdomen when resting, which is most of the time. Adults vary in color, size, and shape. Larvae are found in areas with decaying plants, such as leaf litter, rotting fruit, and fallen trees. A few species have aquatic larvae that feed on algae and tiny invertebrates. Adults are usually found drinking nectar from flowers or feeding on dung close to these larval habitats.

AMY YARGER

GREEN SOLDIER FLY
Hedriodiscus binotatus

Size: 12 mm

Description: Green soldier flies have broad faces with large eyes and distinctive lime green and black coloration. Look for two green spots on the dark background of their thorax.

Habitat: Shortgrass and mixed grasslands, riparian edges; disturbed and developed areas in urban and suburban landscapes

Range: Western North America

Active season: Mid-spring to early fall

Conservation status: None

Plant interactions: Nectar feeders preferring sulfur flower (*Eriogonum* spp.), goldenrod (*Solidago* spp.), and coneflowers (*Rudbeckia* spp., *Echinacea* spp.).

Interesting facts: Omnivorous aquatic larvae feed on tiny invertebrates as well as algae.

Family Syrphidae

Hover or Flower Flies

Syrphids are usually medium-sized, smooth-bodied flies. Many mimic wasps or bees, with bright contrasting yellow, brown, orange, and black stripes or spots. Their wings are usually clear, and they have short antennae and short, unspecialized mouthparts. Adults hover, sometimes silently or sometimes buzzing, over flowers to forage for nectar and pollen. Larvae are soft-bodied, slow-moving, sluglike maggots with tapering heads but have a variety of lifestyles; some species are predators, but others feed on decaying plant matter and other detritus. Female hover flies may lay eggs in moist places or near aphid colonies, which assists in biocontrol for these pests. Hover flies are extremely important pollinators around the world and bioindicators of environmental health but are understudied and underappreciated.

HEIDE KEEBLE

COMMON OBLIQUE SYRPHID

Allograpta obliqua

Size: 6–8.5 mm

Description: Colorful bee mimics with huge red eyes and a white face. Thorax is shiny brown; abdomen has gold and black stripes, with small oblique stripes at the tail.

Habitat: Foothills meadows and forest edges, shortgrass and mixed-grass prairies

Range: Western United States

Active season: Summer to fall in the northern range, year-round in the southwestern United States

Conservation status: None

Plant interactions: Feeds on both nectar and pollen on plants with small, clustered flowers, such as those in the sunflower family (Asteraceae) and onion family (Amaryllidaceae).

Interesting facts: This fly seeks out aphids to drink their honeydew. Females lay eggs in aphid colonies so larvae have a ready food source when they hatch. Larvae eat other agricultural pests, such as mites, caterpillars, mealybugs, and other soft-bodied insects.

COMMON SICKLELEG

SUZANNE IWANICKI

Asemosyrphus polygrammus

Size: 11 mm

Description: Tan flies with fuzzy thoraxes. Males have slender orange abdomens; the abdomens of females are broader and grayish. Eyes are separated in both sexes, with simple eyes (ocelli) close to margins of compound eyes.

Habitat: Prairies and plains; also ditches and old fields

Range: North America from the Rocky Mountains west to the coast, north to British Columbia, and south to Mexico

Active season: Spring to fall

Conservation status: None

Plant interactions: Adults forage from a wide variety of flowering plants, especially in the sunflower family (Asteraceae).

Interesting facts: Larvae are aquatic.

BUMBLEBEE CATKIN FLY

ARNOLD SKEI

Brachypalpus alopex

Size: 18 mm

Description: This fly has a black abdomen with dark wings and black legs. It has a rust-colored or yellow head with large dark eyes.

Habitat: Meadows and wetlands adjacent to aquatic environments

Range: Pacific coast of North America

Active season: Early spring to early summer

Conservation status: None

Plant interactions: This fly drinks nectar from early-emerging flowering species such as manzanita (*Arctostaphylos* spp.).

Interesting facts: Alopex means "fox," referring to the fuzzy, reddish tinge of the thorax.

ORANGE CATKIN SYRPHID

Brachypalpus femoratus

Size: 6–8.5 mm

Description: Medium to large flies with furry thoraxes and large forward-facing eyes, often mistaken for honey bees or bumble bees. Hairs on thorax are yellowish.

Habitat: Shortgrass and mixed-grass prairies

Range: West coast of North America and southwestern states

Active season: Early spring to midsummer

Conservation status: None

Plant interactions: Generalist foragers on many plants with simple flowers, including wildflowers and agricultural crops.

Interesting facts: Flies identified as *B. femoratus* may belong to a complex of species instead of one species; scientists are still learning about these hoverflies. The larval stage of this species prefers damp habitats.

CAROL BLANEY

MEADOW FLY

Chrysotoxum spp.

Size: 14–16 mm

Description: Large flies with yellow faces and broad, convex abdomens with bold stripes of black and yellow. Elongated antennae and red legs are distinctive. Males' eyes touch in the center.

Habitat: Deciduous forest edges in the foothills and mountains, riparian edges

Range: Western United States

Active season: Mid-spring to early fall

Conservation status: None

Plant interactions: Adults visit flowers of black-eyed Susan (*Rudbeckia* spp.) and other aster relatives for pollen and nectar.

Interesting facts: Adult flies are wasp mimics; the predaceous larvae eat aphids.

RICHARD READING

A fly in the genus *Chrysotoxum*

UNDIVIDED LUCENT

Didea fuscipes

YU LIU

Size: 11–14 mm

Description: Large bee mimic flies with dark red eyes; black and broad yellow bands on flattened, downward-pointing abdomen. Distinguished by face markings that look like an upside-down "V."

Habitat: Montane forest edges and meadows

Range: Western North America

Active season: Mid-spring to mid-fall

Conservation status: None

Plant interactions: Generalist forager on flowering plants, including members of the sunflower (Asteraceae) and caper (Capparaceae) families.

Interesting facts: Eyeless and legless larvae are often found in aphid colonies, feeding on aphids. Larval frass is purple and helps the maggots adhere to tree bark.

BLACK-HORNED SMOOTHTAIL

Epistrophe grossulariae

MELINDA FAWVER

Size: 9–12.5 mm

Description: Medium flies with yellow faces below dark, hairy foreheads; dark greenish thorax and dark abdomen with yellow or coppery stripes.

Habitat: Deciduous forest edges and openings in the foothills, wetlands, and riparian forests

Range: Western North America

Active season: Summer

Conservation status: None

Plant interactions: Adult flies forage on many small-flowered species, including thistles, elderberry (*Sambucus* spp.), Queen Anne's lace (*Daucus carota*), blackberries (*Rubus* spp.), and valerian (*Valeriana officinalis*).

Interesting facts: Larvae are predators of aphids and helpful for pest control. This species is distributed across the Northern Hemisphere, including Europe and Asia.

ORANGE-SPOTTED DRONE FLY

Eristalis anthophorina

Size: 11–12 mm

Description: Medium flies with yellow face below a dark hairy forehead; dark greenish thorax and dark abdomen with yellow or coppery stripes.

Habitat: Wetlands, marshes

Range: Western North America

Active season: Mid-spring to mid-fall

Conservation status: None

PETER TERPSTRA

Plant interactions: Adults feed on nectar from a variety of plants, including relatives of the carrot family (Apiaceae).

Interesting facts: *E. anthophorina* is a bumble bee mimic both through appearance and behavior. It's unknown whether this species is native or introduced to North America. Larvae of this species live in water and eat decaying plants.

ORANGE-LEGGED DRONE FLY

Eristalis flavipes

Size: 12–17 mm

Description: Hairy bumble bee mimics with bright yellow abdomens and black legs with orange tips.

Habitat: Found in many habitat types, especially wetlands

Range: Throughout North America

Active season: Spring through early autumn

Conservation status: None

LISA HILL

Plant interactions: Adults visit a wide range of flowers, including goldenrod (*Solidago* spp.), asters, and boulder raspberry (*Rubus deliciosus*), for both pollen and nectar.

Interesting facts: The species name *flavipes* means "yellow-footed." The larval forms of this species are aquatic filter feeders.

DUSKY DRONE FLY
Eristalis obscura

LAURIE J. BREWSTER

Size: 11–12 mm

Description: Medium flies with dark, shiny bodies and pale hairs on the face. Abdomen has a narrow white band; wings have small darkened patches.

Habitat: Found in many habitat types, including wetlands

Range: Northern North America, south to Colorado

Active season: Spring to fall

Conservation status: None

Plant interactions: Adults feed on nectar from a variety of plants, including relatives of the carrot (Apiaceae) and sunflower (Asteraceae) families, as well as chokecherries (*Prunus virginiana*).

Interesting facts: This species of hoverfly also naturally occurs in Siberia and Europe.

YELLOW-SHOULDERED DRONE FLY
Eristalis stipator

CALAIS LEJEUNE

Size: 10–13 mm

Description: Large clear-winged flies with shiny, dark brown bodies with orange-brown markings on abdomen. Males have eyes that meet in the middle.

Habitat: Shortgrass and mixed-grass prairies, stream banks and edges, croplands, developed and disturbed landscapes, gardens

Range: Widespread throughout western North America

Active season: Summer

Conservation status: None

Plant interactions: Adults drink nectar from plants in the sunflower (Asteraceae) and carrot (Apiaceae) families, as well as hoary vervain (*Verbena hastata*), smooth sumac (*Rhus glabra*), raspberry (*Rubus idaeus*), and ninebark (*Physocarpus* spp.).

Interesting facts: Adults feed on aphid honeydew as well as flower nectar. Adults lay eggs in aphid colonies; the larvae then eat aphids before pupating in debris or soil.

BIRD HOVERFLY

Eupeodes volucris

Size: 6–10 mm

Description: Slender, often hovering flies with a white face and reddish legs. Males are black with three ivory bands around abdomen; females have three ivory bands and two thin ivory lines around abdomen.

Habitat: Foothills meadows and shrublands, shortgrass and mixed-grass prairies, wetlands

Range: Western North America

Active season: Mid-spring to mid-fall

Conservation status: None

Plant interactions: Adults drink nectar of plants in the sunflower family (Asteraceae).

Interesting facts: Adults feed on aphid honeydew as well as nectar. Adults lay eggs in aphid colonies; the larvae then eat aphids before pupating in debris or soil.

HEIDE KEEBLE

NARROW-HEADED MARSH FLY

Helophilus fasciatus

Size: 10–15 mm

Description: These flies have vertical stripes on the thorax and interrupted bands of black and gold on the abdomen. Eyes do not touch in the middle.

Habitat: Plains, prairies, as well as ditches and disturbed sites. To reproduce, there must be a freshwater source nearby.

LISA HILL

Range: Widespread throughout United States, southern Canada, and Mexico

Active season: Spring to fall

Conservation status: None

Plant interactions: Adults forage on rabbitbrush (*Ericameria* spp.) and goldenrod (*Solidago* spp.).

Interesting facts: Their active season extends earlier and later than those of most other syrphids. Their name means "marsh lover." Female flies lay their eggs on vegetation overhanging water; the larvae then fall into the water and live on decomposing plant litter.

BROAD-HEADED MARSH FLY

Helophilus latifrons

MARY MENZ

Size: 13–15 mm

Description: These honey bee mimic flies have two vertical stripes of short hairs on their eyes.

Habitat: From the mountains to the prairies. They require a water source to reproduce, so they can inhabit a variety of habitats where there is a standing body of water.

Range: Widespread throughout the United States, Canada, and Mexico

Active season: Fall

Conservation status: None

Plant interactions: Adults drink nectar from a variety of flowers.

Interesting facts: These flies were introduced from Europe before 1874 and are now found all over the world. Male flies are territorial and stay in their territories their whole lives. Larvae, called "rat-tailed maggots" due to their long breathing tube, feed on rotting plants in water. Some theorize that rat-tailed maggots inspired the biblical tales of honey bees spontaneously developing from dead animals.

COMMON LOOPWING APHIDEATER

Lapposyrphus lapponicus

NORMA MCGRAW

Size: 8–14 mm

Description: Bee mimics with white faces; dark abdomens with yellow bands, interrupted in the center. Males have dark red eyes that meet in the center.

Habitat: Coniferous and deciduous forest edges and openings

Range: Western North America

Active season: Mid-spring to late summer

Conservation status: None

Plant interactions: Generalist nectar feeders, often found on flowers in the sunflower family (Asteraceae).

Interesting facts: Adults are often attracted to lights at night.

SYRPHID FLY

Ocyptamus spp.

Size: 9–14 mm

Description: Narrow-bodied flies with long wings; variable amounts of dark pigmentation.

Habitat: Unknown

Range: Widespread through North America

Active season: Throughout the summer

Conservation status: None

Plant interactions: Unknown.

Interesting facts: Larvae feed on aphids and other soft-bodied insects. Members of this genus have been documented feeding on adult flies of other groups.

MATTHEW BERG

O. fuscipennis

THREE-LINED MUDSUCKER

Orthonevra nitida

Size: 9–11 mm

Description: Large flies with hairy faces, long second antennae segments, laterally striped eyes; a longitudinally striped thorax. *O. nitida*, shown here, is part of the *O. bellula* complex.

Habitat: Riparian areas, croplands, urban and suburban areas

Range: Mountains of the western United States

Active season: Spring to fall

Conservation status: None

Plant interactions: Adults feed on nectar and pollen from a variety of flowering plants.

Interesting facts: Larvae that feed on detritus are aquatic, with a modified breathing tube that pierces through aquatic plants for an air supply.

TRACEY FANDRE

BLACK-BACKED GRASS SKIMMER

Paragus haemorrhous

LISA HILL

Size: 2–4 mm

Description: Small flies with large eyes with white rims; an all-black scutellum and red abdomen.

Habitat: Prairies, deserts, agricultural areas, disturbed sites

Range: Scattered throughout central to southern Europe, the Mediterranean Basin. In North America, from the Yukon to Costa Rica.

Active season: Throughout summer

Conservation status: None

Plant interactions: Adults feed on nectar from flowers in the carrot (Apiaceae) and sunflower (Asteraceae) families.

Interesting facts: Larvae eat aphids on many plants.

SEDGESITTER

Platycheirus spp.

ERIN DOYLE

P. trichopus

Size: 5–10 mm

Description: Head and thorax are shiny black; sides of the thorax are hairy. Abdomen is black with pale bands. Male flies have eyes that meet in the center.

Habitat: Areas with grassy vegetation; also edges of high-altitude forests

Range: Western United States and Canada, up to Alaska

Active season: Summer

Conservation status: None

Plant interactions: These flies visit flowers for nectar but will also eat pollen from wind-pollinated plants such as willows (*Salix* spp.) and grasses.

Interesting facts: The genus name comes from the Greek and translates to "flat hands."

PIED HOVERFLY

Scaeva pyrastri

BOB KRUGMIRE

Size: 11–15.5 mm

Description: Flies with white or yellow face and hairy, angular reddish-brown eyes. Thorax and abdomen are shiny blue-black with three sets of interrupted white/yellow bands. The eyes of males touch; the eyes of females are separated.

Habitat: Meadows, riparian edges, agricultural, urban and suburban areas

Range: Widespread throughout North America, Europe, and North Africa

Active season: Spring to fall

Conservation status: None

Plant interactions: These flies feed on nectar from smooth white aster (*Symphyotrichum porteri*) and rabbitbrush (*Ericameria* spp.).

Interesting facts: Adults also feed on aphid honeydew; larvae may eat as many as 500 aphids each. This species is also found in the Old World.

GLOBETAILS

Sphaerophoria spp.

Size: 6–11 mm

Description: Slender flies with elongated abdomens with yellow, gold, or red bands on black background. Males have a white face with eyes that touch; females have separated eyes and a black face with two white stripes.

Habitat: Wetlands, open fields, meadows

Range: Widespread throughout North America

Active season: Spring to fall

Conservation status: None

Plant interactions: Adults visit flowers in the rose family (Rosaceae) for nectar and pollen.

Interesting facts: Larvae feed on aphids.

MARY MENZ

A fly in the genus *Sphaerophoria*

SPATULATE FLY

Sphegina spp.

Size: 5–8 mm

Description: Small delicate flies with bare, concave faces; narrow waists, enlarged abdomens, and long hind legs, often resembling parasitoid wasps.

Habitat: Coniferous and deciduous forest edges in montane and foothills regions, especially areas with dense and damp vegetation

Range: Washington and British Columbia

Active season: Summer

Conservation status: None

Plant interactions: These flies are nectar feeders on pale-colored flowers, often in the carrot family (Apiaceae), but also in rose (Rosaceae), sunflower (Asteraceae), and buttercup (Ranunculaceae) families.

ERIC KNOPF

S. brachygaster

Interesting facts: Larvae are saprophagous and often feed on decaying sap under the bark of trees, especially elms and oaks.

THICK-LEGGED HOVERFLY

Syritta spp.

Size: 6.5–9.5 mm

Description: Narrow-bodied flies with thick black interrupted stripes on abdomen.

Habitat: Developed and disturbed areas, agricultural areas

Range: Widespread throughout North America; introduced from Europe

Active season: Summer to fall

Conservation status: None

Plant interactions: These generalist nectar and pollen feeders are found on a wide variety of small flowers, especially members of the sunflower family (Asteraceae).

Interesting facts: Larvae are often found in damp decaying matter, such as dung.

AMY YARGER

A fly in the genus *Syritta*

HAIRY-EYED FLOWER FLY

Syrphus torvus

Size: 7–15 mm

Description: This fly's body is black with yellow bands that overlap on the sides of abdomen. There are hairs around the eyes.

Habitat: Found in urban areas; also meadows and ditches

Range: Most of North America

Active season: Spring to fall

Conservation status: None

Plant interactions: Adults visit flowers such as curlycup gumweed (*Grindelia squarrosa*) for nectar and pollen.

Interesting facts: This species is also found in northern Europe and Asia.

LISA HILL

MARGINED CALLIGRAPHER

Toxomerus marginatus

Size: 5–6 mm

Description: Delicate flies with thin golden to orange-yellow line around the margin of abdomen. Color varies depending on the environment during pupal development, becoming darker in colder temperatures. Males have rounded abdomens; females' abdomens are pointy on the end.

Habitat: Meadows and savannas, wetland edges, developed and disturbed landscapes

Range: Western North America

Active season: Late spring to mid-fall

Conservation status: None

BOB KRUGMIRE

Plant interactions: These hoverflies are generalist nectar and pollen feeders, visiting many kinds of plants.

Interesting facts: Most other members of the genus are tropical in range. Larvae are predaceous on soft-bodied insects; pupation is in the soil.

LISA HILL

COMMON THICKLEG FLY
Tropidia quadrata

Size: 13 mm

Description: Small dark flies with large reddish eyes, stubby antennae; swollen-looking hind femurs resemble those of some wasps. Banded abdomen narrows and curves downward toward the distal end.

Habitat: Wetlands, drainages

Range: Widespread, including western United States and southern Canada

Active season: Summer

Conservation status: None

Plant interactions: This generalist eats both nectar and pollen from many kinds of flowers, including fleabane (*Erigeron* spp.), swamp milkweed (*Asclepias incarnata*), goldenrod (*Solidago* spp.), foxglove beardtongue (*Penstemon digitalis*), Queen Anne's lace (*Daucus carota*), and meadow anemone (*Anemonastrum canadense*).

Interesting facts: These small flies rarely enter the flowers they visit but instead forage what they can from the surface; for this reason, they are only occasionally effective pollinators. *Tropidia* maggots usually feed on dung and rotting plant material.

Family Tachinidae

Bristle Flies

Bristle flies are medium to large flies with robust bodies and showy bristle patterns on the tip of their abdomens. They have "pad-like" mouthparts for sucking liquid food, such as flower nectar and insect honeydew, as adults. Larvae are parasitoids on other arthropods such as insects, spiders, centipedes, and scorpions but most often caterpillars. You can sometimes see their small oval white eggs on the surface of caterpillars.

BOB KRUGMIRE

FEATHER-LEGGED FLY
Trichopoda pennipes

Size: 5–13 mm

Description: Medium flies with short dark fringe on hind legs; black wings edged in white. Males have orange abdomens; females have dark or dark-tipped abdomens.

Habitat: Agricultural areas, wetland edges, developed landscapes in urban and suburban areas

Range: Widespread throughout western North America

Active season: Late spring to early fall

Conservation status: None

Plant interactions: Adults drink nectar, often found foraging on asters and goldenrod (*Solidago* spp.), as well as Queen Anne's lace (*Daucus carota*) and meadowsweet (*Spiraea* spp.)

Interesting facts: Females hover over plants that harbor hosts for her young, then lays multiple eggs. Only one will survive to drink the body fluids of the host, usually members of the true bug order (Heteroptera). These flies have effectively been introduced as biocontrol in some areas, but they occur naturally throughout much of North America.

Family Buprestidae

Jewel Beetles, Metallic Wood-boring Beetles

Adult jewel beetles are bullet-shaped—elongated, flat, and oval—with hard shiny elytra; usually under 20 mm long with threadlike or serrated antennae. These insects can be shiny and colorful with intricate patterns, sometimes even used as ornaments by humans. Many species are wood-boring in their larval stage, known as flat-headed borers, but some species are stem miners of herbaceous plants. Wood borers often select dead and dying trees or dying branches on healthy trees.

DARLENE VARGA

YELLOW-MARGINED FLOWER BUPRESTID
Acmaeodera flavomarginata

Size: 11–12 mm

Description: Bullet-shaped black beetle with red markings on its elytra; yellow stripes down the side of its abdomen.

Habitat: Urban and suburban areas in gardens, ditches, and disturbed areas; also found in the desert, prairies, and riparian shrublands

Range: New Mexico and Texas, south into Costa Rica

Active season: Fall

Conservation status: None

Plant interactions: Adults forage on members of the sunflower family (Asteraceae, esp. *Bidens* and *Tithonia*). Larvae are wood borers on trees such as *Acacia*, persimmon (*Diospyros*), and mesquite (*Prosopis*).

Interesting facts: This species is believed to be a firefly mimic—the yellow edges and red patches are similar to firefly markings.

Similar species: *A. chiricahuae* is slightly smaller, and the red markings on its elytra are more like red and black dashes than the red band with black spots on *A. flavomarginata*.

FLOWER BUPRESTID

Acmaeodera rubronotata

STEVEN G. MLODINOW

Size: 8–10 mm

Description: Bullet-shaped metallic black beetle with yellow markings on elytra; small red markings along the sides of the abdomen.

Habitat: Montane canyons, foothills scrub and savanna, deciduous forest edge and openings, canyons, and desert sagebrush

Range: Rocky Mountain region, extending into Texas

Active season: Midsummer to early fall

Conservation status: None

Plant interactions: Adults eat pollen and flower petals from many plants. Larvae bore into oaks.

Interesting facts: This genus has over 140 species in North America, with the highest species diversity in the desert southwest of the United States.

GOLDEN JEWEL BUPRESTID

Buprestis aurulenta

ZACHARY KEMP

Size: 19 mm

Description: Large bullet-shaped beetle, brassy green to gold color with copper margins. Adults have five widely spaced ridges on each elytron.

Habitat: Forests

Range: Western United States from the Rocky Mountains to the Pacific coast; southern California north through southern British Columbia

Active season: Mid-spring to mid-fall

Conservation status: None

Plant interactions: Larvae feed on a variety of conifers; adults feed on Douglas fir (*Pseudotsuga menziesii*) foliage before mating but mostly eat pollen from flowers in the sunflower family (Asteraceae).

Interesting facts: Larvae of this species can live for decades in dry wood, even in lumber or furniture.

Similar species: *B. adjecta* is a similar shape and size but more emerald green overall, with fewer colors.

Family Cantharidae

Soldier Beetles

Beetles in the soldier beetle family are sometimes called "leatherwings," because they are somewhat soft-bodied and have wings that don't completely cover the abdomen. Their bold coloration advertises their distastefulness to potential predators. Adults range in size from 2 mm to 28 mm and eat nectar and pollen and may prey on other insects such as aphids. Larvae suck the fluids from snails, insect eggs, and other insect larvae.

RON WOLF

COLORADO SOLDIER BEETLE
Chauliognathus basalis

Size: 9–12 mm

Description: Long and narrow-bodied beetles with long, wiry antennae; black and orange markings on thorax and elytra.

Habitat: Shortgrass and mixed-grass prairies

Range: Rocky Mountain states, extending south into Arizona and east to Texas

Active season: Late summer to frost

Conservation status: None

Plant interactions: Messy pollen eaters of late-blooming plants in the sunflower family (Asteraceae), especially rubber rabbitbrush (*Ericameria* spp.), snakeweed (*Gutierrezia* spp.), and goldenrod (*Solidago* spp.).

Interesting facts: Many soldier beetles can secrete chemicals that make them unpalatable to predators. Black and orange are bold warning colors to remind predators to leave them alone.

MOUNTAIN SOLDIER BEETLE

Chauliognathus deceptus

Size: 9–11 mm

Description: Long and narrow-bodied beetles with long, wiry antennae; dark thorax and elytra with slight reddish markings around edges, mostly in the front half of the elytra.

Habitat: Meadows and shrubland of mountains and foothills

Range: Rocky Mountain states—Arizona, New Mexico, and Colorado

Active season: Late summer to early fall

Conservation status: None

Plant interactions: Adults forage for pollen on gumweed (*Grindelia* spp.) and other members of the Asteraceae family.

Interesting facts: Soldier beetles are important native, late-season pollinators; they are often found in groups mating and pollinating simultaneously.

Similar species: *C. pensylvanicus* and *C. basalis.* All three species are similar in size, shape, and color. However, *C. deceptus* has a greater amount of black than orange on the elytra.

RICHARD READING

GOLDENROD SOLDIER BEETLE

Chauliognathus pensylvanicus

Size: 15–16 mm

Description: Long and narrow-bodied orange beetles with long, wiry antennae. Thorax is orange with black spots; elytra are orange with two black spots.

Habitat: Open fields, prairies, grasslands, parks, roadsides, sand dunes, abandoned fields

Range: Eastern North America, from Colorado to the coast and north into Ontario and Quebec

Active season: Late summer to early fall

Conservation status: None

Plant interactions: Adults feed on pollen and nectar of goldenrod (*Solidago* spp.) and other late-blooming flowers, especially of the aster family (Asteraceae).

Interesting facts: Predaceous larvae eat grasshopper eggs, cucumber beetles and larvae; sometimes found dead on flowers infected with a fungus specific to insects.

Similar species: *C. deceptus* and *C. basalis.* All three species are similar in size, shape, and color. However, *C. pensylvanicus* has two black spots on the orange pronotum, a defining characteristic. In addition, the front half of the elytra (closest to the pronotum) is orange with no black markings.

BOB KRUGMIRE

Family Cerambycidae

Longhorn Beetles

Longhorn beetles are large and showy enough to have collected many common names, including longicorns, capricorns, timber beetles, and sawyer beetles. Adult longhorns carry distinctive long antennae, which may be longer than the beetle's body. Longhorn beetles are considered "primary borers," starting decomposition of wood and biorecycling in forest ecosystems. A few introduced species, such as the Asian long-horned beetle (*Anoplophora glabripennis motschulsky*) can be economic pests on trees and timber.

BOB KRUGMIRE

RED LONGHORN BEETLE
Batyle suturalis

Size: 7–9 mm

Description: Small beetle with red body with black line along elytral suture and another black line between pronotum and wings. Long antennae with eyes that wrap around base of each antenna.

Habitat: Meadows, savanna, deciduous forest edges and shrubland in the foothills, agriculture croplands, urban disturbed sites and roadsides

Range: Rocky Mountain and southwestern states

Active season: Midsummer to early fall

Conservation status: None

Plant interactions: Adults feed on pollen from members of the sunflower family (Asteraceae); larvae are wood-boring, usually in dead or dying trees.

Interesting facts: Bright warning coloration of this beetle protects it by alerting predators to its distastefulness.

GOLDEN FLOWER LONGHORN BEETLE

Lepturobosca chrysocoma

Size: 10–20 mm

Description: Yellow-bodied beetle with black elytra covered in golden hairs. Legs are black; tarsi are orange.

Habitat: Mountains and foothills

Range: From the Rocky Mountains west to the coast; also New England and southern Canada

Active season: Summer

Conservation status: None

Plant interactions: Adults found on yarrow (*Achillea* spp.) and other members of the sunflower family, sticky geranium (*Geranium viscosissimum*), as well as bear grass (*Xerophyllum tenax*) and red-berried elder (*Sambucus racemosa*).

Interesting facts: Larvae eat decaying wood of both hardwoods and conifers. The hairy wings and body of the adult beetle enable better pollen transport.

CHRISTIAN NUNES

LOCUST BORER

Megacyllene robiniae

Size: 11–28 mm

Description: Large beetle with long body, alternating dark and yellow bands, mimicking a wasp or bee; long antennae and orange legs. The metepisternum (region between second and third hind legs) is covered in yellow hairs.

Habitat: Foothills, prairies, agricultural areas, riparian edges, fields, ditches, roadsides

Range: Widespread throughout the United States and southern Canada

Active season: Late summer to mid-fall

Conservation status: None

RON WOLF

Plant interactions: Adults feed on goldenrod (*Solidago* spp.) nectar and other members of the sunflower family (Asteraceae).

Interesting facts: Larvae bore into black locust trees (*Robinia pseudoacacia*); species name refers to this specialized relationship, which determines its range. This beetle is considered a pest of black locust trees. After eggs hatch in the fall, the larvae, also known as "round-headed borers," hibernate under the bark, tunneling through the wood, which can structurally weaken the tree.

Similar species: *Placostemus difficilis*, a mesquite borer, is similar to the locust borer. However, *P. difficilis* is typically darker in color, with smaller, broken yellow bands. *M. caryane* (hickory borer) is also similar, but it's active in the spring compared to *M. robiniae*, which is active in the fall.

Family Chrysomelidae

Leaf Beetles

Leaf beetles belong to one of the most diverse insect families and are found in almost every habitat. Adults are true herbivores, chewing on living flowers and leaves while also drinking nectar and eating pollen. Many will eat just one kind or just a few kinds of plants. The leaf beetle family includes many agricultural pests, including flea beetles, cucumber beetles, bean beetles, and Colorado potato beetles, as well as biocontrols for noxious weeds.

JOHN VAN VELDHUIZEN

GLOBEMALLOW LEAF BEETLE
Calligrapha serpentina

Size: 7–10 mm

Description: Beetle with rounded body; elytra vary in color from yellow, red, or green bands on dark background with a metallic luster. The head and pronotum are black; legs are reddish brown.

Habitat: Deserts

Range: South America north through Central America into Arizona, New Mexico, and Texas

Active season: Midsummer to early fall

Conservation status: None

Plant interactions: Found on members of the mallow family (Malvaceae), esp. globemallows (*Sphaeralcea* spp.).

Interesting facts: Coloration may change from one generation to the next, but also vary within a population.

Similar species: Very similar to *Zygogramma signatipennis*. *C. serpentina* seems to have a more distinct, less blotchy pattern compared to *Zygogramma*.

DOGBANE BEETLE

Chrysochus auratus

Size: 8–11 mm

Description: Beetle with oval body; shiny green iridescent exoskeleton.

Habitat: Riparian edges; also fields, ditches, roadsides

Range: North America, from the Rocky Mountains east to the coast; also southern Canada

Active season: Summer

Conservation status: None

Plant interactions: Adults feed on dogbane (*Apocynum* spp.) and occasionally milkweed (*Asclepias* spp.).

LISA HILL

Interesting facts: Larvae are obligate root feeders.

Similar species: *G. cyanea*. The elytra of *Gastrophysa cyanea* are more roughly punctate than those of *C. auratus*.

SPOTTED CUCUMBER BEETLE

Diabrotica undecimpunctata

Size: 5–9 mm

Description: Abdomen is greenish yellow with eleven black dots on the elytra. Head is dark, with dark antennae.

Habitat: Croplands, urban gardens

Range: Widespread throughout the United States, north into southern Canada and in the central highlands of Mexico

Active season: Mid-spring to mid-fall

Conservation status: None

RON WOLF

Plant interactions: Feeds on plants in the cucumber and squash family (Cucurbitaceae) but will also eat leaves of beans, corn, cotton, and soybean. Also visits various small flowers for nectar.

Interesting facts: Spotted cucumber beetles are common garden and agricultural pests, not only damaging the plants but also spreading diseases among the plants.

Family Cleridae

Checkered Beetles

Beetles in the family Cleridae are commonly called "checkered beetles" due to the bold patterns of colors on their elytra. Their body shape is usually an elongated oval with bright blue, black, yellow, red, or orange coloring. The antennae of most species are clubbed at the end. Most beetles in this family are predaceous, although some are pollen feeders.

JACOB MARTIN

ELEGANT CHECKERED BEETLE
Chariessa elegans

Size: 7–13 mm

Description: Medium-sized beetle with reddish head and thorax; black elytra.

Habitat: Found in the plains and on prairies, commonly associated with oak trees

Range: British Columbia south to California and east to central Texas

Active season: Summer to early fall

Conservation status: None

Plant interactions: Adults feed on pollen of various flowers, especially members of the sunflower family (Asteraceae): goldenrod (*Solidago* spp.), yarrow (*Achillea* spp.), black-eyed Susan (*Rudbeckia* spp.), and Northern bedstraw (*Galium boreale*).

Interesting facts: Larvae feed on eggs, larvae. and adults of longhorn beetles.

Similar species: *Chariessa catalina*, which has a bluer elytra, has a more restricted range that includes the southwestern United States. The elytra of *C. elegans* tends to look more black under direct light.

HANDSOME YUCCA BEETLE

Enoclerus spinolae

Size: 11 mm

Description: Medium-sized beetle with black thorax, red elytra with dark spots. Spots may be variable.

Habitat: Wherever yuccas are found, mostly in desert sagebrush and canyons

Range: North America in the Southwest, southern Rocky Mountains, Great Plains, California, and Texas

Active season: Summer

Conservation status: None

WILLEM VAN VLIET

Plant interactions: Adults are pollen feeders. Found often on soapweed (*Yucca glauca*), sotol (*Dasylirion* spp.), and milkweed (*Asclepias* spp.).

Interesting facts: This beetle has been reported feeding on ladybird beetles and may be able to sequester distasteful compounds from its prey.

RED-BLUE CHECKERED BEETLE

Trichodes nuttalli

Size: 8–10 mm

Description: Beetle with elongated body, black thorax, and an iridescent dark blue elytra with red bands. Fuzz of white hairs on ventral side.

Habitat: Shortgrass and mixed-grass prairie, riparian edges

Range: Northern Rocky Mountains

Active season: Early to midsummer

Conservation status: None

EMILY HJALMARSON

Plant interactions: This generalist pollen feeder visits members of the sunflower family (Asteraceae) such as tickseed (*Coreopsis* spp.), goldenrod (*Solidago* spp.), yarrow (*Achillea* spp.), and sunflower (*Helianthus* spp.); also spotted on bee balm (*Monarda fistulosa*), California lilac (*Ceanothus* spp.), and others.

Interesting facts: More study is necessary to identify the larval hosts of this beetle; they may include the short-horned grasshopper (*Chloealtis conspersa*), bees, and wasps. Checkered beetle eggs may get accidentally picked up by other pollinators and carried back to bee and wasp nests.

RON WOLF

ORNATE CHECKERED BEETLE

Trichodes ornatus

Size: 5–15 mm

Description: Beetle with an elongated body with black thorax; dark elytra with bands of either red or yellow. Males are smaller than females.

Habitat: Montane meadows, shrublands and forest edges, foothill grasslands and shrublands, deciduous forest edges, shortgrass and mid-grass prairie, sagebrush, riparian edges

Range: Western North America

Active season: Late spring to midsummer

Conservation status: None

Plant interactions: This pollen feeder prefers yellow members of the sunflower family, such as yarrow (*Achillea* sp.) but is also found on milkweed (*Asclepias* sp.).

Interesting facts: This beetle is a parasitoid of leafcutter bees. If bees are not available, larvae can feed on pollen. This species is the most common member of the genus in western North America.

Family Coccinellidae

Lady Beetles

Beetles in the family Coccinellidae are commonly called "ladybugs" in North America and "ladybird beetles" in the United Kingdom. In addition to eating flower pests like aphids, these beetles move pollen from flower to flower as they forage on plant material and hunt prey. In North America their bodies are usually black, red, orange, or yellowish in color with white markings and red or black spots on their elytra.

BOB KRUGMIRE

ASIAN LADY BEETLE

Harmonia axyridis

Size: 5–8 mm

Description: Hemispherical beetle; variable in spots and coloration of elytra, often with a white thorax.

Habitat: Widespread in rural and urban areas

Range: Widespread throughout the United States and southern Canada; also South America and Europe. Native to eastern Asia.

Active season: Year-round in many states. Where they do hibernate, it is often in houses and outbuildings.

Conservation status: None

Plant interactions: In the fall they will consume ripe fruit, such as grapes in vineyards.

Interesting facts: Introduced to North America as a biocontrol but now considered less desirable, since there is concern about the decline of native species. Known to gather indoors for shelter, where they can exude an unpleasant odor, making them a winter nuisance in some places. This species is considered a pest in vineyards because they are attracted to overripe grapes and make the wine taste bad.

Similar species: Some variations of *Adalia bipunctata* look like *H. axyridis* but can be distinguished by the extensive orange underside of *H. axyridis* compared to the black underside of *A. bipunctata*.

EUROPEAN SEVEN-SPOTTED LADY BEETLE

Coccinella septempunctata

BOB KRUGMIRE

Size: 7–9 mm

Description: Hemispherical beetle with black and white thorax; red elytra with 3 spots on either wing, with one spot overlapping both wings where the elytra join.

Habitat: Foothills, prairies, riparian zones, urban areas, croplands

Range: Widespread throughout North America. Native to Europe and East Asia.

Active season: Summer to early fall

Conservation status: None

Plant interactions: Feeds from small umbelliferous flowers such as dill (*Anethum graveolens*), parsley (*Petroselinum crispum*), lovage (*Levisticum officinale*), Queen Anne's lace (*Daucus carota*), and fennel (*Foeniculum vulgare*). Sometimes known to visit sunflowers (*Helianthus* spp.), which provide both nectar and pollen.

Interesting facts: Introduced from Europe multiple times as a biocontrol for aphids; not an obligate pollinator.

Similar species: Similar to other *Coccinella* sp. You can distinguish between species by counting the spots—*septempunctata* means "seven dots."

CONVERGENT LADY BEETLE

Hippodamia convergens

RON WOLF

Size: 4–7 mm

Description: Oval-shaped beetle ranging in color from golden orange to red; convergent white lines on a black thorax, which is also outlined in white. Black spots on the elytra, but they are variable in number and pattern.

Habitat: Mountains, foothills, prairies, urban areas, cropland

Range: Widespread throughout North America

Active season: Summer to early fall

Conservation status: None

Plant interactions: Feeds from small umbelliferous flowers such as dill (*Anethum graveolens*), parsley (*Petroselinum crispum*), lovage (*Levisticum officinale*), Queen Anne's lace (*Daucus carota*), and fennel (*Foeniculum vulgare*). Sometimes known to visit sunflowers (*Helianthus* sp.), which provide both nectar and pollen.

Interesting facts: This is the most common lady beetle species in North America and a much-loved predator of aphids and other soft-bodied insects, but it will visit flowers when prey is scarce. This lady beetle shows mass aggregation behavior and is still collected in the wild to provide biocontrol for farmers and gardeners.

Family Curculionidae

Long-nosed Beetles

Beetles in the family Curculionidae are commonly called "true weevils," "snout weevils," or "long-nosed beetles" due to their long rostrum on the front of their head. This nose-like structure is often slender and often curved downward, though this is not representative of all beetles in this family. Their bodies are also typically rounded or oval in shape. Most beetles in this family feed on plants as both larvae and adults, often being garden pests, although some act as pollinators.

CALEB CAMILLERI

BROAD-NOSED WEEVIL
Orimodema protracta

Size: 9.5 mm

Description: A broad-nosed weevil with a long dark body that has a mottled appearance from scattering of pale scales.

Habitat: Herbaceous meadows, shrubland prairies, desert sagebrush

Range: Southwestern United States and Colorado

Active season: Mid- to late summer

Conservation status: None

Plant interactions: Adults are attracted to flowers like curlycup gumweed (*Grindelia squarrosa*). Adults eat flowers, incidentally transporting pollen.

Interesting facts: There is only one species reported in the *Orimodema* genus.

BOB KRUGMIRE

THISTLE HEAD WEEVIL
Rhinocyllus conicus

Size: 5–6 mm

Description: Oval-shaped beetle with mottled black and tan elytra and a short snout.

Habitat: Pastures, rangelands, croplands, along highways

Range: Native to the Mediterranean Basin to central Europe; now widespread in North America except the southeastern United States

Active season: Late spring to late summer

Conservation status: None

Plant interactions: This weevil feeds on thistles. Females lay their eggs on thistle flower heads or buds. Adults and larvae also eat the seeds and buds of native thistles.

Interesting facts: *R. conicus* was introduced from Eurasia as a biocontrol against noxious thistles but is now discouraged due to its herbivory on native thistles.

Family Elateridae

Click Beetles

Beetles in the family Elateridae are called "click beetles" due to their behavior of creating a loud clicking sound when startled. The clicking sound is made by a spinelike growth, which can be quickly moved into a notch by the beetle to make a surprising sound. This clicking also flings the beetle into the air; this movement and sound allow the beetle to scare predators and evade predation. Species in this family tend to be shaped like elongated ovals and may be either colorful or very plain brown and black.

LISA HILL

WESTERN EYED CLICK BEETLE

Alaus melanops

Size: 20–35 mm

Description: Gray beetle with a long body; two distinct eyespots (black ovals with thin white outline) on pronotum. Pronotum also has pointed extensions at the posterior corners, which fit around the elytra.

Habitat: Coniferous forests

Range: Western United States from the Rocky Mountains west to the Pacific Ocean; southern California north through southern British Columbia

Active season: Early to midsummer

Conservation status: None

Plant interactions: Adults feed on a liquid diet of nectar from a variety of flowering plants; larvae bore into dead or dying pine trees and eat other larvae they find there.

Interesting facts: Click beetles have a defense mechanism whereby they can launch themselves up to 6 feet into the air and can flip from their back to their legs this way too.

Similar species: Eastern eyed click beetle (*A. myops*) looks identical but is found only in the eastern and central United States.

Family Melyridae

Soft-winged Flower Beetles

Melyrids have soft bodies that are usually elongated. Many have bright coloration, ranging from reds and yellows to metallic blues and greens. They superficially look like elongated ladybugs. They often predate other flower visitors but may also pollinate as they feed on pollen and move from flower to flower to hunt.

EMIL PETRINIC

FOUR-SPOTTED COLLOPS

Collops quadrimaculatus

Size: 4–6 mm

Description: Small, red, soft-winged flower beetle. Elytra are red with two black spots at the base and two near the thorax. Thorax is red. Male antennae are enlarged at the base. Base of antennae of both females and males is orange-yellow. Adults are sometime referred to as "red cross beetles" because of the red cross the spots create on the elytra.

Habitat: Agriculture areas or croplands

Range: Widespread throughout the United States, less so in the northern states and Great Plains; also throughout Central America

Active season: Summer

Conservation status: None

Plant interactions: Adults graze on pollen and nectar from many plant species when soft-bodied insects are unavailable.

Interesting facts: Adults are predatory on soft-bodied insects such as aphids, mites, and whiteflies. *Collops* beetles are an important biological control for whiteflies in cotton fields.

TWO-SPOTTED MELYRID

Collops bipunctatus

Size: 5–8 mm

Description: Thorax is dull red with two black dots. Elytra are blue-black and hairy and do not quite cover the tip of the abdomen. The head is the same color as the elytra, with yellow-orange mouthparts. Antennae are yellow at base and dull red at tips. Males have enlarged third segment of their antennae.

Habitat: Agricultural areas or croplands

Range: Western United states, from Kansas to the west coast; also southwestern Canada

Active season: Summer

Conservation status: None

HEIDE KEEBLE

Plant interactions: Adults graze on pollen and nectar from many plants when soft-bodied insects are unavailable.

Interesting facts: Adults are predatory on soft-bodied insects. *C. bipunctatus* preys upon crop pests such as the Colorado potato beetle and pea aphids.

Similar species: *C. grandis* has a redder thorax and lacks the two black dots. Also, *C. grandis* has bright red femurs compared to the dull blue-black femurs on *C. bipunctatus*.

NO COMMON NAME

Cradytes serricollis

Size: 4–6 mm

Description: Oval-shaped body is brown and hairy, with the elytra of male beetles lighter brown than head and thorax. Females are entirely dark brown.

Habitat: Desert canyons and shrubland

Range: Southwestern United States

Active season: Early to mid-fall

Conservation status: None

JAMES BAILEY

Plant interactions: Commonly feeds on pollen and nectar from fall-blooming members of the sunflower family (Asteraceae) such as snakeweed (*Gutierrezia* spp.).

Interesting fact: These beetles are sexually dimorphic, which is typically associated with mate selection or territorial behavior in beetles.

LISA HILL

SCARLET MALACHITE BEETLE
Malachius aeneus

Size: 5–7 mm

Description: Head, pronotum, and elytra of these beetles are dark metallic green that sometimes shows only in certain light. Elytra have bright red, wide borders. The pronotum has two small patches of red close to the head/"shoulders."

Habitat: Weedy fields, meadows in the prairie, cropland

Range: Northern United States to Colorado and southern Canada

Active season: Mid-spring to midsummer

Conservation status: None

Plant interactions: Adults feed on a variety of herbaceous plants.

Interesting facts: Introduced to the United States in 1852 and now widespread. Known to cause damage to wheat in Canada.

Similar species: *Anthocomus rufus* is more of a red-orange color, with more red color on the pronotum than *M. aeneus*

Family Meloidae

Blister Beetles

Beetles in the family Meloidae are called "blister beetles" because of the caustic spray, composed of cantharidin, they release when threatened. The larvae of many species parasitize bees, while adults feed on flowers and leaves. Species in this family come in various shapes and sizes, though typically they are elongated or rounded, and some species have noticeably short elytra. Some species have beautiful, colorful markings or are vibrantly metallic.

STEVEN G. MLODINOW

BLISTER BEETLE

Epicauta aspera

Size: 9–13 mm

Description: Narrow but round and soft-bodied beetle; body ash gray and pubescent, with black spots on underside of abdomen; long antennae.

Habitat: Foothills in shrubland and savanna, shortgrass and mixed-grass prairie, desert sagebrush

Range: Southwestern states, extending north to Colorado

Active season: Early spring to midsummer

Conservation status: None

Plant interactions: These beetles are pollen feeders on late-blooming members of the sunflower family, including fleabane (*Erigeron* spp.), smooth white aster (*Symphyotrichum porteri*) and snakeweed (*Gutierrezia* spp.).

Interesting facts: Larvae eat grasshopper eggs; larvae may even be seen running over the ground looking for grasshopper eggs to eat.

RUST-COLORED BEETLE

Epicauta ferruginea

Size: 6–9 mm

Description: A small beetle with an elongated body and rust-colored hairs; dark feet and hairy legs. Eyes have a bulging appearance.

Habitat: Grassy fields, mountain and foothill meadows, open areas

Range: Mostly the central United States; also northern Mexico and south-central Canada. Not found on the east or west coast.

Active season: Midsummer to early fall

Conservation status: None

Plant interactions: This beetle eats the pollen of members of the sunflower family (Asteraceae), such as annual sunflower (*Helianthus annuus*) and curlycup gumweed (*Grindelia squarrosa*).

Interesting facts: *Ferruginea* means "rusty" in Latin, highlighting this beetle's coloration.

HEIDE KEEBLE

DARK BLISTER BEETLE

Epicauta murina

Size: 9–15 mm

Description: Soft-bodied beetle with an elongated body and a rounded abdomen. Its body is dark with sparse gray hairs, resulting in an overall dark gray color.

Habitat: Herbaceous meadows, open prairies

Range: Northeast North America

Active season: Late spring to early summer

PAUL TAVARES

Conservation status: None

Plant interactions: Adults can be a pest on potatoes and alfalfa crops, but they also forage on plants such as spring parsley (*Cymopterus* spp.) and silvery lupine (*Lupinus argenteus*).

Interesting facts: *E. murina* is a mostly northeastern species but extends across the Great Plains.

Similar species: *E. fabricii* has denser hairs, and in females the second and third antennal segments are equal in length. *E. murina* females have a much longer second antennal segment.

BLACK BLISTER BEETLE

Epicauta pensylvanica

Size: 10–15 mm

Description: Soft-bodied, dull black beetle; an elongated and slender body, with few if any hairs.

Habitat: Foothills meadows and shrublands, deciduous forest edge and openings, shortgrass and mixed-grass prairies, riparian edges, agricultural croplands; urban and suburban landscapes, including roadsides, ditches, and gardens.

Range: Western North America

Active season: Mid- to late summer

Conservation status: None

BOB KRUGMIRE

Plant interactions: Adults feed on pollen of sunflowers and their relatives, such as goldenrod (*Solidago* spp.) and rabbitbrush (*Ericameria* spp.); also recorded on sugar beets and alfalfa.

Interesting facts: Still spelled "pensylvanicus" in some sources; aka black aster bug. This species is the most encountered blister beetle in United States, known to form aggregations on hosts. As a defense against predation, they can secrete an irritating chemical that can cause redness or blisters on human skin. Larvae eat grasshopper eggs, needing to consume around twenty-five eggs to fully develop.

SEGMENTED BLISTER BEETLE

Epicauta segmenta

Size: 15–25 mm

Description: Beetle with long, slender body and slightly rounded abdomen. Body, legs, and antennae are black. Abdominal segments are divided by thin white bands.

Habitat: Open, grassy areas, such as prairies

Range: Central United States

Active season: Midsummer to early fall

Conservation status: None

RICH READING

Plant interactions: Adults feed on pollen of sunflowers and their relatives (*Asteraceae*).

Interesting facts: Bold markings and bright colors warn potential predators—this beetle can secrete a noxious chemical if bothered.

Similar species: Similar to black blister beetles such as *E. pensylvanica*, but the white bands on the abdomen are a distinguishing feature.

R. J. BALTIERRA

YAN CHUN SU

STUART'S BLISTER BEETLE

Epicauta stuarti

Size: 8–13 mm

Description: Beetle with long, slender body and slightly rounded abdomen. The body, legs, and antennae are black, covered with golden hairs. Bare areas on elytra look like four large black spots. Abdomen is black and orange striped.

Habitat: Herbaceous and grassy areas, such as meadows and prairies

Range: Great Plains and southwestern United States

Active season: Midsummer to mid-fall

Conservation status: None

Plant interactions: Adults feed on pollen of sunflowers and their relatives, such as golden crownbeard (*Verbesena encelioides*) and broom snakeweed (*Gutierrezia* spp.).

Interesting facts: Individuals of this species often gather on plants but don't necessarily feed on them.

Similar species: Similar to soldier beetles in shape and color, but *E. stuarti* has hairy instead of smooth elytra.

NUTALL'S BLISTER BEETLE

Lytta nuttalli

Size: 7–21 mm

Description: Larger than many of the other blister beetles; elongated body with slightly swollen abdomen and elytra that meet in the middle but do not reach to the end. Purple, black, and green iridescence on body and wings.

Habitat: Mixed-grass prairies, desert sagebrush

Range: In western North America, with southern populations limited to higher elevations

Active season: Midsummer to early fall

Conservation status: None

Plant interactions: Feeds on flowers and foliage of the pea family (Fabaceae), such as silky locoweed (*Oxytropis sericea*), golden banner (*Thermopsis* spp.), and silvery lupine (*Lupinus argenteus*).

Interesting facts: Adults may congregate on food plants. *Lytta* larvae are parasitoids on bee larvae and bee provisions.

Similar species: *L. viridiana* is greener than the purplish *L. nuttalli*.

GREEN BLISTER BEETLE

Lytta viridana

RON WOLF

Size: 10–18 mm

Description: Soft-bodied beetle with elongated and smooth, shiny green body.

Habitat: Mountains and foothills

Range: Southwestern United States

Active season: Late spring to late summer

Conservation status: None

Plant interactions: Feeds on flowers and foliage of the pea family (Fabaceae); also on Rocky Mountain iris (*Iris missouriensis*).

Interesting facts: This beetle species may be found on the same plants as *L. nuttalli*, a species that looks very similar.

Similar species: *L. nuttalli* is more purple than the green *L. viridiana. L. stygica* has broader elytra than *L. viridiana.*

BLACK AND RED BLISTER BEETLE

Megetra cancellata

CONOR FLYNN

Size: 10–15 mm

Description: Soft-bodied black beetle with red netlike markings on sutures and front edges of reduced elytra. A large "humpbacked" rounded abdomen has pointed end.

Habitat: Deserts

Range: Arizona, New Mexico, and Texas; south to Mexico

Active season: Unknown

Conservation status: None

Plant interactions: Feeds on nectar and juices from fruit of native plants, such as succulents.

Interesting facts: Like other members of the family, this brightly colored species advertises its ability to secrete an irritating chemical, cantharidin, from its body when disturbed, causing irritation and blisters. The Navajo term for this insect translates to "water carrier"; others have called this the "football beetle."

BLACK MELOE

Meloe niger

CRAIG ODEGARD

Size: 8–24 mm

Description: Soft-bodied, bluish-black beetle with enlarged ovate abdomen and reduced elytra. Females are larger than males.

Habitat: Foothill and prairie grasslands

Range: Widespread throughout Canada and into the north-central United States (Montana and Wyoming)

Active season: Mid- to late spring

Conservation status: None

Plant interactions: Feed on a variety of grasses and flowering plants.

Interesting facts: Larvae wait on flowers and hitch rides with solitary bees back to their nests. The beetle larvae eat the same food as bee larvae, pupating and emerging the following spring.

BLISTER BEETLE

Nemognatha spp.

LISA HILL

Size: 6–10 mm

Description: Beetles with reddish head; long, thin antenna; and black legs. Elytra can be black or reddish with black sutures.

Habitat: Foothills

Range: Rocky Mountains and southwestern United States

Active season: Late spring to late summer

Conservation status: None

Plant interactions: Adults are nectar feeders on yarrow and other members of the sunflower family (Asteraceae), as well as wild geranium (*Geranium maculatum*).

Interesting facts: Adults slurp nectar through specialized mouthparts called a galeae tube. Female beetles lay eggs on flowers. The larvae then attach themselves to visiting bees and hitch a ride to nests, where they will feed on bee larvae and larval foods.

YELLOW-CRESCENT BLISTER BEETLE

Pyrota insulata

ABIGAIL RECTOR

Size: 10–20 mm

Description: The appearance of this beetle differs across its geographic range. In the south the beetles have black elytra with narrow yellow margins on the outer edges as well as down the center of the elytra; also an apical yellow spot at the base of both elytra. Beetles in the north are more yellow, with two spots of black on the top of the elytra close to the pronotum. Thorax is smaller than the head.

Habitat: Great Plains prairies and grassland

Range: Southwestern-central United States into northern Mexico

Active season: Late winter to early summer

Conservation status: None

Plant interactions: Adults feed on nectar from honey mesquite (*Prosopis glandulosa*).

Interesting facts: If the beetle is agitated or squeezed, it will produce cantharidin, an irritant that causes blisters on human skin. Attracted to light, they may congregate in large numbers near streetlights or other light sources.

DESERT BEETLE

Pyrota bilineata

JAMES BAILEY

Size: 7–9 mm

Description: A beetle with an orange head and pronotum and orange femurs. The pronotum has 2 black spots. Elytra are light yellow with 4 black lines (2 on each elytron) that run the length of the abdomen.

Habitat: Plains, prairies, sandy areas

Range: Southwestern United States

Active season: Late summer to early fall

Conservation status: None

Plant interactions: A generalist that feeds on nectar from a variety of flowering plants.

Interesting facts: Male desert beetles perform elaborate mating rituals to show their fitness to females.

ANDREW MEEDS

IRON CROSS BLISTER BEETLE

Tegrodera aloga

Size: 14–26 mm

Description: Large, striking red beetle with large textured yellow spots on black elytra; elytra markings resemble a black cross.

Habitat: Deserts

Range: Arizona into Mexico

Active season: Mid-spring to early summer

Conservation status: None

Plant interactions: Feeds on spring blossoms, including sand bells (*Nama hispida*) and woollystars (*Eriastrum* sp.), as well as other herbaceous plants.

Interesting facts: Little is known about the larval stage of this insect, but scientists have evidence to suggest that larvae are parasitic on grasshoppers and bees.

Family Scarabaeidae

Scarab Beetles

Many of the most well-known beetles in the world are in the family Scarabaeidae, including rhinoceros beetles, dung beetles, Hercules beetles, Goliath beetles, and June beetles. Beetles in this family are stout bodied and rounded, some being very large. They have club-shaped antennae with fingerlike projections. Many are scavengers that feed on dead animals, plants, and dung; others are known to visit flowers.

AMY YARGER

FLOWER BUMBLE BEETLE
Euphoria inda

Size: 12–17 mm

Description: Large, broad, oval beetle; tan in color, with bristly hairs on the ventral sides.

Habitat: Urban and suburban gardens, disturbed sites, roadsides

Range: Western North America

Active season: Midsummer to early fall

Conservation status: None

Plant interactions: These beetles are pollen eaters on thistles and other members of the sunflower family (Asteraceae). These beetles are also known to eat leaves and fruit or drink sap.

Interesting facts: This bumble bee mimic makes a buzzing sound as it awkwardly flies short distances. Females lay eggs on decaying plant matter.

JAMES GILL

KERN'S FLOWER BEETLE

Euphoria kernii

Size: 8–12 mm

Description: Large, broad, oval beetles. Body coloration is highly variable, ranging from all black to all yellow-orange. Usually the body is pale cream to orange, with irregularly shaped black markings and a large black area on the pronotum. May have blonde hairs on the ventral side.

Habitat: Habitat generalists; often found in fields, meadows, and plains

Range: New Mexico, Colorado, Texas, and Mexico in the west

Active season: Late spring to midsummer

Conservation status: None

Plant interactions: This species feeds on a variety of plants. They have been particularly observed on prickly poppies (*Argemone* spp.), prickly pear cacti (*Opuntia* spp.), thistle (*Cirsium* spp.), yucca (*Yucca* spp.), mesquite (*Prosopis* spp.), winecups (*Callirhoe involucrata*), wheat (*Triticum* spp.), and roses (*Rosa* spp.).

Interesting facts: Often found eating in large congregations on flower plants. (The larvae of this beetle are often found in nests of burrowing rodents such as pocket gophers or pack rats.)

Family Andrenidae

Mining Bees

The Andrenidae family contains small to medium-sized bees that are solitary ground nesters. They tend to be very specialized in the plants they forage on, some only foraging on a single plant species. They can be identified by the presence of two subantennal sutures on the face (best observed under magnification). Many species also have hairy grooves by the inner margins of the eyes, though this is not a characteristic solely of andrenids.

ANDREW NEWMARK

CHERRY LEAF MINER BEE
Andrena cerasifolii

Size: 8–13 mm

Description: A dark blue-black metallic bee with white hairs covering the abdomen and thorax. Clear wings; long antennae.

Habitat: Open habitats such as meadows and forest edges

Range: Central and North America—Utah, New Mexico, Arizona, Oregon, California, and British Columbia

Active season: Late winter to summer

Conservation status: None

Plant interactions: This bee is known for pollinating cherry plum trees (*Prunus cerasifera*); hence its other common name, "cherry plum miner bee."

Interesting facts: This species nests in the ground.

Similar species: The cherry leaf miner bee closely resembles the blue orchard bee (*Osmia lignaria*); however, the cherry leaf miner bee has a longer, thinner abdomen and is less hairy compared to the blue orchard bee.

KRIS ETHINGTON

MILWAUKEE MINING BEE

Andrena milwaukeensis

Size: 8–11 mm

Description: This small bee varies in appearance depending on location. In general, rust-orange hairs cover the thorax and part of the abdomen. Females' hind legs have long, black shaggy hairs, where they collect pollen.

Habitat: Woodlands

Range: Western North America

Active season: Early spring to summer

Conservation status: None

Plant interactions: Pollinates a wide variety of crops, including blueberries, cranberries, apricots, pears, currants, and apples. Wild food sources include dogwood (*Cornus* spp.), viburnum (*Viburnum* spp.), chokecherry (*Prunus virginiana*), claytonia, snowberry (*Symphoricarpos occidentalis*), bush honeysuckle (*Lonicera tatarica*), native bittersweet (*Celastrus scandens*), spirea, squill (*Scilla* spp.), buffaloberry (*Shepherdia argentea*), and violets (*Viola* spp.).

Interesting facts: Discovered in 1903 by entomologist Sigmund Graenicher, who named it for his hometown, Milwaukee.

Similar species: *A. milwaukeensis* is distinguished from similar bees by the shaggy black hairs on the hind legs. Similar species include rufous-backed cellophane bee (*Colletes thoracicus*), which has short hairs on its hind legs; Clark's mining bee *(A. clarkella)*, which has orange hairs on its hind legs; and Dunning's miner *(A. dunningi)*, which has blond hairs on its hind legs.

C. puellea

CALLIOPSIS BEES

Calliopsis spp.

Size: 5–9 mm

Description: Small bees with broad heads. The abdomen has yellow and black stripes; legs and wings are long. Male *Calliopsis* species have broad yellow stripes on their head; females have narrow yellow stripes.

Habitat: Habitat generalists, favoring open and sunny areas; nest in disturbed soil

Range: North, Central, and South America from Canada to Chile

Active season: Late spring to fall

Conservation status: None

Plant interactions: Most species in this genus are oligolectic or monolectic, meaning they are extreme specialists: They collect pollen from a few related species or just one species. There are four distinctive subgenera associated with four plant families: the pea family (Fabaceae), the spurge family (Euphorbiaceae), the sunflower family (Asteraceae), and the verbena family (Verbenaceae).

Interesting facts: Male-male contests involve a rapid spiraling-upward flight, often followed by physical aggression after the pair tumbles to the ground. Females build solitary nests in dense soil; nests are often located in dense aggregations.

Similar species: Similar to nomad bees (genus *Nomada*), fairy bees (genus *Perdita*), and Crabronid wasps (family Crabronidae). Also similar to yellow-masked bees (genus *Hylaeus*) but with broader heads and generally hairier.

JAMES BAILEY

M. latior

GOBLIN BEES

Macrotera spp.

Size: 2–16 mm

Description: Very small bees with wide faces and broad heads (especially males). Abdomens are usually pointed at the end. Males have different size classes, and males and females of the same species may have different coloration of the abdomen and thorax. Body is frequently all black or a black thorax with a red abdomen. Some species, like *M. mellea*, are mostly yellow.

Habitat: Arid grasslands and deserts

Range: Mexico and the southwestern United States—California, Nevada, Utah, Colorado, Arizona, New Mexico, Texas, and Oklahoma

Active season: Spring to fall

Conservation status: None

Plant interactions: Most species are extreme specialists, meaning they will only collect pollen from a few closely related species of plants, particularly globe mallows (*Sphaeralcea* spp.) and cacti (family Cactaceae). Many species are found on prickly pear cacti (*Opuntia* spp.).

Interesting facts: Goblin bees are ground nesters. Some species, like *M. portalis*, have been found to share communal nests. Two to twenty-nine females will share the nest tunnels burrowed into the ground, but each female will construct and provision only her own brood cells with pollen balls.

Similar species: Similar bees such as nomad (genus *Nomada*) and fairy (genus *Perdita*) bees are best distinguished by facial and wing characteristics not easily seen with the naked eye. In general, nomad bees are smaller; are slender; are wasp-like with red, black, and yellow colors; and lack pollen-carrying scopa. Fairy bees are smaller, often brightly colored, with sparse scopal hairs.

BRIAN WRIGHT

P. interrupta

FAIRY BEES

Perdita spp.

Size: < 2–10 mm

Description: Small, brightly colored bees; often white or yellow with metallic markings. Some are mostly black, but usually have yellow markings.

Habitat: Deserts

Range: North and Central America, Canada to Costa Rica

Active season: Spring to fall

Conservation status: None

Plant interactions: Most species in this genus are extreme specialists on plants such as spurges (Euphorbiaceae) and poppies (Papaveraceae).

Interesting facts: Perdita is one of the most speciose bee genera, with many undescribed species. The smallest known species of bee in the world, *P. minima*, is in this genus.

Similar species: Similar bees such as nomad (genus *Nomada*) and goblin (genus *Macrotera*) bees are best distinguished by facial and wing characteristics not easily seen with the naked eye. In general, nomad bees are slender and wasp-like with red, black, and yellow colors, and lack pollen-carrying scopa. Goblin bees are larger, black or reddish in color, with a pointed abdomen.

Family Apidae

Honey Bees, Bumble Bees, Digger Bees, Carpenter Bees, etc.

The family Apidae contains some of the most well-known bees, including honey bees, bumble bees, and carpenter bees. Many are solitary nesters, laying their brood in plant stems or in tunnels underground; though some, such as honey and bumble bees, live together in social nests. Bees in this family come in a wide variety of sizes and colors. They can generally be identified by the presence of three submarginal cells on the forewing, a long tongue, a body covered in hairs, and the presence of a pollen-carrying segment on their hind leg; although these characteristics are difficult to identify with the naked eye.

JORDAN SATLER

BUMBLE BEE MIMIC DIGGER BEE
Anthophora bomboides

Size: 12–15 mm

Description: A medium-sized, hairy bee. Coloration varies by location and often mimics local bumble bee species. Its body is black with bands of white, yellow, or orangish hairs that mimic the patterning of bumble bees. Males have yellow markings on the face. They carry pollen using long black or orange hairs on the hind legs.

Habitat: Nest in areas of sandy banks, coastal bluffs, and other areas of exposed soil

Range: North America

Active season: Late spring to summer

Conservation status: None

Plant interactions: Gathers pollen and nectar from a wide variety of flowering plant species.

Interesting facts: This species nests in large aggregations in clay, so they are often found near rivers.

Similar species: These bees superficially resemble many bumble bee species. Males can be separated from bumble bees by their broad, yellow mask on the face. Females can be distinguished by their flight pattern, antennae originating higher up on the head, and generally thinner body shape and protruding face compared to bumble bees.

NORMA MCGRAW

WESTERN HONEY BEE
Apis mellifera

Size: 12 mm

Description: Medium sized, hairy bees. The abdomen has iconic bands of dark black-brown and yellow-orange hairs. These bees store pollen in "pollen baskets" called the corbicula on their hind legs. Males (drones) have large, stout bodies and large eyes. Workers (females) are smaller than males. The queen (female) has a long, shiny abdomen that distinguishes her from the worker bees.

Habitat: Habitat generalists

Range: Worldwide except Antarctica

Active season: Spring to fall

Conservation status: None

Plant interactions: The western honey bee is a generalist pollinator of a wide variety of crops and native and non-native plants. Forager bees collect pollen from flower anthers and transfer the pollen back to the hive using a "pollen basket" on their hind legs. The worker bees mix the pollen with saliva and honey and use it to feed the larvae. Foragers also collect nectar from flowers in a specialized honey stomach and fly it back to the hive, where workers mix the nectar with enzymes and fan it using their wings to reduce the moisture content to below 18 percent, ultimately turning the nectar into honey, which can feed the whole colony through winter or drought seasons when flowers are not in bloom.

Interesting facts: Honey bee colony activities are organized by complex communications through pheromones and dance. They are a highly social species that exhibit cooperative brood care, overlapping generations of adults within the colony, and a division of labor between reproductive and nonreproductive adults. *A. mellifera* is one of eight surviving species of honey bees in the world and one of only two honey bee species (*A. mellifera* and *A. cerana*) that are kept as domesticated species by humans. *A. mellifera* has a variety of subspecies, such as the Italian honey bee (*A. mellifera ligustica*) and the Cape honey bee (*A. mellifera capensis*), and has been bred into many hybrid types to suit various needs for pest and disease control, weather hardiness, and temperament.

Similar species: Similar bees such as nomad (*Nomada*) and goblin (*Macrotera*) bees are best distinguished by facial and wing characteristics not easily seen with the naked eye. In general, nomad bees are slender and wasp-like with red, black, and yellow colors and lack pollen-carrying scopa. Goblin bees are larger, black or reddish in color, with a pointed abdomen.

BRIAN WRIGHT

CROTCH'S BUMBLE BEE
Bombus crotchii

Size: 14–18 mm

Description: Large, short- or medium-tongued, social bumble bee. Hair short and even. Face and head black except on top in the back, where it is yellow. Thorax yellow at the front, maybe on the sides, otherwise black. Tergum 1 (T1) is black; T2 mostly yellow with a black notch, small to large, in the middle toward the front. T3–T6 mostly reddish or reddish orange. Alternatively, T3–T6 may be all or mostly black. Nests underground or at ground level.

Habitat: Montane, foothills, and prairie open grassland and scrub

Range: Moderately common in southern California, where it ranges from the coast to the Central Valley, including desert areas but excluding the mountains. Less common in western Nevada.

Active season: Spring to fall

Conservation status: Endangered

Plant interactions: Nectar and pollen feeder; buzz pollinator. Food plants include snapdragon (*Antirrhinum* spp.), milkweed (*Asclepias* spp.), dusty maiden (*Chaenactis* sp.), *Clarkia*, bush poppy (*Dendromecon* sp.), California poppy (*Eschscholzia* sp.), wild buckwheat (*Eriogonum* spp.), lupines (*Lupinus* spp.), alfalfa (*Medicago sativa*), *Phacelia*, and *Salvia*.

Interesting facts: Once abundant in California's Central Valley, known for its agriculture, it is now scarce.

Similar species: Similar to *B. occidentalis* but distinguished by its reddish-orange tail tip.

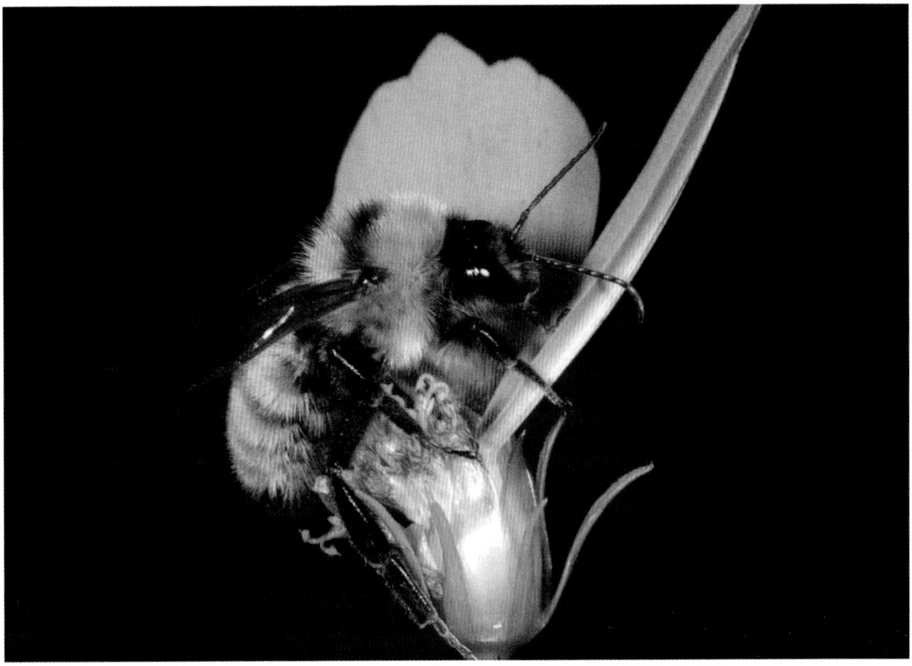

BOB KRUGMIRE

GOLDEN NORTHERN BUMBLE BEE

Bombus fervidus

Size: 14–20 mm

Description: Medium-sized, social bumble bee. Widespread and common in its range. Emerges relatively late in the season. Face and head mostly black, thorax yellow with black band across body between wings, abdomen mostly yellow, wings dark and smoky colored; T1–T4 mostly yellow, T5 black. Males perch or hover outside nest entrances in search of queens. Considered synonymous with California bumble bee (*B. californicus*). Previously the lighter coloration in the eastern United States was deemed *B. fervidus* and the darker in the west identified separately as *B. californicus*. Some still argue for this distinction. Nests established spring through summer, usually at ground surface but sometimes underground, within 50 meters of food source. Forages in heat of day.

Habitat: Forest openings, meadows, and scrubland from prairie to montane; urban agricultural areas; roadsides

Range: Throughout western North America except for west of the Sierra-Cascade Crest

Active season: Summer to fall

Conservation status: Vulnerable

Plant interactions: Nectar and pollen feeder on a wide range of plants including those in sunflower (Asteraceae), carrot (Apiaceae), mint (Lamiaceae), rose (Rosaceae), and pea (Fabaceae) families and more. Long-tongued, generalist. Performs buzz pollination when required, such as tomatoes, peppers, blueberries, and other plants in the nightshade family (Solanaceae).

Interesting facts: Perform dances to communicate the location of food or possible danger. Make small amounts of honey, used to feed the queen and young. Parasitized by *B. insularis* and *B. suckleyi*. Known to sometimes act more aggressively than other bumble bees.

Similar species: *B. pensylvanicus* is yellow at front of thorax, black between wings, mostly black at back of thorax, T1–T3 yellow. B. nevadensis thorax is mostly to all yellow, black band between wings strongly intermixed with yellow reducing band to black dot, if it exists at all. T1 usually yellow, T2–T3 yellow.

JESSICA GOLDSTROHM

BROWN-BELTED BUMBLE BEE

Bombus griseocollis

Size: 10–23 mm

Description: Medium-sized body, medium-long tongue; social bumble bee. Widespread and abundant in its range. Hair short and even. Face and top of head are predominantly black, sometimes with sparse yellow hairs. Thorax yellow with small to medium black spot between the wings, entirely yellow on the sides. T1 yellow; T2 yellow with black edges for queen, black with some brown for workers; T3–T5 black; palest color patterns occur in the west.

Habitat: Habitat generalist from plains to montane zones, including developed landscapes. Typically nests at ground surface, sometimes underground.

Range: Throughout western North America, except for large parts of southern California, Nevada, Arizona, New Mexico and Texas

Active season: Spring to fall

Conservation status: Least concern

Plant interactions: Nectar and pollen feeder; buzz pollinator, generalist. Food plants include milkweed (*Asclepias* spp.), coneflowers (*Echinacea* spp.), bee balm (*Monarda* spp.), goldenrod (*Solidago* spp.), clover (*Trifolium* spp.), *Verbena*, alfalfa (*Medicago sativa*), thistle (*Cirsium* spp.), and sunflower (*Helianthus* spp.).

Interesting facts: Males known to prefer high perches and have been found at the top of the Empire State Building in New York.

Similar species: Resembles *B. nevadensis* but has the distinct black spot on the thorax between the wings and yellow T3.

CLIFF DEJONG

HUNT'S BUMBLE BEE

Bombus huntii

Size: 9–20 mm

Description: Medium-sized, social bumble bee. Face and head mostly yellow with sparse black hairs; thorax yellow on top and sides with black between the wings; T1 yellow, T2–T3 orange, T4 yellow, and T5 black. Hair length medium and even.

Habitat: Habitat generalist from deserts and grasslands up to forest openings in the foothill and montane zones; rarely above tree line. Nests mostly underground.

Range: Throughout western North America

Active season: Spring to fall

Conservation status: Least concern; population considered stable

Plant interactions: Nectar and pollen feeder on a wide range of plants, including those in sunflower (Asteraceae), carrot (Apiaceae), mint (Lamiaceae), rose (Rosaceae), and pea (Fabaceae) families and more. Medium-long tongued, generalist. Performs buzz pollination when required, such as tomatoes, peppers, blueberries, and other plants in the nightshade family (Solanaceae).

Interesting facts: Males patrol circuits in search of mates.

Similar species: Similar to *B. sylvicola* and *B. melanopygus*. Unlike *B. sylvicola*, found at lower elevations and T5 is all black. Unlike *B. melanopygus*, black band between wings on thorax is distinct and T5 is all black.

ANDREA CARPIO

BLACK-TAILED BUMBLE BEE

Bombus melanopygus

Size: 10–19 mm

Description: Small, medium-long-tongued, social bumble bee. Hair short and even. Face and head yellow. Thorax yellow in the front with black hairs sparsely to densely intermixed, forward edge of black band indistinct, back of thorax yellow sometimes with black along the midline. T1 yellow, T2–T3 red, sometimes with black hairs in the middle and/or to back edge; T4–T5 black often with some yellow. If T2–T3 mostly black instead of red, T4–T5 mostly yellow, sometimes with small amount of black at center of midline and black at the back.

Habitat: Habitat generalist from rocky slopes and tundra in the alpine zone down to grasslands on the plains and deserts, as well as developed landscapes in cities and farms.

Range: Common throughout western North America

Active season: Late winter to fall

Conservation status: Least concern; population stable

Plant interactions: Nectar and pollen feeder on a wide range of plants, including those in the heath (Ericaceae), rose (Rosaceae), pea (Fabaceae), and aster (Asteraceae) families and more. Medium-long-tongued, generalist. Performs buzz pollination when required, such as tomatoes, peppers, blueberries, and other plants in the nightshade family (Solanaceae).

Interesting facts: This bumble bee, like most, nests underground or aboveground in man-made structures. One of the earliest bumble bees to emerge and start nesting.

Similar species: Similar to *B. sylvicola* and *B. huntii.* Distinguished from both because the lines between the yellow portions of the thorax and the black band between the wings is not clearly defined. Appears at higher elevations than *B. huntii.*

CINDY NEWLANDER

BLACK AND GOLD BUMBLE BEE

Bombus nevadensis

Size: 15–25 mm

Description: Large-bodied, long-tongued, social bee. Head and face black with very few yellow hairs. Thorax predominantly yellow, with yellow strongly intermixed in the black spot or band between the wings, if it exists. Sides of thorax mostly black. T1 usually yellow, especially on sides, maybe some black at center; T2–T3 yellow, T4–T5 black. While color patterns vary somewhat within the species, they are more consistent than body size, which can vary greatly.

Habitat: Open grassy prairies and meadows from the plains to the foothills

Range: Moderately common in its range, especially at higher elevations throughout western North America

Active season: Spring to fall

Conservation status: Least concern; population stable

Plant interactions: Nectar and pollen feeder on a wide range of plants, including those in the sunflower (Asteraceae), mint (Lamiaceae), pea (Fabaceae), rose (Rosaceae), and plantain (Plantaginaceae) families and more. Long-tongued, generalist. Performs buzz pollination when required, such as tomatoes, peppers, blueberries, and other plants in the nightshade family (Solanaceae).

Interesting facts: Used somewhat commercially to pollinate highbush blueberry (*Vaccinium corymbosum*) in southern British Columbia. Nests mostly underground, infrequently aboveground. Late-emerging species. Males perch and chase moving objects searching for mates.

Similar species: Similar to *B. griseocollis*, *B. pensylvanicus*, and *B. fervidus*. Unlike *nevadensis*, *griseocollis* has brown on T2 or yellow with black edges. T3 is black.

WESTERN BUMBLE BEE

Bombus occidentalis

Size: 9–21 mm

Description: Medium-sized, short-tongued, social bee. Hair short to medium and even. Typically nests underground. Colonies relatively larger than other species. Many color variations. First variant is found from northern California north to British Columbia and east to Montana. Face and head mostly black with some yellow hairs mixed in. Thorax yellow except for a central black spot or band where the wings attach. T1 black, T2–T3 black or yellow, T4 often white, T5 usually white; T6 may appear black in spite of the sparse white hairs. Another variant from the central California coast has yellow hairs on the sides of T2, all of T3, and reddish-brown hair on T5. A third variant, in the Rocky Mountains, has yellow behind the wings on the thorax, yellow on posterior of T2, and yellow on all of T3.

Habitat: Shrublands, savannas, and forest openings in the montane and foothills zones; also observed in developed landscapes in urban areas

Range: Distributed throughout western North America but usually rare

Active season: Early spring to late fall

Conservation status: Vulnerable

Plant interactions: Nectar and pollen feeder; buzz pollinator, generalist. Food plants include a wide range of flowers in the aster (Asteraceae), pea (Fabaceae), mint (Lamiaceae), and rose (Rosaceae) families such as thistle (*Cirsium* spp.), lupines (*Lupinus* spp.), brambles (*Rubus* spp.), *Agastache*, and more.

Interesting facts: Short-tongued bumble bees may rob nectar and pollen from long tubular flowers when they cannot otherwise reach them. Although bumble bee populations are vulnerable to pesticides, climate change and habitat loss, abrupt population declines for *B. occidentalis* in the 1990s are believed to have been caused by exposure to disease during attempts to commercialize the species for agricultural pollination services. May pollinate the fairy slipper orchid (*Calypso bulbosa*).

Similar species: Similar to *B. crotchii* and *B. franklini*. On *B. occidentalis*, unlike *B. crotchii*, T4–T5 are white to somewhat white; unlike *B. franklini*, the thorax is yellow at both the front and the back.

RICH READING

AMERICAN BUMBLE BEE

Bombus pensylvanicus

Size: 13–26 mm

Description: Large-bodied, long-tongued, social. Hair is short and even. Hair on the face and dorsal head always black. Thorax yellow at the front, black on the side and between the wings, black with some yellow mixed in at the back. T1 yellow, at least at midline. T2–T3 yellow, T4 black. Males congregate outside nest entrances in search of mates.

Habitat: Dry, desert-like areas of the western United States

Active season: Spring to fall

Conservation status: Vulnerable

Plant interactions: Nectar and pollen feeder, generalist; buzz pollinator. Feeds on a wide variety of flowers, especially those in the aster (Asteraceae), pea (Fabaceae), and mint (Lamiaceae) families and more. Nests most often at ground surface in long grass, less often underground.

Interesting facts: While this species is vulnerable and populations are documented as declining, this was once one of the most widespread species in the United States; hence its common name. Some argue *B. pensylvanicus* spp. sonorus is a western, distinct subspecies, but the separation is not currently accepted.

Similar species: Similar to *B. fervidus* and *B. nevadensis*. Unlike *B. nevadensis*, on *B. pensylvanicus* the hair on the face and dorsal head is always black, T1 is yellow (at least at the midline), T2–T3 yellow, T4 black. Unlike *B. fervidus*, the *B. pensylvanicus* thorax is yellow at the front, black on the side and between the wings; T1 is mostly yellow, T2–T3 yellow, T4 black.

JESSICA GOLDSTROHM

MOUNTAIN BUMBLE BEE

Bombus sylvicola

Size: 10–17 mm

Description: Small social bee with a medium-long tongue. Emerges later in the season. Hair is long and uneven, causing it to appear larger than it is. Hair on face and dorsal head is black, with yellow patches at base of antennae. Thorax yellow at the front with few black hairs, if any; black band across the body at the wings is sharply defined at its front edge. Thorax also yellow to the back, into which a black notch may extend from the center black band. T1 yellow; T2 reddish orange, sometimes with black notch at center pointing to its tail. T4–T5 mostly yellow, maybe some black toward the middle; T6 black. An alternate form within the species found in the Sierra Nevada range has less to no reddish hair on T2–T3, which instead are black with some yellow; then T4 yellow, T5 black with yellow low on the sides. Males patrol circuits in search of mates.

Habitat: Alpine tundra; boreal-alpine species primarily found at higher elevations. Open grassy areas and mountain meadows, including forest edges and openings. Nests mostly underground, sometimes on the surface.

Range: Uncommon in its range—Alberta, British Columbia, California, Colorado, Idaho, Montana, Nevada, Oregon, Utah, Washington, and Wyoming

Active season: Late spring to mid-fall

Conservation status: Least concern

Plant interactions: Nectar and pollen feeder; buzz pollinator, generalist. Food plants are limited to those growing at higher altitudes, including species of ragwort (*Senecio* spp.), willowherb (*Chamerion* spp.), lupines (*Lupinus* spp.), sandwort (*Arenaria* spp.), and others in the aster (Asteraceae) and pea (Fabaceae) families and more.

Interesting fact: There is genetic evidence for *B. sylvicola* and the northern European/Asian *B. lapponicus* complex being closely related.

Similar species: Similar to *B. melanopygus* and *B. huntii*. *B. sylvicola* overall hair is long and uneven, whereas the others' is short and even; facial hair and head is mostly black, whereas the others' is mostly yellow; the line between the yellow front of thorax and black band between the wings is sharply defined, whereas it is indistinct in the others. Frequents higher elevations than *B. huntii*.

LISA HILL

YELLOW-FACED BUMBLE BEE
Bombus vosnesenskii

Size: 8–21 mm

Description: Social bumble bee with medium-sized body, medium tongue length. Hair length is short to medium and even. Yellow hair on head and face, thorax yellow at the front, black band in the middle between wing bases, black at thorax back. T1–T3 black, T4 yellow with sparse black hairs at midline, T5–T6 black. A distinctive and easily identifiable color pattern. Nests belowground; colonies relatively larger than other species.

Habitat: Habitat generalist from shrublands and forest openings in the montane zone to grasslands in the plains, including agricultural and developed landscapes.

Range: Found in the Pacific states, where it is not only one of the most common bumble bees at lower elevations but may be increasing. Present from the coast eastward to the Sierra-Cascade crest. Uncommon but present in Nevada.

Active season: Midwinter to late fall

Conservation status: Least concern

Plant interactions: Nectar and pollen feeder; buzz pollinator, generalist. Food plants include manzanita (*Arctostaphylos* spp.), thistle (*Cirsium* spp.), wild buckwheat (*Eriogonum* spp.), California poppy (*Eschscholzia*), lupines (*Lupinus* spp.), *Phacelia*, *Clarkia*, and other flowers in the aster (Asteraceae), borage (Boraginaceae), heath (Ericaceae), pea (Fabaceae), and mint (Lamiaceae) families and more.

Interesting facts: Historically, *B. occidentalis* was the most common bumble bee in this range; however, its populations have decreased dramatically since the late 1990s. Evidence supports that *B. vosnesenskii* populations may be both increasing and decreasing depending on the habitat and may, in some cases, be filling the gap left by *B. occidentalis*. *B. vosnesenskii* is used commercially for agricultural pollination services, including greenhouse tomatoes, where disease exposure risk is higher. This can, in turn, negatively impact wild populations when they are exposed to commercial populations that have been released.

Brachymelecta californica

BRACHYMELECTA DIGGER CUCKOO BEES

Brachymelecta spp.

Size: 9–12 mm

Description: The three species in this genus in our region all have characteristic thick, black, antennae that do not get thinner at the ends. No long scopal hairs on the hind legs. *B. larreae* is all black with black wings and bright red hairs on the thorax, similar to a velvet ant. *B. californica* is black bodied with clear wings, fluffy white hairs on the thorax, and distinctive bands of short white hair on the abdomen that do not meet in the middle. *B. interrupta* is black bodied with black wings, fluffy orange hairs on the thorax and face, and bands of short orange hair that do not meet in the middle of the abdomen.

Habitat: Habitat generalists

Range: Throughout western North America

Active season: Spring to fall

Conservation status: None

Plant interactions: Generalist feeder; commonly seen on members of the sunflower family (Asteraceae).

Interesting facts: This genus was formerly classified as *Xeromelecta* until 2021. These bees are kleptoparasites of other digger bees, with females laying their eggs in digger bee nests.

Similar species: The thick antennae and lack of scopal hairs are characteristic of this genus.

DARLENE VARGA

CAESALPINIA OIL-DIGGER

Centris caesalpiniae

Size: 20–22 mm

Description: Females are distinguished by their bright red eyes and red facial plate. Females are black with dense, short yellow hair covering the face, thorax, and top of the abdomen. Female legs have long black hairs. Males are covered in white to yellow hairs with a yellow facial plate and bright yellow eyes. Males and females have black abdomens and may have small bands of white hair.

Habitat: Deserts

Range: Colorado, New Mexico, Arizona, Texas, northern Mexico

Active season: Spring to summer

Conservation status: None

Plant interactions: Members of this genus mainly visit plants of the Barbados cherry family (Malpighiaceae) to collect oil, but also visit others such as those in the plantain (Plantaginaceae), calceolara (Calceolariaceae), and krameria (Krameriaceae) families. They are commonly observed on desert-willow (*Chilopsis* spp.), paloverde (*Parkinsonia* spp.), and other plants, such as sunflowers (*Helianthus* spp.), mallows (Malvaceae), and snoutbean (*Rhynchosia* spp.).

Interesting facts: The females use their first two pairs of legs to collect oil from plants, which they use to line their nests. They transfer the oil to their hind legs. They also collect pollen using their long hind leg hairs.

Similar species: Very similar to the red-legged oil-digger (*Centris rhodopus*); however, the Caesalpinia oil-digger is about 5 mm larger and does not have red legs. The red-legged oil-digger also has a more western distribution.

BRIAN WRIGHT

RED-LEGGED OIL-DIGGER
Centris rhodopus

Size: 12–15 mm

Description: Females are black with bright red eyes, facial plate, and legs. Short, dense yellow to white hairs cover the thorax, face, and top of abdomen. Hind and middle legs are long with long black hairs. Males are black with bright yellow-green eyes and facial plate with short, dense white to yellow hairs covering the face, thorax, and top of abdomen. The hind legs of males also have long white to yellow hairs. Abdomen of males and females are black and may have small bands of white hair.

Habitat: Deserts

Range: California, Nevada, New Mexico, Arizona, Texas, northern Mexico

Active season: Spring to fall

Conservation status: None

Plant interactions: Members of this genus mainly visit plants of the Barbados cherry (Malpighiaceae) family to collect oil, but also visit others such as those in the Plantaginaceae, Calceolariaceae, and Krameriaceae families. They are commonly observed on desert-willow (*Chilopsis* spp.), paloverde (*Parkinsonia* spp.), and other plants, such as sunflowers (*Helianthus* spp.), mallows (Malvaceae), and snoutbean (*Rhynchosia* spp.).

Interesting fact: The Latin name of this species describes its most distinguishing characteristic from the ancient Greek *rhodo*, meaning "rose-colored" or "red," and the suffix "pus," meaning "foot."

Similar species: Very similar to the caesalpinia oil-digger (*C. caesalpiniae*); however, the caesalpinia oil-digger does not have red legs and is about 5 mm larger. The red-legged oil-digger also has a more western distribution.

C. arizonensis

SMALL CARPENTER BEES
Ceratina spp.

Size: < 8 mm

Description: Small, dark, shiny bees with sparse hair. Many are metallic greens and blues.

Habitat: Habitat generalists

Range: Worldwide distribution

Active season: Late spring into fall

Conservation status: None

Plant interactions: Generalist pollinators.

Interesting facts: Some species exhibit unique brood care and mating relationships; for example, males in some species will guard the brood nests of females they hope to mate with, even though the brood being guarded is not their own. Some species can reproduce through parthenogenesis (reproducing without males). In some species, nests are founded by two females—one that is a passive guard of the nest and the other that reproduces and forages.

Similar species: The small carpenter bees are commonly mistaken for sweat bees (family Halictidae), orchid bees (tribe Euglossini), or cuckoo wasps (family Chrysididae), which are also often metallic blue and green. They are separated from sweat bees (Halictidae) by inspection of the tongue length and the hindwing lobe. They are generally smaller than orchid bees and cuckoo wasps.

BINDWEED TURRET BEE

Diadasia bituberculata

NICOLE DESNOYERS

Size: 13 mm

Description: Thorax and face covered in gray-white hairs. Abdomens are mostly hairless and black, with thin white hair bands. Legs are black with white hairs.

Habitat: Deserts and grasslands with hard-packed and sandy soils

Range: Central and North America; California, Oregon, and Nevada

Active season: Spring to late summer

Conservation status: None

Plant interactions: Feed particularly on flowers from the false bindweed (*Calystegia* spp.) and bindweed (*Convolvulus* spp.) genera.

Interesting facts: These bees frequently surround the opening of their soil nests with a long tubelike "chimney" or turret (hence their common name), the purpose of which has not been agreed upon.

Similar species: Often confused with digger bees (tribe Anthophorini) and bumble bee species.

GLOBE MALLOW BEE

Diadasia diminuta

JESSICA GOLDSTROHM

Size: 7–9 mm

Description: Body and legs are black, with the thorax and face covered in long, white-blond hairs. The abdomen with dispersed white-blond hairs and distinct bands of short white-blond hairs on the ends of the abdominal segments. Females have long, plumose hairs on their hind legs for transporting pollen.

Habitat: Habitat generalists. Nests are frequently located in very compacted soil, particularly along dirt roads.

Range: Western United States, Canada, and Mexico

Active season: Mid-spring to mid-fall

Conservation status: None

Plant interactions: Specialize on globe mallow plants (*Sphaeralcea* spp.).

Interesting fact: Globe mallow bees are in the chimney bee tribe (Emphorini) that build turrets on the outside of their ground nests.

Similar species: Similar in appearance to digger bees (tribe Anthophorini) and other chimney bees (tribe Emphorini)

ELENA OEY

CACTUS BEE

Diadasia rinconis

Size: 11–12 mm

Description: Body densely covered in yellow-gold hairs. Abdomen with bands of dense yellow-gold hairs and bands of less dense yellow-black hairs, with long golden hairs on hind legs. Eyes appear blue. Black antennae.

Habitat: Deserts and arid grasslands

Range: Southwestern United States (Arizona, California, New Mexico, Texas) and Mexico

Active season: Late winter to summer

Conservation status: None

Plant interactions: Feeds on a variety of plants, especially prickly pear cacti (*Opuntia* spp.).

Interesting facts: Males can often be found sleeping in aggregations inside cactus flower blossoms in the early mornings. Males also form "mating balls" in which they intensely grapple for a chance to mate with females.

Similar species: Often mistaken for other digger bees (tribe Anthophorini) and bumble bees (genus *Bombus*).

A bee in the genus *Melissodes*

MELISSODES LONGHORN BEES

Melissodes spp.

Size: 7–18 mm

Description: Medium to large, robust bees. Usually densely hairy and black or white. Often have bands of pale hair on abdomen. Densely hairy rear legs. Females carry pollen in scopa on hind leg. Males often have yellow coloration on the face and long antennae.

Habitat: Habitat generalists

Range: North, Central, and South America

Active season: Spring to fall

Conservation status: None

Plant interactions: Generalist pollinators of a variety of plants.

Interesting fact: Males can often be found sleeping in aggregations within flowers.

Similar species: Bumblebees (*Bombus* spp.) lack the long antennae and the hairy rear legs. Other bees in the Eucerini tribe, *Peponapis* spp. and *Xenoglossa* spp., specifically visit squash and melon plants in the gourd family (Cucurbitaceae), while *Svastra* spp. are found on sunflowers (*Helianthus* spp.)

STEVEN G. MLODINOW

TWO-SPOTTED LONGHORN BEE

Melissodes bimaculatus

Size: 11–15 mm

Description: Females are larger than males. Males have blond hairs and yellow coloration on the face and white-blond hairs on the middle and hind legs. Females have black coloration on the face and long white-blond hairs only on the hind legs. The antennae are black on top, with light coloration on the bottom. The antennae of males are long; females have shorter antennae. The females have a black abdomen and thorax with two white spots (sometimes difficult to see) located near the tip of the abdomen; males are completely black on the abdomen and thorax. The wings are a shiny black-blue.

Habitat: Habitat generalists, including meadows, deserts, forest edges, and developed landscapes

Range: Mostly located in the eastern United States, this bee has been found in eastern Wyoming, Colorado, New Mexico, and Texas.

Active season: Spring to early fall

Conservation status: None

Plant interactions: These bees are generalist pollinators and feed on a variety of plant species, including garden crops like beans and cucumbers.

Interesting facts: Larvae of this species are parasitized by another bee, the lunate longhorn-cuckoo bee (*Triepeolus lunatus*).

Similar species: Often confused with carpenter bees (*Xylocopa*) and bumble bees (*Bombus*). The two-spotted longhorn bee can be determined by the presence of the two white spots on the abdomen, the long antennae on males, and the hind legs with long blond hairs.

A bee in the *Nomada* genus

NOMAD BEES

Nomada spp.

Size: 8–10 mm

Description: Small, wasplike bees. The coloration is usually red, red and black, or yellow and black. Antennae are often red or yellow as well. Nomad bees usually have very little hair and no scopa.

Habitat: Habitat generalists

Range: All of western North America and much of the rest of the world

Active season: Spring to late summer

Conservation status: None

Plant interactions: Adults feed on nectar from a variety of plants. However, because females do not collect their own pollen to feed their brood, they lack pollen-carrying structures that many other bees have and therefore are not very efficient pollinators.

Interesting facts: Nomad bees are kleptoparasites, meaning the females lay their eggs in the nests of other bees, thereby stealing the resources the other bees had collected for their brood. Because this behavior resembles the nest parasitism behavior of cuckoo birds, these bees are commonly referred to as "cuckoo bees."

Similar species: It can be difficult to distinguish these bees from wasps in the field. Nomad bees strongly resemble the small square-headed wasps in the family Crabronidae. Unlike wasps, these bees have branched hairs (must be viewed under a microscope) and have beelike wing venation.

JESSICA GOLDSTROHM

EASTERN CUCURBIT (PRUINOSE SQUASH) BEE

Peponapis pruinosa

Size: 11–14 mm

Description: Medium-sized, robust bees. Females are slightly larger than males. The body is black with dense, short white to yellow hairs on the face and thorax. The abdomen is black with bands of short white hairs. The legs have shaggy golden-orange hairs. Females have scopa on their hind legs to carry pollen. Males have a yellow plate on their face.

Habitat: Habitat generalists, but especially found near gourd crop fields

Range: All the western US states south of Washington, Montana, and northern Idaho; south into Mexico

Active season: Late spring to early fall

Conservation status: None

Plant interactions: This bee specializes in feeding on plants in the cucurbit, aka gourd, family (Cucurbitaceae), such as cucumbers, melons, squash, and pumpkins.

Interesting facts: Because they specialize in gourds, these bees frequently spend their lives in crop fields and therefore face threats from pesticides, tillage, and other agricultural practices. It is believed that the planting of gourds by humans has expanded the range of these bees. Males are frequently found sleeping in the closed blooms of squash plants.

Similar species: *Melissodes* spp., also in the Eucerini tribe, are generalists and visit a wide variety of flowers. *Xenoglossa* spp., also a gourd family specialist, is larger.

AMY YARGER

OBLIQUE LONGHORN BEE

Svastra obliqua

Size: 14–16 mm

Description: Females are dark black with patches of orange hair on the face, dorsal thorax, hind legs, and bands on the lower abdomen. There are two forms—one with more prominent bands of hairs and the other with few hairs, or dark hairs that make them look much darker. Males are more covered in lighter blond hairs in the same areas as females and have green eyes and long antennae.

Habitat: Habitat generalists and ground nesters

Range: Washington, California, Utah, Arizona, Colorado, Las Vegas, New Mexico, Texas, Mexico; few sightings in Montana, Wyoming, and Idaho

Active season: Summer

Conservation status: None

Plant interactions: Pollen specialist on the plant family Asteraceae, including the genera *Helianthus* (sunflowers), *Vernonia*, *Cirsium* (thistles), and *Borrichia*. Also found on the genera *Curcubita* (gourds) and *Helenium* (sneezeweeds) and the pea family (Fabaceae), among others.

Interesting facts: Also called the sunflower longhorn bee; however, this name is confusing due to other similar bees that also frequent sunflowers.

Similar species: Unlike other longhorn bees (tribe Eucerini), female *Svastra* spp. have a tuft of long hairs on the metanotum.

T. verbesinae

TRIEPEOLID CUCKOO BEES

Triepeolus spp.

Size: 8–16 mm

Description: Small and stout bees with broad heads, very wasplike. Mostly black bodies with bands of short white or yellow hairs marking the body. Often the bands are incomplete across the abdomen. Many species in this genus have smiley face–shaped markings on the thorax. Legs are often red.

Habitat: Meadows and forests

Range: Throughout North and Central America; limited sightings in other continents

Active season: Late spring to early fall

Conservation status: None

Plant interactions: Bees in this genus feed on a variety of flower nectars; they can particularly be found around the food plants of the bee species they parasitize.

Interesting facts: These cuckoo bees are kleptoparasites of bees in the tribe Eucerini, especially the *Svastra* and *Melissodes* genera. They lay their eggs in other bees' nests, allowing their offspring to feed on the brood provisions left by other bees.

Similar species: Fairy bees (genus *Perdita*) are similar but possess pollen-collecting hairs on their rear legs. Nomad bees (Genus *Nomada*) have a pitted thorax.

A bee in the genus *Xenoglossa*

LARGE SQUASH BEES

Xenoglossa spp.

Size: 15–20 mm

Description: Large, robust, hairy bees. Males have mostly yellow on their faces; females have more black. Body is black or golden. The hairs on the thorax and abdomen are yellow-orange. Hairs on abdomen are often banded. Hairs on hind legs are long and yellow-orange.

Habitat: Desert, arid and semiarid, and coastal areas where xerophytic Cucurbita species are found

Range: Southwestern United States (California, Arizona, New Mexico, Texas); Mexico into Central America

Active season: Late spring to fall

Conservation status: None

Plant interactions: These bees only collect pollen from the plant genus *Cucurbita*, which includes pumpkins and squash.

Interesting facts: Males are often found sleeping in closed gourd flowers, which open in the morning and close later in the day. Females visit the flowers earlier in the day, so they are not trapped inside the closed flowers and are rarely observed more than two hours after sunrise.

Similar species: These bees look similar to other squash bee genera such as *Peponapis*; however, *Peponapis* bees have black on their mandibles, whereas *Xenoglossa* have yellow markings on the mandibles. *Peponapis* bees are also much more common than *Xenoglossa* species.

ELLIOT LIU

WESTERN CARPENTER BEE

Xylocopa californica

Size: 20–25 mm

Description: Large, black bees. The body is shiny with blue-green reflections. Dense, short black hairs cover much of the thorax and lower area of the face. Females have smoky-brown wings; males have black wings. Males also tend to have white hairs on the thorax and parts of the abdomen, while females are all black. There are three subspecies of western carpenter bee, which also vary slightly in appearance.

Habitat: Mountain foothills, forests, meadows, deserts

Range: Oregon, Nevada, California, Utah, Arizona, New Mexico, and Texas; south into northwestern Mexico. They may also be found in Washington and Montana, although infrequently.

Active season: Late winter to late fall

Conservation status: None

Plant interactions: Western carpenter bees have been observed acting as nectar robbers by chewing holes in the sides of flowers to get to nectar without touching the pollen parts of flowers. They will take nectar from a variety of plants but are more discerning about collecting pollen from specific plants like creosote (*Larrea tridentata*) and honey mesquite (*Prosopis glandulosa*). These bees also make T-shaped nests in plant stems, particularly in yucca and agave plants.

Interesting facts: Western carpenter bees can fly in extremely hot temperatures (over 48°C/118°F), which would kill other bee species; however, they cannot withstand temperatures lower than 10°C (50°F), hence their restricted range. These bees, like bumble bees, also perform a special type of pollination called sonication that other bees, like honey bees, cannot. During pollination, western carpenter bees grab onto a flower's anthers using their mandibles and rapidly vibrate their body to loosen the pollen grains from the flower. The pollen grains fall onto the bee's body, get trapped in its hairs, and are then transported to other flowers for pollination. Western carpenter bees can even adjust the frequency of their vibrations based on plant species.

Similar species: This species resembles other carpenter bees (*Xylocopa*) in the region. The distinguishing characteristic of the western carpenter bee is its metallic blue-green shine compared to other carpenter bees without the shine. The males of the western carpenter bee are black; the males of the valley carpenter bee (*Xylocopa sonorina*) are golden with green eyes.

VALLEY CARPENTER BEE

Xylocopa sonorina

Size: 25 mm

Description: Large bees. Females are all black with black hair and dark black wings. Males are a golden brown with green eyes and clear brown wings.

Habitat: Valleys and foothills with deciduous forests

Range: Oregon, Nevada, California, Utah, Arizona, New Mexico, and Texas; south into Mexico

Active season: Spring to late fall

Conservation status: None

Plant interactions: Valley carpenter bees feed on a variety of plants. They perform a special type of buzz pollination called sonication in which they grasp male flower parts and vibrate their bodies to knock pollen loose from the flowers. They may also steal nectar without performing pollination by chewing through closed flowers and bypassing pollen-carrying parts of the flower.

MIKE YOSHIHARA

X. sonorina female

WILSON YAU

X. sonorina male

Interesting facts: Male valley carpenter bees produce pheromones to attract females. Males mark their territories by rubbing on leaves, and females have been observed pausing in areas where males have left their pheromones.

Similar species: The females of this species resemble other carpenter bees (*Xylocopa*) in the region. The distinguishing characteristic of the valley carpenter bee is an all-black body with no metallic shine, whereas western carpenter bees are black with a metallic blue-green shine.

NANCY OVERHOLTZ

HORSEFLY CARPENTER BEE
Xylocopa tabaniformis

Size: 12–18 mm

Description: Female bees are all black with black hairs on the thorax and the abdomen bare. Males have a black abdomen with yellow hairs on the face and thorax with green-blue eyes. The wings are lighter than other species of carpenter bees in the area.

Habitat: Habitat generalists; can be found nesting in dead wood.

Range: Oregon, California, New Mexico, Arizona, Colorado, Utah, Texas, and Nevada; Mexico into Central America

Active season: Early spring to late fall

Conservation status: None

Plant interactions: Generalist pollinator that visits many plant species, including Salvia (*Salvia* spp.), Penstemon (*Penstemon* spp.), lupines (*Lupinus* spp.), wisteria (*Wisteria* spp.), and berberis (*Berberis* spp.).

Interesting facts: There are ten subspecies of the horsefly carpenter bee, two of which are found in the western United States and Mexico: the foothills carpenter bee (*Xylocopa tabaniformis orpifex*) and the pale male carpenter bee *(Xylocopa tabaniformis androleuca*).

Similar species: Horsefly carpenter bees look similar to other carpenter bees in the area, valley carpenter bee (*Xylocopa sonorina*) females, and western carpenter bee (*Xylocopa californica*) males and females; however, horsefly carpenter bees are about half the size of the other two species. Western carpenter bees are also black with a metallic blue-green shine; horsefly carpenter bees have no blue-green metallic shine to them.

JAKE NITTA

SPOTTED MINI-DIGGER-CUCKOO

Zacosmia maculata

Size: 5–9 mm

Description: Small bees. The body of males and females is black with short, patchy patterns of white hairs on the face, thorax, legs, and abdomen. Black and brown patches also cover the body. Two white spots are on each abdominal segment. The most distinctive characteristic of this species is the thick, black fusiform (meaning spindle shaped and tapered at both ends) antennae in males, which are different than most bees or wasps. Females have straight, brown to black antennae, though they do have a noticeable thickness.

Habitat: Open grasslands and deserts

Range: Throughout western North America, with documented sightings in southern Canada, California, New Mexico, Nevada, Utah, and northern and central Mexico

Active season: Spring to fall

Conservation status: None

Plant interactions: Noted to feed on plants in the sunflower (Asteraceae), mustard (Brassicaceae), spurge (Euphorbiaceae), mint (Lamiaceae), mallow (Malvaceae), and tamarisk (Tamaricaceae) families.

Interesting facts: This species is kleptoparasitic on *Anthophora* bees. The females will break into *Anthophora* cells, insert their own eggs, and reseal the cell.

Similar species: The fusiform antennae of the males set this species apart from other bees. This species is unique in its white patterning and is the only species in its genus.

Family Colletidae

Plasterer Bees

Bees in the family Colletidae are commonly referred to as "plasterer" or "polyester" bees due to their behavior of lining their nests with cellophane-like secretions from their mouthparts. These bees are best identified under a microscope, as their distinguishing characteristics are in their wing cell sizes, having one subantennal suture, and the short length of the tongue. However, the masked bees in the genus *Hylaeus* are more easily identified by their yellow facial features and lack of body hair.

JESSICA GOLDSTROHM

A bee in the genus *Colletes*

CELLOPHANE BEES

Colletes spp.

Size: 7–16 mm

Description: Generally, the body of this bee is black, the thorax and face are densely covered in white-yellow (and sometimes orange) hairs, and the abdomen is black with bands of white-yellow hairs. Thickness of the abdominal banding varies by species, but most have thin bands. The face is heart-shaped. The tongue is short and forked at the tip. On the forewings, the second and third submarginal cells are about the same size, and the second recurrent vein has a strong "S" shape. They carry pollen on their hind legs.

Habitat: Habitat generalists, nesting in dry soils in open areas

Range: All of western North America and much of the rest of the world

Active season: Different species are active in either spring or fall; sometimes both spring and fall. Cellophane bees are less common in summer.

Conservation status: None

Plant interactions: Some species are specialists on plants in families like the sunflower (Asteraceae) and pea (Fabaceae) families; others will visit a variety of flowers.

Interesting facts: These bees get their common names "cellophane bees," "polyester bees," and "plasterer bees" from the fact that these solitary ground-nesters line their brood nests with an actual polyester secretion that comes from a gland on their abdomen.

Similar species: Almost indistinguishable from Andrenidae bees without microscopic examination

JESSICA GOLDSTROHM

A bee in the genus *Hylaeus*

MASKED BEES

Hylaeus sp.

Size: 4–7 mm

Description: Very small, wasplike bees. These bees have no pollen-collecting hairs and instead store pollen and nectar in an internal stomach for transportation. These bees tend to have black (or sometimes red) bodies with no metallic sheen. May have yellow or white markings on the legs, thorax, or abdomen. Females have yellow or white facial markings besides the eyes; males have yellow or white markings that extend across the lower face. They have two submarginal cells, with the first submarginal cells being larger than the second.

Habitat: Forests and woodlands

Range: Worldwide distribution

Active season: Late spring to early fall

Conservation status: No status as a genus; however seven species (*Hylaeus anthracinus, H. assimulans, H. facilis, H. hilaris, H. kuakea, H. longiceps*, and *H. mana*) endemic to Hawaii were listed as endangered under the US Endangered Species Act in 2016 due to habitat loss and invasive plants and animals degrading native habitat. The listing was the first time that any bee species have been protected under the Endangered Species Act.

Plant interactions: Generalist pollinators. Some plants they have been observed visiting include golden Alexander (*Zizia aurea*), swamp milkweed (*Asclepias incarnata*), common boneset (*Eupatorium perfoliatum*), goldenrod (*solidago* spp.), and Queen Anne's lace (*Daucus carota*) and other members of the carrot family (Apiaceae). They burrow into plant stems or wood to build nest cells.

Interesting facts: These bees are also commonly called "yellow-faced bees"; however, many species also have white face masks, so the common name is deceptive.

Similar species: These bees closely resemble small black and yellow wasps in the family Crabronidae, especially those in the Crabronini tribe. Under microscopic inspection, it can be seen that masked bees have branched hairs, whereas wasp hairs are not branched.

Family Halictidae

Sweat Bees

Bees in the family Halictidae are commonly referred to as "sweat bees" due to their attraction to perspiration on humans. Many species in this family are small and often mistaken for flies. Most bees in this family are ground nesting. This family exhibits various levels of sociality among the species, with some species having rigid divisions of labor with queen and worker castes to others being completely solitary.

JESSICA GOLDSTROHM

A bee in the genus *Agapostemon*

STRIPED SWEAT BEES

Agapostemon spp.

Size: 7–15 mm

Description: The thorax is metallic green; body is covered in small white hairs. Males have a black and yellow–striped abdomen. Females may also have a black and yellow– or white-striped abdomen, although in some species the female abdomen is all green. Legs have yellow and/or black markings, pollen-carrying hairs on the hind legs.

Habitat: Habitat generalists; ground nesters

Range: Southern Canada throughout the United States; south into Central and South America

Active season: Late spring to fall

Conservation status: None

Plant interactions: Generalist pollinators that visit plants including but not limited to members of the sunflower (Asteraceae), mustard (Brassicaceae), pea (Fabaceae), and rose (Rosaceae) families and many others. The genus name *Agapostemon* means "stamen loving," referring to their habit of pollen collection. They have short tongues and are therefore restricted to taking nectar from shallow flowers.

Interesting facts: Some species nest communally, with females sharing the same nest entrance but building their own nest cells. This communal nesting helps defend the brood from kleptoparasitic cuckoo bees, which may try to enter the nest if a female is not around to guard the entrance.

Similar species: Other metallic green bees in the family Halictidae, mason bees (*Osmia* genus), and small carpenter bees (*Ceratina* genus)

A bee in the genus *Augochlorella*

PERIDOT SWEAT BEE
Augochlorella pomoniella

Size: 7–9 mm

Description: Small metallic green-blue bees. Body is covered in small white hairs. Legs and antennae are black. Females carry pollen on hind legs.

Habitat: Habitat generalists; ground nesters

Range: California, Nevada, Utah, Arizona, Texas, and New Mexico

Active season: Early spring to fall

Conservation status: None

Plant interactions: Generalist pollinators.

Interesting facts: These bees are considered to be "primitively eusocial," in that a group of females may produce young and nonreproductive bees assist with nest care. This species will often have a mix of solitary and social nest founders.

Similar species: Similar bees are other metallic green sweat bees in the genera *Agapostemon* and *Augochlora*. These bees can only be differentiated from *Augochlora* using microscopic examination.

BOB KRUGMIRE

A bee in the genus *Halictus*

FURROW BEES

Halictus spp.

Size: 5–14 mm

Description: Small bees. Body is usually black or brown. Some species have a dark metallic greenish tint. Thorax and face are generally covered in short white or yellow to orange hairs. Generally the abdomen is black, with distinct bands of short white hairs on the apical sections (outer edges) of the abdominal sections. Some species have less-distinct hair bands on the abdomen. Pollen is carried on the hind legs.

Habitat: Habitat generalist; ground nesters

Range: All of western North America and much of the world

Active season: Mid-spring to mid-fall

Conservation status: None as a group. However, the Xerces Society considers *Halictus harmonius*, which has only been found in the foothills of the San Bernardino and San Jacinto Mountains in southern California, to be critically imperiled due to development in its habitat.

Plant interactions: Generalist pollinators. Especially found on composite type flowers, like plants in the sunflower family (Asteraceae).

Interesting facts: Almost all species are semi-social, meaning the daughters stay in the nest to help care for the young. They nest in the ground in groups of up to 200 individuals.

Similar species: Similar to bees in the genus *Lasioglossum*; however, bees in the genus *Halictus* have abdominal hairs on the apical portion (outer edge) of the abdominal segments, whereas bees in the genus *Lasioglossum* have the hairs on the basal portion (inner edge) of the abdominal segments. *Halictus* bees also have stronger wing veins, whereas bees in *Lasioglossum* have weaker wing venation.

CHARLES HOLSTEIN

A bee in the genus *Lasioglossum*

LASIOGLOSSUM SWEAT BEES

Lasioglossum spp.

Size: 2–8 mm

Description: Slender black, green, or blue bodies. Short white hair covers the body. Bands of short white hair on the basal (innermost) end of the abdominal segments.

Habitat: Habitat generalists from plains to montane zones. Most nest in the ground, but some nest in rotten wood.

Range: Throughout western North America and much of the world

Active season: Spring to fall

Conservation status: None

Plant interactions: There are generalist and specialist species in this genus. Among the specialist species, some are attracted to genera such as *Oenothera* spp. and *Clarkia* spp. in the evening primrose family (Onagraceae).

Interesting facts: Sociality is variable across species. Some are solitary; others are primitively eusocial, with small divisions of labor and cooperative brood care. Some live in colonies with a queen and a few to more than 400 workers.

Similar species: These bees closely resemble bees in the genus *Halictus*; however, the genera can be identified based on the placement of hair bands on the abdomen. In *Halictus* the hairs are on the outermost edge of the abdominal segments, whereas in *Lasioglossum* the hairs are located on the innermost edge of the abdominal segments. *Lasioglossum* bees also have weaker wing venation compared to *Halictus*.

AMY CAMPION

A bee in the genus *Sphecodes*

BLOOD BEES

Sphecodes spp.

Size: 5–10 mm

Description: Small bees. Usually head and thorax are black, with red abdomen. Sometimes males are all black. White hairs on the face and outer thorax.

Habitat: Habitat generalists

Range: Western North America and much of the rest of the world

Active season: Spring to fall, with a dip in summer

Conservation status: None

Plant interactions: Not efficient pollinators because they mostly visit flowers to drink nectar, although females may visit for some pollen after they first emerge.

Interesting facts: Bees are kleptoparasitic, laying their eggs in the cells of other sweat bees so that their brood can eat the pollen collected by other bees.

Similar species: Look similar to nomad bees in the genus *Brachynomada*, which have similar black thoraxes with red abdomens. May resemble small wasps with red abdomens, but *Sphecodes* bees have branched hairs while wasps do not.

Family Megachilidae

Leafcutter and Mason Bees

Bees in the family Megachilidae are commonly referred to as "leafcutter" and "mason" bees, reflecting the types of materials they collect to build their nests. Bees in this family carry pollen on the underside of their abdomen, often making it look like their abdomens have fuzzy orange or yellow hairs, although the coloration comes from the pollen they are carrying. Some species in this family are kleptoparasitic, meaning they steal pollen from other species rather than collect it on their own.

JESSICA GOLDSTROHM

A bee in the genus *Anthidiellum*

ROTUND RESIN BEE
Anthidiellum sp.

Size: 5–10 mm

Description: Smallish black, stocky, relatively hairless solitary bee. May have yellow, orange, cream, or red markings. Anterior of thorax partially extends over the posterior abdomen.

Habitat: Habitat generalist. Distinctively build their nests on rocks or plant stems using plant resin, sometimes combined with small pebbles.

Range: Western United States; primarily California, Arizona, New Mexico, Utah, and Colorado

Active season: Mid-spring to late fall

Conservation status: None

Plant interactions: Observed to be generalists, possibly preferring plants in the sunflower family (Asteraceae).

Interesting facts: While more than sixty species are described worldwide, only three live in North America. *A. notatum* is found in the west.

JESSICA GOLDSTROHM

A bee in the genus *Anthidium*

WOOL CARDER BEES

Anthidium spp.

Size: 6–19 mm

Description: A robust black bee with distinctive yellow abdominal stripes that may be broken in the middle. Sometimes mistaken for a wasp. It has a flat, straight body and large, prominent mandibles with teeth that are visible without a microscope. Exhibits fly-like hovering behavior. Females transport pollen on the scopa beneath their abdomen. Unusually, males are larger than females and display territorial behavior, particularly around food sources.

Habitat: Dry and desert areas

Range: More common in western North America, with the widest variety occurring in the Great Basin and on the Colorado Plateau

Active season: Late spring through summer

Conservation status: None

Plant interactions: Some *Anthidium* are generalists; others are specialists. Preferred plants are in the waterleaf (Hydrophyllaceae), pea (Fabaceae), and aster (Asteraceae) families.

Interesting facts: Solitary cavity-nesting bees that utilize preexisting openings in old wood, trees, or plant stems for nesting; some also dig holes in sandy soil. Females collect hairs from fuzzy-leaved plants to line their nests, leading to their common name. Notably, male eggs are deposited at the back of the nest, a departure from the usual practice in other bee species, possibly due to the larger size and longer development time of these male bees.

Similar species: While thirty-six *Anthidium* species are native to North America, the European species *Anthidium manicatum* is now widespread across the entire United States. Unlike native varieties, it is more active later in the season.

JESSICA GOLDSTROHM

EUROPEAN WOOL CARDER

Anthidium manicatum

Size: 11–17 mm

Description: These solitary bees are yellow and black, but mostly black with only a few yellow dots or incomplete stripes on the outer margin of their abdomen. Adults have yellow legs and large mandibles. Males distinctly larger than females.

Habitat: Grasslands, agricultural lands, disturbed sites, sagebrush, and forests in the foothills. Nest in cavities.

Range: Widespread throughout the United States but absent from the most southern states; native to Europe

Active season: Early summer through early fall

Conservation status: None

Plant interactions: Females collect hairs/wool from plants to line nest cavities. Individual bees collect nectar from a wide variety of flowers.

Interesting facts: Unintentionally introduced into North America in the 1960s, where it is now established. Males are territorial and will aggressively attack other bees. Females collect woollike material from downy plants to line their nests.

Similar species: Appear similar to yellowjackets, but stouter and hairier.

LISA HILL

Dianthidium curvatum spp. *sayi*

SONYA ANDERSON

Dianthidium nest

PEBBLE BEES

Dianthidium spp.

Size: 7–10 mm

Description: Small bees with broad heads and stout bodies. Bodies are typically black with yellow, white, or red markings that resemble yellowjacket wasps and with few hairs. Face may have distinctive geometric yellow markings similar to yellow-masked bees (*Hylaeus*). The abdomen is often curled under the body.

Habitat: Habitat generalists

Range: Throughout western North America

Active season: Late spring to early fall

Conservation status: None

Plant interactions: Generalists, but often found on sunflower family (Asteraceae).

Interesting facts: These bees construct nests using pebbles glued together with resin. The nests are located on twigs, the sides of rocks or dug into the ground and attached to roots or other burrows.

Similar species: Appear similar to carder bees (Anthidium) They can be distinguished by the thinness of the pronotal (shoulder area above the wings) lobes. Appear similar to yellowjackets but are much smaller. Facial markings are similar to yellow-masked bees (*Hylaeus*), but the *Dianthidium* bodies are much stouter.

JESSICA GOLDSTROHM

A bee in the genus *Lithurgopsis*

NORTHERN CACTUS WOODBORER BEES

Lithurgopsis spp.

Size: 7.5–20 mm

Description: Robust bees. The female face has a raised, bulbous hornlike ridge. Bodies are generally black with white hairs on face, thorax, and legs. Abdomens taper abruptly. Abdomen is black with bands of white hairs. Females carry pollen on scopa on the underside of their abdomen. One species, *L. apicalis*, often has an orange tuft of hair at the end of the abdomen.

Habitat: Wood nesting in open, arid habitats

Range: Texas, Colorado, New Mexico, Utah, Arizona, Nevada, California, Idaho, and Mexico

Active season: Mid-spring through summer

Conservation status: None

Plant interactions: Collect nectar and pollen from pink prickly poppies (*Argemone Chisoensis*) and prickly pear cacti (*Opuntia* spp.).

Interesting facts: Only four species are well documented in the United States—*L. apicalis, L. echinocacti, L. gibbosa*, and *L. littoralis*—with *L. apicalis* and *L. echinocacti* being in the Southwest.

Similar species: Very similar to *Megachile* leafcutter bees; however, the tibia of the hind leg of *Lithurgopsis* has distinct raised bumps (difficult to see in live specimens), and the females have the bulbous protrusion on the face.

JAMES BAILEY

PARALLEL LEAFCUTTER

Megachile parallela

Size: 12–14 mm

Description: Medium-large solitary bee with a dark, robust body and wide face. They carry the pollen they collect on the underside of their bellies with modified hairs called scopa instead of in pollen baskets on their legs. Females' last abdominal segment appears upturned.

Habitat: Prairie and plains; ground nester. Tunnel into dead twigs and cavities in wood or the ground to build their nests.

Range: Throughout the western United States and north into Alberta and British Columbia

Active season: Summer to fall

Conservation status: None

Plant interactions: Pollen specialist on the sunflower family (Asteraceae); will also visit members of the mustard (Brassicaceae), pea (Fabaceae), and verbena (Verbenaceae) families.

Interesting facts: Leafcutter bees are important pollinators of commercial crops, including alfalfa, carrots, onions, blueberries, and cranberries, among many others. Females cut leaf pieces and use them to line the cells of their nests. The holes they leave in leaves are strikingly even and well-shaped.

JESSICA GOLDSTROHM

WESTERN LEAFCUTTER

Megachile perihirta

Size: 12–14 mm

Description: Black bee with long yellow-white hair and light bands across the abdomen. Also known as the furry leafcutter bee. Females are distinguished by the large mandibles used to cut leaf pieces for lining their nests.

Habitat: Desert, grasslands, and forest edges, as well as agricultural fields and urban areas. Ground nester, unlike other leafcutter bees.

Range: Throughout the western United States north into Alberta and British Columbia

Active season: Summer to fall

Conservation status: None

Plant interactions: A generalist, visiting a wide range of flowers, especially members of the sunflower (Asteraceae) and pea (Fabaceae) families.

Interesting facts: Solitary bee that may nest gregariously. Important pollinator of wildflowers as well as agricultural crops, including alfalfa (Medicago sativa).

BOB KRUGMIRE

PUGNACIOUS LEAFCUTTER BEE
Megachile pugnata

Size: 11–18 mm

Description: Medium, stocky bee with distinctively large mandibles. Striking lines of hairs crossing their abdomens. Carry pollen on their bellies or undersides. Also known as sunflower leafcutter bee or feisty leafcutter bee.

Habitat: Open, sunny areas such as gardens, farms, meadows, and forest edges. Cavity nester utilizing abandoned tunnels in logs or stumps as well as tunnels in artificial bee nests.

Range: Throughout United States into southern Canada; absent from the Great Basin

Active season: Summer to fall

Conservation status: None

Plant interactions: Primarily feed on members of the sunflower family (Asteraceae), especially sunflowers (*Helianthus* spp.). Females cut leaf pieces to line nests.

Interesting facts: Can be significant crop pollinators. Their name is the result of the female bees' intense defense of their nests.

JESSICA GOLDSTROHM

ALFALFA LEAFCUTTER BEE

Megachile rotundata

Size: 7–9 mm

Description: Smallest leafcutter bee. Dark gray with white bands across top of abdomen and white scopa on underside of abdomen for carrying pollen.

Habitat: Open sunny areas including farms and gardens. Cavity nester using rotting wood and flower stems and will adapt to artificial bee nests.

Range: Worldwide distribution, including temperate regions of North America

Active season: Early to late summer

Conservation status: None

Plant interactions: Feed on plants in the sunflower (Asteraceae) and pea (Fabaceae) families.

Interesting facts: Native to Asia and southeastern Europe, they were introduced to North America to increase alfalfa crop production. Alfalfa crop production is believed to have more than doubled as a result.

HEIDE KEEBLE

BLUE ORCHARD BEE
Osmia lignaria

Size: 9–11 mm

Description: Dark metallic blue-green and almost-black bees. Densely hairy. Females have more black hairs and males have more white hairs on the face and thorax. Females are larger. Pollen is mostly carried under the abdomen.

Habitat: Woodlands and forest edges

Range: Throughout the United States and north into southern Canada

Active season: Spring to early summer

Conservation status: None

Plant interactions: Visit flowers of orchard species in the rose family (Rosaceae) like cherries, pears, apples, quince, and almonds. Also visit the golden chain tree (*Laburnum* spp.) and blueberries. This species is cultivated to pollinate crops; however, attempts to move them outside of their natural range have not been successful, likely due to the species' need for cooler temperatures.

Interesting facts: Larvae build cocoons in their brood cells in early summer then pupate. They then go into diapause and stay inside the cocoon over winter. The adult bees emerge in spring. The females continue their life cycle by laying thirty to forty eggs, each inside its own brood cell and provisioned with pollen.

Similar species: Similar to other *Osmia* species. However, this species is distinctively dark, almost black, in its coloration.

MATTHEW A. MULVEY

CURRANT ORCHARD BEE

Osmia ribifloris

Size: 9–12 mm

Description: Metallic-blue bee; sometimes appears metallic green as well. Covered in black hairs. Antennae and legs are black. Sometimes dense whitish hairs on the face. Females are larger. Pollen is mostly carried under the abdomen.

Habitat: Woodlands and forest edges

Range: Oregon, California, Nevada, Utah, Arizona, New Mexico, and Texas; northern Mexico

Active season: Spring

Conservation status: None

Plant interactions: Gathers pollen from plants in the heath family (Ericaceae). Manzanita (*Arctostaphylos* spp.) is its preferred host plant.

Interesting fact: This bee species is sometimes used to pollinate blueberry plants.

Similar species: Two subspecies exist in the West: *Osmia ribifloris* ssp. *ribifloris* is a brilliant blue and more eastern (Texas, New Mexico, Mexico, Utah, California); *Osmia ribifloris* ssp. *biedermannii* is greener and more western (California, Nevada, New Mexico, Arizona). They are not as dark as *Osmia lignaria.*

Family Melittidae

Melittid Bees

Melittidae are considered one of the most ancient bee families. The oldest-known bee fossil contains a member of this family and is believed to be about one hundred million years old. They are small to medium in size, ground nesters, and oligolectic. Including both short-tongued and long-tongued bees, they are uncommon to rare in the United States but most prevalent in the Southwest.

GEORGE WILLIAMS

Hesperapis regularis

EVENING BEES

Hesperapis spp.

Size: 7–15 mm

Description: Small, solitary bees with an abdomen that is flat with grayish or black hairs. Head is oval, slightly longer than wide, and covered in short hairs. The wing has two submarginal cells, and identification usually requires a microscope. Diurnal, despite its common name.

Habitat: Arid deserts and grasslands

Range: Southwestern United States

Active season: Early spring through fall

Conservation status: None

Plant interactions: Most are pollen specialists, although the chosen plants differ widely from each other.

Interesting facts: Solitary ground nesters seeming to prefer loose, sandy soil, leaving a small mound at their nest entrance. Although with many ground-nesting bees, the parent waterproofs the lining of the egg nest, with some *Hesperapis* species, it's believed the larvae do this themselves. Strikingly, their nest tunnels can be up to 3 feet deep with multiple branches, each leading to just one to a few cells.

Family Crabronidae

Square-headed Wasps

Wasps in the family Crabronidae are often referred to as the "square-headed wasps," with some species specifically being called "sand wasps." As their common name implies, they are often distinguished from other wasps by their square-shaped heads, with little room between the head and thorax. Many species closely resemble bees, such as nomad bees, and can only be distinguished through microscopic inspection. Wasps in this family are often sleek and black with red, white, or yellow markings.

CALAIS LEJEUNE

A wasp in the genus *Bembix*

SAND WASPS
Bembix spp.

Size: 15–24 mm

Description: Large wasps, often with large green-blue eyes. Usually a black abdomen with large, wavy bands of yellow, white, or blue that meet at the dorsal midline. Often with yellow legs and black thorax.

Habitat: Open, sandy habitats, such as deserts, grasslands, and banks of streams. Nests are made in the sand.

Range: Throughout western North America and much of the world

Active season: Spring through fall

Conservation status: None

Plant interactions: Visit a variety of flowers to drink nectar; hunt flies to provision their brood.

Interesting facts: Females progressively provision their brood with multiple flies to feed on as they develop from larvae to adults.

Similar species: The wavy bands of yellow, white, and blue are fairly distinctive, though these wasps may be confused with yellowjacket wasps (*Vespula*), which are similarly sized and colored. They also appear similar to other genera in the same subtribe (Bembicini).

LISA HILL

WESTERN CICADA KILLER

Sphecius grandis

Size: 30–50 mm

Description: Large wasps. Body is red and black, with yellow and red markings on the abdomen. Short hairs on thorax. Legs are red and spinose. Wings are a smoky red-brown. Face has yellow plates. Antennae have red base and fade into black.

Habitat: Habitat generalists; prefer to nest in sandy, well-drained soil

Range: Across western North America except Wyoming, Montana, and Canada

Active season: Late spring to early fall

Conservation status: None

Plant interactions: Generalist nectar feeders; occasional pollinators.

Interesting facts: The common name of this species comes from their behavior of using their venom to paralyze cicadas, which they bring back to their nests for their brood to consume. Males emerge earlier than females and live only a few days to mate. Females live up to a year and spend that time mating and provisioning their brood.

Similar species: The western cicada killer is most common in the West; however, they do overlap in areas with the eastern cicada killer (*Sphecius speciosus*) and the Pacific cicada killer (*Sphecius convallis*). Eastern cicada killers have more black coloration on the abdomen; Pacific cicada killers are generally redder, with more yellow markings on the abdomen compared to western cicada killers. They may also be confused with yellowjacket wasps (*Vespula*) and hornets (*Vespa*), although they are usually much larger.

Family Ichneumonidae

Ichneumonid Wasps

Ichneumonid wasps vary greatly in size, from 3 mm to 40 mm, and are characterized by a narrow wasp waist, often elongated abdomen (longer than rest of body), and long antennae. They range in color from yellowish to brown or black, often with bold stripes and bands on their bodies. Unlike predaceous wasps, these parasitoids do not usually have their ovipositors modified into a stinger at the end of their abdomen. Even though they look scary, only a few species have been documented as stinging humans, or even having ovipositors capable of penetrating skin.

HOVERFLY PARASITOID
Diplazon laetatorius

DAMON TIGHE

Size: 4–7 mm

Description: Small, rounded wasp with black and red body markings and long tan antennae. Hind legs have a distinctive white band.

Habitat: Wetlands, agricultural crops, and developed landscapes, including disturbed sites and roadsides

Range: Distributed globally, including western North America

Active season: Summer through early fall

Conservation status: None

Plant interactions: Adult wasps drink nectar from small flowers, such as members of the sunflower (Asteraceae) and carrot (Apiaceae) families.

Interesting facts: This species has a worldwide distribution and was likely spread via agriculture. This parasitoid wasp lays eggs in flies, especially syrphid flies. Adults have also been documented eating syrphid eggs. Some reports say that this wasp parasitizes up to 75 percent of syrphid larvae. Because this wasp often reproduces with unfertilized eggs, males are extremely rare.

CHRISTIAN NUNES

NORTON'S GIANT ICHNEUMON
Megarhyssa nortoni

Size: 23–75 mm

Description: Large, slender wasp with bright yellow, red, and black body markings and yellow legs. Females are larger than males and have a distinctive long ovipositor.

Habitat: Forest edges and openings in montane areas, foothills, and wetlands; also developed parks in urban and suburban areas

Range: Western North America

Active season: Summer through early fall

Conservation status: None

Plant interactions: Adult wasps drink nectar from small flowers, such as members of the sunflower (Asteraceae) and carrot (Apiaceae) families.

Interesting facts: This wasp is a parasitoid on horntails—look for females on tree trunks or fallen wood as they search for horntail larvae to lay eggs in. The female wasps find horntail larvae by smelling the wood-eating fungi the horntails use to predigest wood pulp, then lay eggs with their ovipositor. The ovipositor is often as long as the entire insect.

BETH BURROUS

ICHNEUMON WASP
Spilopteron vicinum

Size: 10–20 mm

Description: Slender wasps with black thorax and banded, narrow abdomen that appears to be elevated. Females have distinctive long ovipositors. Clear wings have dark tips; dark antennae have pale bands.

Habitat: Deciduous forest openings and edges in foothills and wetlands, disturbed sites such as fields and ditches, developed parks and gardens in urban and suburban areas

Range: Northern North America, including Intermountain West south to Texas

Active season: Summer through early fall

Conservation status: None

Plant interactions: Adult wasps drink nectar from small flowers, such as members of the sunflower (Asteraceae) and carrot (Apiaceae) families.

Interesting facts: This wasp is a parasitoid of longhorn beetle grubs, and females can often be observed searching for the larvae inside tree trunks.

Family Pompilidae

Spider Wasps

Pompilids are medium to large, solitary, charismatic wasps with robust bodies and long, spiny legs. They are usually dark and metallic in color and often have smoky or amber-colored wings. Adults are usually spotted visiting flowers in the summer to drink nectar or walking along the ground searching for spiders. These spiders, once paralyzed and brought to a specially constructed nest, will provide food for the wasp's larvae as they grow. Females are famous for their potent sting, but these insects are generally shy around humans, making interactions rare.

RICH READING

A wasp in the genus *Pepsis*

TARANTULA HAWK

Pepsis sp.

Size: 15–44 mm

Description: Large, slow-flying wasp with velvety, almost iridescent, black body and orange wings that fade with age. Females tend to be larger; the smaller males have straight antennae.

Habitat: Desert sagebrush and canyons, occasionally developed urban gardens

Range: Throughout western North America

Active season: Mid-spring to mid-fall

Conservation status: None

Plant interactions: Milkweeds (*Asclepias* spp.) and other flowering plants with umbels are a favorite nectar source for adult wasps.

Interesting facts: State insect of New Mexico. Parasitoid of tarantulas—females will disturb the webbing of tarantula burrows to entice the tarantula out, then paralyze it as provision for wasp larvae. This wasp is shy, but is notorious for having one of the most painful stings of any insect.

LUANN WRIGHT

WESTERN RED-TAILED SPIDER WASP
Tachypompilus unicolor

Size: 11–23 mm

Description: Medium, robust, active wasp with rusty-red body, sometimes with dark markings; teardrop-shaped abdomen, long legs, and shiny blue-black wings. These wasps vibrate their wings constantly.

Habitat: Open dry areas such as sagebrush and desert canyons, as well as developed landscapes and fields in urban and suburban areas

Range: Western North America

Active season: Late spring through mid-fall

Conservation status: None

Plant interactions: Adult wasps drink nectar from many kinds of plants, including the carrot family (Apiaceae), small-flowered members of the sunflower family (Asteraceae), and the buckwheat family (Polygonaceae), among others. Also documented on milkweed (*Asclepias* spp.) and bridal veil (*Clematis paniculata*).

Interesting facts: Generalized spider hunters, usually of large wolf spiders. Females may use chinks or gaps in stone walls for nest sites and can be observed making "orientation flights" to later find the correct nest.

Family Sphecidae

Thread-waisted Wasps

Wasps in the family Sphecidae are commonly called "thread-waisted wasps" due to the narrow front part of their abdomen. Their bodies are typically black (possibly with metallic blue or green sheen), sometimes with red or yellow markings. Adults feed on nectar from flowers and nectaries of plants and sometimes body fluids from their prey. They feed paralyzed arthropods to their young.

RICH READING

COMMON THREAD-WAISTED WASP
Ammophila procera

Size: 25–38 mm

Description: Slender, delicate black wasp with elongated "thread-waist" and silver markings on side of thorax. Slightly bulbous abdomen is red-orange with a black tip. Some localities have color variations with less red-orange or with additional black spots. Females are larger than males.

Habitat: Open, sunny areas such as meadows, prairies, sagebrush, and savannas; also fields, gardens, roadsides, and developed landscapes in urban and suburban areas

Range: Widespread across North America

Active season: Summer through early fall

Conservation status: None

Plant interactions: Adult wasps drink nectar from many kinds of plants, including bee balm (*Monarda* spp.), sage (*Salvia* spp.), mountain mint (*Pycnanthemum* spp.), and sulfur flower (*Eriogonum umbellatum*), especially members of the sunflower family (Asteraceae) like goldenrod (*Solidago* spp.), ragwort (*Senecio* spp.), Joe-Pye weed (*Eupatorium purpureum*), and rabbitbrush (*Ericameria* spp.).

Interesting facts: *Ammophila* females dig burrows in the earth, often in compacted sand, and paralyzes a moth caterpillar (often larger than she is) to provision her young. The larva stays in the nest, eating the caterpillar, until it pupates and emerges as an adult. Mating often occurs while the female is foraging on flowers. There have been observations of female *Ammophila* chirping; the hypothesis is that females chirp to signal they are ready to mate.

RICH READING

COMMON BLUE MUD-DAUBER

Chalybion californicum

Size: 9–23 mm

Description: Shiny, bluish-black wasp with short thread-waist, long black legs, short black hairs, and dark, shiny wings. Females are larger than males.

Habitat: Open, sunny areas such as mountain and foothill meadows, prairies, sagebrush, and savannas; also forest openings, fields, gardens, roadsides, and developed landscapes in urban and suburban areas

Range: Widespread across North America

Active season: Spring through fall

Conservation status: None

Plant interactions: Adult wasps drink nectar from many kinds of plants, including plants with umbels or clusters of small flowers, such as barberry (*Berberis vulgaris*), Queen Anne's lace (*Daucus carota*), dill (*Anethum graveolens*), and golden Alexander (Zizia aurea).

Interesting facts: Females hunt on the ground (or occasionally lure spiders from their webs) for black widows and other spiders to feed their young. They build mud nests aboveground in sheltered areas or often use old nests from other wasps and bees. Offspring pupate and overwinter in the nests and emerge the following spring. These are shy wasps and sting only if harassed. Occasionally, adults gather in a "sleeping aggregation," which may assist in connecting potential mates.

AMY YARGER

THREAD-WAISTED WASP

Prionyx thomae

Size: 15–20 mm

Description: Medium black wasp with black head and thorax, threadlike waist, and bulbous red-orange abdomen.

Habitat: Shortgrass and mixed-grass prairies, urban/suburban gardens, old fields, and roadsides

Range: Throughout western North America

Active season: Late spring to early fall

Conservation status: None

Plant interactions: Adult wasps drink nectar from members of the sunflower family (Asteraceae), especially coneflowers (*Rudbeckia* spp.) and goldenrod (*Solidago* spp.).

Interesting facts: Female wasps hunt and paralyze grasshoppers to provision young with food during their larval development.

Family Vespidae

Yellowjackets, Hornets, Paper Wasps, Potter Wasps, and Mason Wasps

Wasps in the family Vespidae comprise almost all of the known eusocial wasps, although some species in this family are solitary. In the eusocial species, the queens hibernate alone over winter and restart the colonies every year by producing more female workers and male drones. Many species are pollen collectors for their young and nectar feeders as adults; others are solely predators of other arthropods.

LISA HILL

COMMON YELLOW AERIAL YELLOWJACKET

Dolichovespula arenaria

Size: 10–12 mm

Description: A medium-sized social wasp with a hairy face and long black antennae. Its thorax is mostly black; its striped abdomen is blunt at the tip.

Habitat: Forests and forest edges, as well as developed landscapes, provide sites for aerial nest building.

Range: Throughout western North America

Active season: Spring to fall

Conservation status: None

Plant interactions: These wasps visit many kinds of plants, especially those with small, shallow flowers, to obtain nectar, which fuels their hunting activity.

Interesting facts: These wasps hunt live arthropods of a wide variety, including grasshoppers, crickets, caterpillars, spiders, flies, lacewings, and even lady beetles to bring back to their nests to feed larval wasps. Yellowjacket queens overwinter alone underground and emerge in spring to start laying colonies of workers.

Similar species: Other yellowjacket species and hornets nest in the ground; however, the aerial yellowjacket builds its nest in trees, shrubs, or other overhangs up high.

BALD-FACED HORNET

Dolichovespula maculata

ROBIN AGARWAL

Size: 12–20 mm

Description: Large black yellowjacket with black and white markings, sparse hair, and smoky-colored wings.

Habitat: Woodlands and forests, as well as developed areas with trees, which are necessary for these wasps to nest

Range: Throughout western North America

Active season: Early spring to fall

Conservation status: None

Plant interactions: Generalist nectar feeders that also feed on a variety of invertebrates. Commonly feed chewed-up insects and spiders to their young. In the spring these wasps visit flowers such as chokecherry (*Prunus virginiana*) and snowberry (*Symphoricarpos* spp.) to drink nectar.

Interesting fact: These social wasps have smaller colonies than yellowjackets, and colonies are active only until midsummer.

Similar species: This species is larger and more robust and differs from the yellow-and-black patterns of other vespids.

GOLDEN PAPER WASP

Polistes aurifer

SONYA ANDERSON

Size: 10–25 mm

Description: This species appears differentially black or brown, based on geography. Body is predominantly black with yellow markings, accented with rusty-brown wings and antennae. The abdomen is mostly a dull yellow.

Habitat: Prefers sheltered locations such as developed areas and woodlots

Range: Throughout western North America

Active season: Early spring to fall

Conservation status: None

Plant interactions: This paper wasp visits a wide range of flowers, especially those with small, shallow blooms such as goldenrod (*Solidago* spp.) and milkweed (*Asclepias* spp.). They may also be observed gathering plant fibers from leaves to build their nests.

Interesting fact: Although it resembles the more-defensive western yellowjacket, this is a relatively gentle and nonaggressive species.

Similar species: European paper wasp (*Polistes dominula*). *P. aurifer* has more yellow and rusty brown in its markings, especially on the abdomen.

BOB KRUGMIRE

EUROPEAN PAPER WASP

Polistes dominula

Size: 20 mm

Description: Slender-bodied black wasp with yellow markings. This wasp has brown wings and black antennal bases that turn orange at the tips.

Habitat: Grasslands and meadows; also developed landscapes, such as roadsides, gardens, and agricultural areas

Range: Throughout western North America

Active season: Early spring to fall

Conservation status: None

Plant interactions: These wasps are generalist nectar feeders while hunting for invertebrate prey to feed their larvae.

Interesting facts: This native wasp of Mediterranean Europe was introduced to North America in 1978. Only females overwinter.

Similar species: None; other paper wasps lack the distinctive yellow color of the antennae.

Pseudomasaris edwardsii

POLLEN WASPS

Pseudomasaris spp.

Size: 10–20 mm

Description: Species are variable in appearance, but they have a common vespid appearance of black bodies with yellow, white, and red bands on the abdomen and markings on the body. The most unique trait of this genus is the club-shaped antennae.

Habitat: Semiarid environments with rocks

Range: Southwestern Canada through the western United States and into northern Mexico

Active season: Early spring to summer

Conservation status: None

Plant interactions: They feed their brood nectar and pollen from a variety of plants, though many are specialists that feed on *Phacelia* spp., yerba santa (*Eriodictyon californicum*), waterleafs (family Hydrophyllaceae), beardtongue (*Penstemon* spp.), tansies (*Tanacetum* spp.), or borage (*Borago* spp.). Some even pollinate rare plants, such as the blowout beardtongue (*Penstemon haydenii*), an endangered plant species.

Interesting facts: Unlike other wasps in the Vespidae family, which are predators, adults of this genus feed solely on nectar and pollen. They are also solitary and build their mud nests on rocks or twigs.

Similar species: The clubbed antennae differentiate this genus from other Vespid wasps, such as yellowjackets.

JUVIA HEUCHERT

GERMAN WASP

Vespula germanica

Size: 13 mm

Description: This introduced social wasp looks like a common black and yellow, stout yellowjacket, but the workers have three tiny black dots on the clypeus that distinguish them from other wasps.

Habitat: Found in open sunny areas in almost every lowland habitat, but especially common in urbanized landscapes such as roadsides, gardens, and agricultural areas.

Range: Throughout western North America

Active season: Early spring to fall

Conservation status: None

Plant interactions: These wasps have a varied diet; they not only feed on a wide variety of flowers for nectar but also drink sweet fluids from aphid secretions and fruit. Also scavengers and predators of other arthropods.

Interesting facts: This species, native to Europe, northern Africa, and Asia, now can be found on every continent except Antarctica. Their rapid global spread is attributed to humans accidentally transporting hibernating queens.

Similar species: Unlike the common wasp (*V. vulgaris*), this species has three small dots on the front of its face, or clypeus.

BOB KRUGMIRE

WESTERN YELLOWJACKET

Vespula pensylvanica

Size: 10–16 mm

Description: Medium-sized, stout-bodied social wasps with bold yellow and black striping on their abdomen and slender legs. Eyes are surrounded by a yellow band. These wasps have sparse hairs, especially compared to honey bees, with which they are often confused.

Habitat: These ground nesters are found wherever people are—parks, gardens, near buildings, open fields, as well as in woodlands and forest openings. They usually nest underground or in cavities.

Range: Throughout western North America

Active season: Early spring to fall

Conservation status: None

Plant interactions: Visit many kinds of flowers to get energy for their relentless scavenging. Western yellowjackets are scavengers of everything from dead insects to picnic lunches; the animal material collected is used to feed their young.

Interesting facts: Western yellowjackets build a paper nest in sheltered spaces, such as abandoned rodent burrows and crevices in structures. Their populations increase dramatically during warm, dry springs and summers, when they are often considered a nuisance.

Similar species: This species of yellowjacket has a distinctive yellow ring around each eye.

Family Erebidae

Erebid Moths

These moths are a speciose family, inclusive of some of the most recognized groups of moths, including tiger moths, wasp moths, tussock moths, and the black witch moth. Species in this group vary highly in size, as this group is inclusive of some of the smallest as well as largest of the moths. Their color and form are also widely variable, ranging from dull and highly cryptic to brightly colored and conspicuous. Just like the adults, caterpillars in this family are not characterized by a single unifying trait; they may be fuzzy, like the well-known woolly bears (*Pyrrharctia isabella*), to smooth and patterned. Representatives of this group are found in every continent except Antarctica.

YELLOW-COLLARED SCAPE MOTH

Cisseps fulvicollis

Size: 30–37 mm

Description: Slender moth with a distinct bright orange or dark yellow collar. Forewing is dark brown to black. Hindwing is black with a clear or grayish proximal patch, which is usually obscured from view. The thorax and abdomen are black and may display blue iridescence.

Habitat: Open meadows and grasslands as well as riparian habitats; occasionally in open urban or suburban spaces

Range: Western North America

Active season: Late spring to autumn

Conservation status: None

Plant interactions: Adults are nectar feeders and frequently visit milkweeds and asters. Caterpillars of this moth feed on grasses, bonesets (*Eupatorium* spp.), and goldenrods (*Solidago* spp.).

STEVEN G. MLODINOW

Interesting facts: Day-flying moth. This moth will take nectar from *Eupatorium* plants, which are rich in toxic alkaloids; males may pass toxins to females as a nuptial gift. The toxins may be used to protect their vulnerable eggs from predators. These moths may be mimics of wasps or distasteful beetles, which grants them additional protection from predators.

Similar species: Adult grapeleaf skeletonizer moth (*Harrisina americana*) is a similar species. The end of the abdomen curls upward and expands to a broader tip. Adult Virginia ctenucha moth (*Ctenucha virginica*) is larger and wider, with distinct blue iridescence on the thorax that starts under the collar.

RICH READING

POLICE CAR MOTH
Gnophaela vermiculata

Size: 50–55 mm

Description: Moderately sized black and white tiger moth. Forewings are broad and squared, colored black, translucent patches and cells with a white, yellowish, or greenish tone. Hindwings similar to forewings. Head and thorax are black with white dots. Base of front legs has a bright orange patch. Abdomen is blue-black with slight iridescence and white dots on each side. Antennae are bipectinate, markedly in males and lightly in females.

Habitat: Mid-elevation mountain ranges, forest edges, and herbaceous spaces

Range: Western North America as far east to New Mexico, especially in the Rocky Mountain region

Active season: Late summer through early fall

Conservation status: None

Plant interactions: Caterpillars feed on bluebells (*Mertensia* spp.), puccoon (*Lithospermum* spp.), and stickseed (*Hackelia* spp.). Adults are nectar feeders from herbaceous flowers such as thistles (*Cirsium* spp.) and goldenrods (*Solidago* spp.).

Interesting facts: Day-flying moth.

Similar species: Adult Langton's forester moths (*Alypia langtoni*) are smaller, with black wings with four visible white circular patches uninterrupted by black veins. Adult wild forget-me-not moths (*Gnophaela latipennis*) are smaller, with smaller light patches. Found only in California and Oregon.

Family Geometridae

Geometer Moths

Geometer moths are variable moths with usually slender bodies and delicate, broad wings. They are often patterned with wavy lines that cross the length of their wings. When resting, they often hold their wings spread flat. Their caterpillars are generally small and smooth, with a reduced number of prolegs; usually only have two pairs of false legs at the tail end of their body. Their distinctive movement gives the caterpillars the name "loopers"; they contract and extend their bodies to move, forming a loop-like shape. Some species in this group may be considered agricultural pests of fruit crops and forest trees.

ROSE LUDWIG

CHICKWEED GEOMETER MOTH
Haematopis grataria

Size: 19–25 mm

Description: Brightly colored pink and yellow geometer moth. Forewings are yellow with pointed tips; hindwings also yellow. Each forewing has a centered pink dot and two pink bands running below. When at rest, forewings are usually held wide open and the forewing bands appear to run continuously with the hindwing bands. Males have distinctly feathery, plumose antennae; females have thin, filiform antennae.

Habitat: Grasslands, meadows, and open fields; common in urban and suburban areas, including lawns, gardens, fields, and roadsides

Range: Rocky Mountain region

Active season: Mid-spring to mid-fall

Conservation status: None

Plant interactions: Adults visit flowers. Caterpillars feed on low plants, including chickweed (*Stellaria* spp.), knotweeds (*Polygonum* spp.), and clovers (*Trifolium* spp.).

Interesting facts: This day-flying moth is the only North American representative of its genus.

Scopula junctaria

GEOMETRID MOTH

Scopula spp.

Size: 17–30 mm

Description: A variety of shapes and sizes, but typically light brown to pale white with wavy traverse lines; sometimes clearly darker postmedial and medial lines through the fore- and hindwings.

Habitat: Many different habitats, from developed gardens to shrubs, grasslands, and mixed forests

Range: Worldwide

Active season: Late spring to early fall

Conservation status: None

Plant interactions: Larvae are generalists and feed on a variety of woody and herbaceous plants, including bedstraw (*Galium* spp.), clover (*Trifolium* spp.), and meadowsweet (*Filipendula* spp.). Adults sip nectar from a variety of flowering plants.

Interesting facts: There are more than 700 species in this genus; 24 species in North America.

Family Noctuidae

Owlet Moths

Noctuids are a variable group of moths. Their antennae are generally threadlike. Coloration is often drab; their bodies are stocky and may be fuzzy. Many individuals in this group have front wings in various shades and patterns of mottled browns and grays; hindwings usually differ from the forewings in color. Caterpillars are often dull and smooth, with reduced or lost prolegs. Some species in this group, like the miller moth (*Euxoa auxiliaris*), may be considered agricultural pests in their caterpillar form. Noctuids are found in every continent with the exception of Antarctica. Juveniles are commonly referred to as cutworms or army worms.

EIGHT-SPOTTED FORESTER
Alypia octomaculata

CHRISTIAN NUNES

Size: 30–37 mm

Description: Forewings are black with two pale yellow spots and metallic blue bands. The hindwings are black with white spots. The body is black with prominent pale yellow stripes on the shoulders and on the dorsal side of the abdomen. Front and middle legs have orange hairlike scales. Antennae are thickened at the tips. Mature larvae are black and white–striped with orange bands, which have black dots and white spots laterally.

Habitat: Open areas with flowers, near woodland edges where host plants grow

Range: Maine and southern Quebec to Florida; west to the Rockies

Active season: Early spring to midsummer; second brood in August in the South

Conservation status: None

Plant interactions: Larval hosts include grapes (*Vitis* spp.), pepper vine (*Nekemias arborea*), and Virginia creeper (*Parthenocissus quinquefolia*). Adults feed on nectar from a variety of plants.

Interesting facts: Daytime flyer. Their flight pattern and coloring create a strobe-like effect. Often mistaken for a butterfly.

Similar species: The six-spotted Forester (*Alypia langtoni*) is smaller than *A. octomaculata*; the female has six spots, and males have eight spots. Males have distinctive white rings at the base of the antennal shafts. Larvae feed on fireweed (*Chamaerion angustifolium*). *A. langtoni* is more common in the north and west; *A. octomaculata* is an eastern species.

JOHN SULLIVAN

MACCULLOCH'S FORESTER MOTH

Androloma maccullochii

Size: 10–13 mm forewing length

Description: Wings are black with pale yellow spots. The two spots on top of forewings are oblong; a third adjacent spot is round. The bottom of the forewing has a row of yellow spots divided by fine black lines. The hindwings are black with two yellow spots toward the top and a row of yellow spots at the bottom, divided by fine black lines. The body is black with yellow shoulders and orange hairs on the front legs. There are additional yellow bands across the back of the abdomen.

Habitat: Open habitats such as meadows, clear-cuts, and disturbed roads, as well as burned areas of coniferous forests; also common in dry canyonlands

Range: Rocky Mountains west to the coast and north through British Columbia

Active season: Late spring to summer; most found in late spring

Conservation status: None

Plant interactions: Larvae feed on fireweed (*Chamerion angustifolium*); adults drink nectar from a variety of flowering plants.

Interesting facts: Only two *Androloma* species are found in North America north of Mexico.

Similar species: *Alypia ridingsii* is a similar species, but *A. maccullochii* has hairy yellowish "shoulder pads."

MILLER MOTH

Euxoa auxiliaris

DAVID RANKIN

Size: 17–22 mm forewing length

Description: Hindwings are light gray. Forewings are brown and gray; many varied patterns of lighter browns, grays, blacks, and whites, with a lighter spot toward the middle of each wing and a larger light spot below those.

Habitat: Open grassland and agricultural habitats. Found at high altitudes, including alpine tundra in the summer. Found in disturbed areas and urban or riparian areas in the fall.

Range: Widespread throughout North America, occurring as far east as Michigan and Texas

Active season: Spring to fall

Conservation status: None

Plant interactions: Larvae feed on sixteen plant families but prefer cereal grasses. Caterpillars are also known as army cutworms because they snip growing plants at the base. Adults feed on nectar from a variety of flowering plants.

Interesting facts: Migrating miller moths provide significant protein resources to emerging bears in the spring. Adults are capable of flying long distances and for long periods of time.

OWLET MOTH

Mesogona olivata

PENNI EATWELL

Size: 15–19 mm forewing length

Description: Forewings are brown, sometimes mixed with gray, red, or yellow, depending on location. Accented with smooth lines, irregularly shaped spots and a scalloped margin. Overall color is darker in wetter habitats, but lighter where dryer. Head and thorax color similar to the wings. Distinctly identified by claws on front legs.

Habitat: Ranges from wetter forests to semiarid steppe habitats up to 7,000 feet.

Range: Mostly found along the west coast of North America, north into British Columbia and east to Colorado and Wyoming

Active season: Late summer to fall

Conservation status: None

Plant interactions: Larvae feed on many woody plants, including oak (*Quercus* spp.), poplar (*Populus* spp.), hazel (*Corylus* spp.), antelope bitterbrush (*Purshia tridentata*), currants (*Ribes* spp.), and roses (*Rosa* spp.). Adults feed on nectar and fermenting fruit.

Interesting facts: Adults are most active in the fall, when foliage is changing.

Similar species: Similar to *M. rubra* and *M. subcuprea*, but *M. rubra* is more reddish and *M. subcuprea* is lighter. Both have shinier and more colorful hindwings.

YELLOW UNDERWING MOTH

Noctua pronuba

CAMILLE STEPHENS

Size: 21–26 mm

Description: Adult has yellow hindwings with a black marginal band. Forewing varies in color, darkness, and contrast, including browns, reds, or grays, with kidney-shaped spot in the middle and a dark spot on front edge of wing toward the tip. Nocturnal.

Habitat: Open areas, lawns, agricultural fields, urban and disturbed areas

Range: Introduced to eastern Canada in the 1970s; now widespread throughout the United States, Canada, and into northern Mexico

Active season: Summer to early fall

Conservation status: None

Plant interactions: Larvae feed on weedy and cultivated herbaceous plants, including plants in the nightshade (Solanaceae), goosefoot (Chenopodiaceae), mustard (Brassicaceae), and grape (Vitaceae) families. Adults are nectar generalists.

Interesting facts: Native range is Eurasia and Africa. It was introduced from Europe to Nova Scotia in 1979 and has since spread to the Arctic and Pacific Oceans.

Similar species: *N. comes* is similar; however, *N. pronuba* lacks a dark discal spot on the hindwing, which is present in *N. comes*.

ARCIGERA FLOWER MOTH

Schinia arcigera

STEVEN G. MLODINOW

Size: 22–25 mm

Description: Forewing is dark brown and velvety at the base and edged in white. Median and terminal areas are grayish brown and also bordered with white. Head and body are dark brown, usually with a purple or red tint. Male hindwing is yellow at the base with a dark spot and black on the outer half. Female hindwing is dark brown to black with pale fringe. Nocturnal.

Habitat: Prairies and grasslands

Range: North America east of the Rocky Mountains

Active season: Midsummer through early fall

Conservation status: None

Plant interactions: Larvae feed on leaves from members of the sunflower family (Asteraceae). Adults feed on nectar.

Interesting facts: Adults lay their eggs on the flowers of the host plant, instead of on the leaves.

Similar species: Jaguar flower moth (*S. jaguarina*) has pale yellow and light reddish-brown coloring on the forewing. Ragweed flower moth (*S. rivulosa*) has similar forewing patterns, but is light gray and found more to the east.

RICH READING

BLANKET FLOWER MOTH
Schinia masoni

Size: 22 mm

Description: Head and thorax are yellow-orange. Wings are cherry red, with white and yellow patterns providing camouflage on their similarly colored host plant, blanketflower (*Gaillardia* spp.). Larvae are pale, with brown to dark red vertical striping patterns.

Habitat: Edges of coniferous forests

Range: Flight area is in the ponderosa pine belt in the Rocky Mountain Front Range, southeastern Wyoming south to central Colorado.

Active season: Early to midsummer

Conservation status: None

Plant interactions: *Gaillardia* flowers are host to larvae. Larvae feed on blanketflowers and seeds; the nectar is food for adults.

Interesting fact: This moth is known for its distinctive upside-down resting position.

Similar species: *S. masoni* and *S. volupia* are very difficult to distinguish but have slightly different ranges, with *S. volupia* more eastward in the Great Plains states.

MEAD'S FLOWER MOTH

Schinia meadi

CHRISTIAN NUNES

Size: 10–13 mm forewing length

Description: Forewing is light yellow and green with silver lines and dark accent lines along the olive patterns; fringe of the forewing is white and dark stripes. Hindwing is dark brown with white spots.

Habitat: Grasslands, prairies, deserts

Range: From the Rocky Mountains west to the coast; north into southern Canada

Active season: Late spring to late summer

Conservation status: None

Plant interactions: Larvae thought to eat members of the pea family (Fabaceae), such as prairie turnip (*Pediomelum esculentum*) and clover (*Trifolium* spp.) In the Pacific Northwest, adults are seen flying by thick stands of *Pediomelum* during the day.

Interesting facts: Like other flower moths, the larvae of this species primarily eat the buds and flowers of plants instead of the leaves.

BINDWEED MOTH

Tyta luctuosa

HEIDE KEEBLE

Size: 11 mm forewing length

Description: Dark in color, with two white spots on the lateral sides of the forewings and two elongated spots on the hindwings.

Habitat: South-facing slopes and open fields

Range: Western North America; native to the Old World

Active season: Late spring to late summer

Conservation status: None

Plant interactions: Larvae feed on field bindweed (*Convolvulus arvensis*); adults drink nectar from a variety of flowering plants.

Interesting facts: Also goes by the name "four-spotted moth." Introduced as a biological control for bindweed.

Family Sesiidae

Clearwing Moths

Clearwing moths are a diurnal and unique group of lepidopterans. They often mimic wasps in shape, coloration, and even behavior of several wasp species. Most species in this group have noticeable transparent patches in their wings and an elongated abdomen with a tuft toward the end; abdomen often has bright yellow or orange rings. These excellent wasp mimics lack stingers.

KEVIN KREBS

SYNANTHEDON MOTH

Synanthedon myopaeformis

Size: 18–28 mm

Description: Black body with an orange band around the second segment of the abdomen and a black tuft at the base of the abdomen. Wings are clear with black margins and veins.

Habitat: Agricultural areas such as apple orchards

Range: Recorded in British Columbia and southeastern Canada, as well as the New England states

Active season: Late spring to late summer

Conservation status: None

Plant interactions: Larvae bore into the bark of fruit trees, causing damage. Adults are attracted to showy milkweed (*Asclepias speciosa*) flowers.

Interesting facts: A pest of apple trees, this moth was introduced from Europe.

Family Prodoxidae

Yucca Moths

Yucca moths are small, generally day-flying moths. Many genera are found in dry regions of North America. They are typically colored in whites or grays.

JESSICA GOLDSTROHM

A moth in the genus *Tegeticula*

YUCCA MOTH
Tegeticula sp.

Size: 11–23 mm

Description: Adults are white, resembling the color of the yucca flowers they visit, sometimes with black dots and small spines covering their wings. Day-flyers, they will be found on yucca blooms. Head with rough scales, simple antennae, no ocelli, and a short proboscis.

Habitat: Chaparral and sagebrush—wherever yucca plants grow

Range: Throughout the western United States. As yucca has increased in popularity as an ornamental, the range of the yucca moth has also expanded.

Active season: Spring to summer

Conservation status: None

Plant interactions: Different species of yucca plants have corresponding species of yucca moths as their pollinators. This includes the yucca plant of the American Southwest known as the Joshua tree (*Yucca brevifolia*). Female yucca moths pollinate the flowers of their related yucca species by gathering and rolling pollen from the flowers and flying to a different flower, where they deposit eggs and the pollen mass, pollinating the plants in the process. This leads to the plant producing the seeds her offspring exclusively require. Yucca moth larvae burrow into yucca and agave stems and emerge when the plants flower to feed on the seeds. The moth and the yucca plant depend on each other for survival. Adult yucca moths do not eat.

Interesting facts: Female yucca moths will not lay more eggs on a yucca plant than it can support. Since adult females are short-lived and do not feed, they do not have a long tongue. They use tentacles to gather and move pollen between flowers of different plants. This is a family of primitive Monotrysian lepidoptera.

Family Sphingidae

Sphinx Moths

Sphinx moths, or hawk moths, are medium to large moths. Powerful and agile flyers, they are among the fastest insects. Most species are crepuscular or nocturnal, but some are active during the day. They can hover midair while visiting flowers, as hummingbirds do, earning them the occasional nickname of "hummingbird moths"; this hovering behavior is unique among moths. Their body is thick and hairy, often pointed at the end. Hindwings are much smaller than forewings and may be brightly colored. When wings are held at rest, they often resemble a flat triangle. Caterpillars of this group are often called hornworms; they are large and colorful, often bright green, with a small horn at the end of their body. Their prolegs are thick and strong.

ACHEMON SPHINX

Eumorpha achemon

Size: 87–97 mm

Description: Body is tan with dark patches on the "shoulders." Dorsal side of forewings is tan with a pinkish hue, with darker patches at the middle of the inner margin and at the outer tips. The dark patch at the inner margin is squarish. There is a small dark spot at the wing base near the "shoulders." Hindwings are pink, edged in black with a tan marginal band. Often mistaken for a dried-up leaf. Nocturnal.

Habitat: Found in a range of habitats, including gardens, suburban areas, and scrub where host plants are available

Range: Throughout the western United States; missing or less common in Washington, Idaho, Oregon, Montana, and Nevada

Active season: Late spring to summer; only one flight to the north, two to the south

ASHLEY STRAIT

Conservation status: None

Plant interactions: Larval host plants include grape (*Vitis* spp.), Virginia creeper (*Parthenocissus quinquefolia*), and peppervine (*Ampelopsis* spp.). Adults feed on nectar from flowers.

Interesting facts: When numerous, they can damage vineyard crops.

SNOWBERRY CLEARWING

Hemaris diffinis

BRIONNA MCCUMBER

Size: 32–50 mm

Description: Adults resemble bumble bees and are active during the day. Wings are clear and framed in black to red-brown; the forewing cell is undivided. Dorsal side of thorax is yellow, sometimes with a green hue; abdomen is light yellow with some black. Ventrally it is mostly black, with some light yellow on the thorax and black and light yellow edges on the abdomen. Legs are black.

Habitat: Wide variety of open habitats—streamsides, fields, gardens, and suburban areas

Range: East of the Continental Divide

Active season: Spring to summer

Conservation status: None

Plant interactions: Larval host is snowberry (*Symphoricarpos* spp.), honeysuckle (*Lonicera* spp.), dogbane (*Apocynum* spp.), and dwarf bush honeysuckle (*Diervilla lonicera*). Caterpillars pupate in leaf litter at the base of host plants. Adults feed on nectar from flowers of host plants plus thistles (*Cirsium* spp.), lilac (*Syringa* spp.), and Canada violet (*Viola canadensis*).

Interesting facts: Look for young caterpillars by turning over host plant leaves with small holes from feeding.

Similar species: May overlap geographically with *H. thetis* just east of the Continental Divide but is distinguished by central yellow hairs on the dorsal abdomen, where *H. thetis* is completely black. Distinguished from *H. thysbe* by its black legs.

BRIAN WRIGHT

ROCKY MOUNTAIN CLEARWING

Hemaris thetis

Size: 32–55 mm

Description: Adults resemble a bumble bee and are active during the day. The wings are clear and framed in blackish gray, changing to reddish brown toward the base, with a red spot at the forewing's apex. The forewing cell is undivided. Dorsally, head and thorax are greenish yellow; abdomen is mostly black, with a couple lighter yellow segments at the bottom and a black and yellow tufted "tail" at the end. Ventrally, the thorax is mostly black, and the yellow abdominal segments are visible. Legs are black.

Habitat: Open areas of forests, grasslands, and streamsides

Range: Throughout west of the Continental Divide to just east of it in Colorado and Alberta

Active season: Spring to fall, with one flight in northern areas and two flights in southern

Conservation status: None

Plant interactions: Larval hosts include plants in the honeysuckle (Caprifoliaceae) family. Adults feed on nectar from flowers, including manzanita (*Arctostaphylos* spp.) and lupines (*Lupinus* spp.).

Interesting facts: Previously classified as *H. senta*.

Similar species: May overlap geographically with *H. diffinis* just east of the Continental Divide but is distinguished by some completely black body segments, where *H. diffinis* is centrally yellow. Distinguished from *H. thysbe* by its black legs.

ROBERT G. BROWN

HUMMINGBIRD CLEARWING

Hemaris thysbe

Size: 40–55 mm

Description: Adults resemble hummingbirds and are active during the day. Wings are clear and framed in dark brown. Dorsal side of thorax is greenish yellow or tan; abdomen has a couple reddish-brown segments, followed by a couple greenish-yellow to tan segments, ending in a yellow, brown, and black tuft. Ventrally, the thorax is yellow and the abdomen is black, with two longitudinal parallel brown stripes and some light yellow visible toward the end. Legs are brown to red-brown.

Habitat: Meadows and open forests

Range: Rare in western North America; widespread and common in the East

Active season: Summer

Conservation status: None

Plant interactions: Larval hosts include honeysuckle (*Lonicera* spp.), snowberry (*Symphoricarpos* spp.), hawthorns (*Crataegus* spp.), cherries and plums (*Prunus* spp.), and European cranberry bush (*Viburnum opulus*). Adults drink nectar from a variety of flowers, including Japanese honeysuckle (*Lonicera japonica*), bee balm (*Monarda* spp.), red clover (*Trifolium pratense*), lilac (*Syringa* spp.), snowberry (*Symphoricarpos* spp.), cranberry (*Vaccinium* spp.,) vetch (*Vicia* spp.), and thistles (*Cirsium* spp.).

Interesting facts: Wings are initially covered with scales that fall off with use, creating the clear windowpane effect.

Similar species: Distinguished from *H. thetis* and *H. diffinis* by its brown to reddish-brown legs and divided forewing cell.

DOUG MACAULAY

SPURGE HAWKMOTH

Hyles euphorbiae

Size: 64–77 mm

Description: Body is a warm brown with few black and white markings on the sides of the dorsal abdomen. Dorsal side of forewings are pale brown, darker brown at base and at center of the costa, with darker brown marginal band. Margins are pinkish gray. Hindwings black with pink median band.

Habitat: Disturbed open areas where leafy spurge is found growing

Range: Northern United States and southern Canada

Active season: Spring to summer

Conservation status: None

Plant interactions: Larval host plants include species in the spurge family (Euphorbiaceae). Adults feed on flower nectar.

Interesting facts: The spurge hawkmoth was introduced to Canada to control various weedy spurges and has since moved into the United States.

STEVE VAN LOH

WHITE-LINED SPHINX

Hyles lineata

Size: 60–90 mm

Description: Thorax is striped brown and white. Abdomen is brown with black and white markings. Dorsal side of forewings is brown with a yellow or tan longitudinal stripe, perpendicular white veins, and gray terminal band. Dorsal side of hindwings is black with a pink median band. Ventrally, body and wings are light brown to tan. Antennae are club-like. Usually nocturnal, but will fly during the day. Often referred to as "hummingbird moths." Larva is green with black and orange markings and a yellow-orange horn.

Habitat: Open habitats such as deserts, meadows, suburbs, and gardens

Range: Throughout the United States, extending into southern Canada and northern Mexico; also Eurasia and Africa

Active season: Spring to fall

Conservation status: None

Plant interactions: Larval hosts consist of a wide variety of plants in the evening primrose (Onagraceae) and rose (Rosaceae) families, including willow weed (*Chamerion* spp.), four o'clock (*Mirabilis* spp.), apple (*Malus* spp.), evening primrose (*Oenothera* spp.), elm (*Ulmus* spp.), grape (*Vitis* spp.), tomato (*Lycopersicon* sp.), purslane (*Portulaca* spp.), and fuchsia (*Fuchsia* spp.). Adults feed on nectar from a variety of deep-throated flowers, including columbines (*Aquilegia* spp.), larkspurs (*Delphinium* spp.), honeysuckle (*Lonicera* spp.), lilac (*Syringa* spp.), clovers (*Trifolium* spp.), thistles (*Cirsium* spp.), and jimsonweed (*Datura meteloides*).

Interesting facts: Caterpillars are sometimes pests that damage grapes, tomatoes, and other garden crops.

Similar species: White veins on thorax and forewings distinguish it from other *Hyles* species.

BRIONNA MCCUMBER

CAROLINA SPHINX

Manduca sexta

Size: 95–120 mm

Description: Body is brown with white markings and six yellow-orange spots along each side. Dorsal side of forewing is brown with subtle black, brown, and white markings. Dorsal side of hindwing has black zigzag median lines with some white in between. Nocturnal. Caterpillars are green with seven white lateral stripes and a red horn.

Habitat: A wide variety of habitats, including fields, agricultural areas, and vegetable gardens

Range: Southern portion of the western United States; not found in the Pacific Northwest, Montana, or the Dakotas

Active season: Spring to fall

Conservation status: None

Plant interactions: Larval host plants include potatoes, tobacco, tomatoes, and other plants in the nightshade family (Solanaceae). Adults feed on nectar from deep-throated flowers, often white, that bloom at night.

Interesting facts: Caterpillars are called tobacco hornworms and are considered pests on tobacco, tomato, and other solanaceous crops.

Similar species: Similar to *M. quinquemaculata*, which usually has five orange-yellow spots on either side of its body instead of six.

M. quinquemaculata (lower left); *M. sexta* (upper right)

FIVE-SPOTTED HAWKMOTH

Manduca quinquemaculata

Size: 90–135 mm

Description: Brownish gray in color overall. Body is brown with white markings, and usually five yellow-orange spots along each side. Dorsal side of forewings is a heathered brownish gray, fringed in gray. Hindwings are lighter, with darker, distinctive zigzag lines. Nocturnal. Caterpillars are green with eight V-shaped yellow markings and a black horn.

Habitat: Agricultural fields, vegetable gardens, meadows, and grasslands

Range: Throughout most of the western United States; sometimes southern Canada

Active season: Spring to fall

Conservation status: None

Plant interactions: Larval host plants include tomatoes, peppers, eggplant, potatoes, and other plants in the nightshade family (Solanaceae). Adults feed on nectar from deep-throated flowers such as honeysuckle (*Lonicera* spp.), petunia (*Petunia hybrida*), and *Phlox* spp.

Interesting facts: Caterpillars, called "tomato hornworms," have a black horn at the end of their abdomen and are considered pests on tobacco, tomato, and other solanaceous crops.

Similar species: Similar to *Manduca sexta,* which has six yellow-orange spots on each side of the body instead of five.

DONA HILKEY

POPLAR SPHINX

Pachysphinx occidentalis

Size: 108–148 mm

Description: Two color forms exist. In the pale form, dorsal wings are yellow-brown with a scalloped edge; in the dark form they are dark gray. In both forms, lines and bands are distinct. Dorsal hindwings are reddish with tan and two bluish-black parallel lines that are somewhat arrow-shaped. Larva is large, green, with seven white diagonal stripes; the stripe leading to the horn is thicker.

Habitat: Riparian areas and suburbs

Range: Throughout the western United States, extending south into Mexico

Active season: Spring to fall, with two broods in the south and one in the north

Conservation status: None

Plant interactions: Larval hosts are cottonwood, poplar (*Populus* spp.), and willow (*Salix* spp.). Adults do not feed.

Interesting facts: Caterpillars pupate and overwinter in shallow burrows in the ground.

Similar species: The two black lines on the hindwing for *P. occidentalis* are similar in color and shape, whereas for *P. modesta* the anterior black line on the hindwing is darker and more triangular than the posterior black line.

SCOTT DENKERS

BLINDED SPHINX MOTH

Paonias excaecata

Size: 55–95 mm

Description: Large sphinx moth. Dorsal side of forewings are light gray with reddish-brown mottling and are strongly scalloped at the outer margins with white fringe in concave areas of scallops (unique to genus). Hindwings are pink bordered by tan, subtly scalloped. Blue and black false eyespots lacking "pupils" inside the blue; hence the common name "blinded sphinx moth." Body is brown with darker brown stripe down the middle. Nocturnal. Caterpillars are green with red-purple random splotches, seven white diagonal streaks; the last white streak ends in a green horn.

Habitat: Deciduous woods, forest edges, clearings, and gardens

Range: Throughout the United States and southern Canada but more common to the east. In the western United States, found primarily in the northwest and along the Rockies.

Active season: Mid-spring to late fall depending on location, with multiple broods to the south and only a couple in the north

Conservation status: None

Plant interactions: Larval hosts are deciduous trees, including basswood (*Tilia* spp.), willow (*Salix* spp.), birch (*Betula* spp.), hawthorn (*Crataegus* spp.), poplar (*Populus* spp.), oaks (*Quercus* spp.), ocean spray (*Holodiscus* spp.), and cherry (*Prunus* spp.). Adults do not feed.

Interesting facts: Flies like a hummingbird. Eggs hatch eight days after being laid.

Similar species: *Smerinthus cerisyi*, which possesses the "pupil" in the eye spot, and *P. myops,* whose hindwing is yellow, not pink.

SUE ELWELL

CLARK'S SPHINX

Proserpinus clarkiae

Size: 30–38 mm

Description: Dorsal forewings are greenish brown with two bands of lighter green. Hindwings are yellow to orange with a black margin and white fringe. Body is similar in color to forewings. Ventral forewings, hindwings, and body are much lighter in color. Adults are active during the day.

Habitat: Open grasslands in high-mountain meadows to sagebrush steppe in foothills

Range: Southern British Columbia to southern California west of the Continental Divide

Active season: Mid-spring to early summer

Conservation status: None

Plant interactions: Larval host plants are in the evening primrose family (Onagraceae), including satin flower (*Clarkia* spp.) and evening primrose (*Oenothera* spp.). Adults feed on flower nectar of heartleaf milkweed (*Asclepias cordifolia*), golden currant (*Ribes aureum*), blue dicks (*Dichelostemma capitatum*), fairy fans (*Clarkia* spp.), vetches (*Vicia* spp.), thistles (*Cirsium* spp.), and hedge nettles (*Stachys* spp.).

Interesting facts: Caterpillars pupate under stones or other heavy objects. Species named for Lewis and Clark expeditioners.

Similar species: *P. juanita* is very similar but found farther to the east.

NORMA MAURICE

YELLOW-BANDED DAY SPHINX

Proserpinus flavofasciata

Size: 39–51 mm

Description: Head and thorax yellow; abdomen black with yellow tufted "tail." Dorsal forewings are dark brown to black, with pale to distinct white median band from the costal edge to inner margin. Dorsal hindwings are black with broad orange-to-yellow band. Uncommon to rare. Active during the day. Larva is jet black, with an eyespot instead of a horn.

Habitat: Subalpine meadows in coniferous forests

Range: Alaska south through British Columbia to Washington, Oregon, Idaho, Montana, Wyoming, and Colorado

Active season: Spring to summer

Conservation status: None

Plant interactions: Larval hosts include willow weed (*Epilobium* spp.) and possibly thimbleberry (*Rubus parviflorus*). Adults feed on nectar from flowers including dandelion (*Taraxacum* spp.), cherry (*Prunus* spp.), and currants (*Ribes* spp.).

Interesting fact: This moth is a bumble bee mimic.

ELINOR GATES

PACIFIC GREEN SPHINX

Proserpinus lucidus

Size: 48–61 mm

Description: Dorsal forewings are green with pink and gray areas in between. Dorsal hindwings are pink with darker submarginal band and beige fringe on the outer margin. Body is green. Active during the day. The larvae are either green or black with white subdorsal stripes, and a yellow circle outlined in black where the horn once was (this happens in the fifth instar stage). Larvae are considerably variable.

Habitat: Oak woodlands and grasslands at lower elevations west of the Cascades. East of the Cascades they are found in ponderosa pine forests and juniper woodland at moderate elevation and sagebrush steppe at lower elevations.

Range: Washington, Idaho, Oregon, and California

Active season: Midwinter to early spring

Conservation status: None

Plant interactions: Larval host plants are in the evening primrose family (Onagraceae), including evening primrose (*Oenothera* spp.) and satin flower (*Clarkia* spp.). Adults do not feed.

Interesting facts: Distinguished by its very early flight season.

JESSICA GOLDSTROHM

ONE-EYED SPHINX
Smerinthus cerisyi

Size: 62–90 mm

Description: Dorsal body is marbled in varying shades of brown, gray, and cream. Forewing edges are more deeply scalloped, sometimes straight. Dorsal hindwing is reddish pink and tan with a blue-and-black eyespot. Ventral forewings are rose colored. Sphinx moth whose appearance can be quite variable.

Habitat: Valleys and streamsides

Range: Throughout western North America

Active season: One flight from late spring to late summer

Conservation status: None

Plant interactions: Larval hosts include willow (*Salix* spp.) and poplar (*Populus* spp.). Adults do not feed.

Similar species: Twin-spotted sphinx (*S. jamaicensis*) has two blue bars in the black diamond on the hindwing rather than blue eyes.

FINN MCGHEE

SOUTHWESTERN EYED MOTH
Smerinthus ophthalmica

Size: 68–94 mm

Description: Large sphinx moth is light brown overall, with shades of darker browns and gray. Variable. Wing edges scalloped. Hindwings are pink and have blue and black eyespots connected to wing's edge by a black line. Blue ring around "pupil" is distinctive. Thorax with light brown "shoulders."

Habitat: Valleys and streamsides

Range: Southern British Columbia south; does not occur east of the Rocky Mountains

Active season: Mid-spring to summer

Conservation status: None

Plant interactions: Larval hosts include willows (*Salix* spp.), cottonwoods (*Populus* spp.), and quaking aspen (*P. tremuloides*). Adults do not feed.

Similar species: Formerly a synonym of *S. cerisyi*, currently distinguished as a separate species.

JESSICA GOLDSTROHM

NESSUS SPHINX MOTH

Amphion floridensis

Size: 37–55 mm

Description: Large moth that resembles a hummingbird. Brownish overall with reddish or russet overtones. Wings generally brown, with darker median stripe on front wings and orange-red median band on hindwings that can be pale or even absent. Wing edges scalloped and lined in white. Two bright yellow stripes on the dorsal side of the abdomen and a fringed tuft at the end. Active from day to dusk. Caterpillars emerge from underground chambers they construct. One to several broods, depending on location.

Habitat: Forests, streamsides, suburbs, disturbed areas, barrens

Range: Colorado and Texas; most common in the Midwest and along the East Coast of United States

Active season: Summer in the north, mid-spring to fall in the south, year-round farther south

Conservation status: None

Plant interactions: Larval hosts include both native and non-native plants: grape (*Vitis* spp.), Virginia creeper (*Parthenocissus quinquefolia*), ampelopsis (*Ampelopsis* spp.), and peppers (*Capsicum* spp.). Adult drink nectar from lilac (*Syringa vulgaris*), herb-Robert (*Geranium robertianum*), beauty bush (*Kolkwitzia amabilis*), mock orange (*Philadelphus coronarius*), and *Phlox* spp.

Interesting facts: Larvae build underground chambers when ready to pupate.

Similar species: Previously known as *Amphion nessus* (Nessus sphinx moth)

Family Hesperiidae

Skippers

Skippers are small to medium-sized plump butterflies. They are named for their rapid and erratic, darting flight pattern, giving them the appearance of "skipping" along the grasses. They are generally colored in rusty or deep browns or dull oranges. Skippers generally hold their forewings at an angle above their hindwings, giving them a distinctive, well-defined triangular shape. Their most distinctive trait is the hooked tip in the antennae of most skippers. Caterpillars in this group are dull and generally green or brown, with a pronounced narrow collar just behind the head. They often create shelters out of folded, rolled, or tied leaves.

CHRISTIAN NUNES

SILVER-SPOTTED SKIPPER

Epargyreus clarus

Size: 45–67 mm wingspan

Description: The silver-spotted skipper is a large skipper with dark brown wings. The forewings are triangular, with a large yellow-orange medial patch spanning three to five cells that can be seen ventrally or dorsally. Forewings of males are more pointed than those of females. The dark brown hindwings have a large silver patch that can be seen ventrally.

Habitat: Swamps, forests, brushy areas, and riparian areas in low elevations

Range: Widespread across the United States and southern Canada and into Mexico and south-central America; not found in the Great Basin or western Texas

Active season: Mid-spring to mid-fall

Conservation status: None

Plant interactions: *E. clarus* caterpillars consume leaves of herbs, vines, shrubs, and trees in the pea family (Fabaceae). Adults drink nectar from everlasting pea (*Lathyrus latifolius*), common milkweed (*Asclepias syriaca*), red clover (*Trifolium pratense*), buttonbush (*Cephalanthus occidentalis*), blazing star (*Liatris* spp.), and thistles (*Cirsium* spp.).

Interesting facts: One of the largest and most widespread skippers in North America. They prefer blue, red, pink, and purple flowers over yellow flowers. Also prefer to fly in the shade.

LYLE ROSBOTHAM

DUSKYWINGS

Erynnis spp.

Size: 25–45 mm

Description: Small, darkly colored skippers; often with white spots, that somewhat resemble moths. Their dark colors lead to dour common names like "funereal" or "mournful." Usually perch with both sets of wings open but will close them when it's hot. Antennae are short and wider at the end. Southwestern species tend to have white fringe on their hindwings.

Habitat: Open areas or forest edges in montane and foothills, prairies and plains, streambanks, gardens, and disturbed sites

Range: Throughout the western United States

Active season: Early spring to fall

Conservation status: None

Plant interactions: Larval food ranges from oaks (*Quercus* spp.) to *Ceanothus* to herbaceous members of the pea family (Fabaceae), depending on the species. Adults avidly feed on flower nectar.

Interesting facts: *Erynnis* species are found in Europe, Asia, and North and Central America, but the most, seventeen species, occur in North America. These skippers have a habit of roosting with their wings wrapped around dead flower heads at night or in overcast weather.

Similar species: Adults in this genus can be very similar and difficult to tell apart without a microscope. A good strategy is to narrow down the species by location, habitat, and host plant presence and then compare with correctly identified images. Further identification requires a microscope.

SHIRAN HERSHCOVICH

WESTERN BRANDED SKIPPER
Hesperia colorado

Size: 22–30 mm

Description: Adult pattern varies by location. However, many individuals have yellow-brown fore- and hindwings with white markings on the underside. Forewing tips are pointed and bright orange on the dorsal side. The body has yellow-green, dusty hairs.

Habitat: Prairies, mountain forests, grasslands, meadows, riparian edges, and urban areas

Range: Western United States from Nebraska to the coast

Active season: Late spring to mid-fall

Conservation status: None

Plant interactions: Adults feed on nectar from a variety of flowers, including asters (*Symphyotrichum* spp.), goldenrods (*Solidago* spp.), and blazing star (Liatris spp.). Larvae feed on species of muhly grass (*Muhlenbergia* spp.), feather grass (*Stipa* spp.), big bluestem (*Andropogon* spp.), and ryegrass (*Lolium* spp.), as well as other grasses.

Interesting facts: Males will perch near host plants or even on top of hills to wait for females.

Similar species: Common branded skipper (*H. comma*) is similar but is more commonly found in southern Canada and the eastern United States.

CHRISTIAN NUNES

PAWNEE MONTANE SKIPPER

Hesperia leonardus montana

Size: 32–45 mm

Description: Adults are brownish yellow with white spots on the outer margins of their wings. Bodies are whitish brown, with large black eyes on a white head.

Habitat: Open ponderosa pine forests between 6,000 and 7,500 feet high in soils from the Pikes Peak Granite formation with minimal understory

Range: Colorado

Active season: Adults fly from midsummer to mid-fall

Conservation status: No International Union for Conservation of Nature (IUCN) status but listed as "threatened" on the federal endangered species list. At risk due to development of its small range.

Plant interactions: Larvae feed on grasses, primarily blue grama (*Bouteloua gracilis*). Adults mostly feed on flower nectar from prairie gayfeather (*Liatris pycnostachya*) but will also take nectar from smooth asters (*Aster laevis*), bee balm (*Monarda* spp.), and sunflower (*Helianthus* spp.), as well as a few others.

Interesting facts: Endemic to the South Platte River drainage of Colorado.

Similar species: Similar to the two other subspecies of *H. leonardus*: the Pawnee skipper (*H. leonardus pawnee*) and Leonard's skipper (*H. leonardus leonardus*). However, *H. leonardus montana* is found only in Colorado.

ANDREA CARPIO

FIERY SKIPPER

Hylephila phyleus

Size: 26–32 mm

Description: Antennae are very short. Male wings are orange or yellow in color; females tend to be dark brown. There are dark brown margins on the dorsal side of the hindwing, with dark brown spots on the hindwing and forewing.

Habitat: Open grassy areas, such as meadows, gardens, or lawns

Range: Widespread throughout the United States and into eastern Canada, except the Rockies and the Great Basin

Active season: Spring to fall in cooler areas; year-round where warmer

Conservation status: None

Plant interactions: Larvae feed on various grasses including Bermuda grass (*Cynodon dactylon*), crab grass (*Digitaria*), and St. Augustine grass (*Stenotaphrum secundatum*). Adults are generalist nectar feeders.

Interesting facts: Fiery skippers are pests of turfgrass.

Similar species: Woodland skipper (*Ochlodes sylvanoides*) is found in a different range, including the Rockies and the Pacific Northwest.

LYLE ROSBOTHAM

WOODLAND SKIPPER
Ochlodes sylvanoides

Size: 25–32 mm

Description: Dorsal side of both hindwing and forewing is orange with dark brown, toothed borders. Male forewing with a black stigma in a dark diagonal band; females with band but lack stigma. Large reddish patch on the hindwings. Underside of both forewings and hindwings is yellow, red, and brown; underside may not have markings or may have distinct white banding.

Habitat: Prairies and grasslands

Range: Western United States, excluding the Southwest; continuing north through Canada

Active season: Early summer to mid-fall

Conservation status: Imperiled in Alberta and Saskatchewan, but not listed in the United States

Plant interactions: Larvae feed on various grass (Poaceae) species; adults are nectar generalists.

Interesting facts: The common name is a misnomer. This species prefers open, grassy areas.

Similar species: Fiery skipper (*Hylephila phyleus*) is more orange with dark brown margins on the dorsal forewings, and umber skipper (*Poanes melane*) is reddish brown with pale orange spots.

GRANT MARR

UMBER SKIPPER
Poanes melane

Size: 31–36 mm

Description: Dorsal side of wings is reddish brown. Forewings have some pale orange spots; hindwing has a light yellow-brown band. Female is larger and lighter colored. Underside looks similar to the dorsal side, but the spots are larger and lighter.

Habitat: Desert foothills, oak woodlands, streamsides, grassy areas

Range: Arizona, California, and Texas

Active season: Early spring to fall

Conservation status: None

Plant interactions: Larvae feed on various grasses (Poaceae). Adults visit a variety of plants, including yerba santa (*Eriodictyon californicum*), dogbane (*Apocynum* spp.), milkweed (*Asclepias* spp.), thistles (*Cirsium* spp.), California buckeye (*Aesculus californica*), and coyote brush (*Baccharis pilularis*).

Interesting facts: Scientists have yet to document which grass species feed the larvae of the umber skipper; the degree of host plant specialization determines how extensive the range of this insect can be.

Similar species: Fiery skipper (*Hylephila phyleus*) is more orange with dark brown margins on the dorsal forewings, and woodland skipper (*Ochlodes sylvanoides*) is orange with dark brown, toothed borders.

TAXILES SKIPPER

Poanes taxiles

Size: 32–43 mm

Description: Adult males have orange wings with narrow black borders and a thin orange outer margin. Dorsal side of the female is dark orange-brown with pale orange patches on the forewing and central hindwing. Underside of the hindwing is violet-brown with a pale band of spots and a patch of gray scales near the outer margin.

Habitat: Forest clearings and grasslands in the plains and foothills

Range: Central North America

Active season: Late spring to late summer

Conservation status: None

Plant interactions: Caterpillars feed on grasses; adults are nectar generalists.

Interesting facts: This butterfly is still active in cloudy weather, when most butterflies will be absent.

BRIONNA MCCUMBER

Similar species: Umber skipper (*Poanes melane*), Zabulon skipper (*Poanes zabulon*), and woodland skipper (*Ochlodes sylvanoides*) are similar in appearance.

PECK'S SKIPPER

Polites peckius

Size: 19–27 mm

Description: Dark brown and orange small skippers with fringed wings. Ventrally, both sexes have a light brown patch in the middle of the hindwing. Males are lighter than females and have a stigma (round or oval mark) on the forewing. Both sexes have light-colored postmedian spot bands on the underside of the forewings.

Habitat: Prairies and plains, marshes and roadsides

Range: Northern United States and southern Canada; absent from the West Coast and less common in the southern United States

CHRISTIAN NUNES

Active season: Late spring to mid-fall

Conservation status: None

Plant interactions: Larvae feed on grasses (Poaceae). Adults will nectar from a variety of flowers including clover (*Trifolium* spp.), vetch (*Vicia* spp.), alfalfa (*Medicago sativa*), coneflowers (*Echinacea* spp.), teasel (*Dipsacus* spp.), blazing star (*Liatris* sp.) and thistles (*Cirsium* spp.). Adults also sip on mud from moist soil.

Interesting facts: Peck's skippers fly rapidly close to the ground.

GERRY SNYDER

COMMON CHECKERED-SKIPPER

Burnsius communis

Size: 19–32 mm

Description: Dorsal male wings are bluish gray, females black, with white in a checkered pattern. Large white spots create median bands across forewings and hindwings. Fringe is checkered at least partway. Marginal white spots are small; submarginal white spots are larger. Ventral wings are cream with dark gray or olive bands.

Habitat: Wide range of habitats, from mountains to prairies, woods, pastures, roadsides, and areas with low vegetation

Range: Widespread throughout the United States and Canada

Active season: Mid-spring to early fall

Conservation status: Vulnerable in British Columbia; not listed in the United States

Plant interactions: Larvae feed on plants in the mallow family (Malvaceae).

Interesting facts: The common checkered-skipper is the most common skipper in North America. Formerly known as *Pyrgus communis*.

Similar species: White checkered-skipper (*B. albescens*) and desert checkered-skipper (*B. philetas*) are similar in appearance.

Family Lycaenidae

Gossamer-winged Butterflies (Hairstreaks, Blues, and Coppers)

The slight and fragile nature of these butterflies earns them the name "gossamer-winged butterflies." Their wings come in different shades of iridescent blues, coppers, and grays; more rarely, purples and greens. This group is easily identified by their small and distinctive shape and antennae with alternating rings of black and white. Gossamer-winged butterflies are speciose, with over 6,000 species worldwide. Identification down to species may be difficult in this group.

RON WOLF

WESTERN PYGMY BLUE
Brephidium exilis

Size: 13–19 mm

Description: Very small; common in its range. Dorsal wings are copper, fringed in white with muted blue base. Ventral wings are copper with marginal black spots, white at base with three black spots.

Habitat: Salty marshes, deserts, alkaline and other disturbed areas, plains, foothills

Range: Throughout the western United States except Montana and Wyoming

Active season: Midsummer to early fall in the north; year-round in warmer areas

Conservation status: None

Plant interactions: Larval hosts include pigweed (*Chenopodium album*), saltbush species (*Atriplex* spp.), winterfat (*Krascheninnikovia lanata*), and others in the amaranth family (Amaranthaceae). Adults feed on flower nectar. Females lay eggs on host plants, especially upper side of leaves. Caterpillars will eat any part of the plant.

Interesting facts: Some of the smallest butterflies in the world are blues, and this may be the smallest in North America. Introduced and spreading in the Middle East.

WESTERN GREEN HAIRSTREAK

Callophrys affinis

MICHAEL J ANDERSEN

Size: 25–30 mm

Description: Ventral side of the forewing and hindwing are yellow-green to green, with white dashes on the margins and medially through the wing. Dorsal side of the wings is typically gray to orange. There are no tails on the hindwings.

Habitat: Chaparral, woodland, scrubland

Range: Western United States and Canada, from Rocky Mountains to the west coast of North America

Active season: Late spring to midsummer

Conservation status: None; could be rare at the periphery of its range

Plant interactions: Larvae feed on flowers and immature fruit of sulfur flower (*Eriogonum* spp.), canary clover (*Lotus* spp.) and *Ceanothus* spp. Adults feed on nectar.

Interesting facts: This species overwinters as a chrysalis.

LOTUS HAIRSTREAK

Callophrys dumetorum

HEIDE KEEBLE

Size: 25–32 mm

Description: Undersides of the wing have small white spots in a postmedian line. Hindwings have no tails. Dorsal wings are gray for males and yellowish for females. Eggs are laid on flower buds and underside of foliage.

Habitat: Coastal scrub and foothill canyons.

Range: Coastal Washington, Oregon, and California

Active season: Active throughout spring.

Conservation status: None

Plant interactions: Caterpillars eat foliage and flowers; adults feed on nectar. Larval hosts are coast buckwheat (*Eriogonum latifolium*); chrysalids hibernate in debris at the base of the host plant.

Interesting facts: Inhabits coastal areas, rarely inland.

WESTERN PINE ELFIN

Callophrys eryphon

LYLE ROSBOTHAM

Size: 25–35 mm

Description: Underside of wings of adults is reddish brown with irregular dark bands. Ventral side of the wings is reddish black with no bands. Hindwings lack tails. Males wait near host plants for females. Females will lay eggs on young needles and catkins. Chrysalids hibernate; adults emerge in spring.

Habitat: Coniferous pine forests

Range: Mostly found in the western United States from the Rocky Mountains to the West Coast and north into British Columbia; some sightings recorded in the Midwest

Active season: Late spring through early summer

Conservation status: None, though sometimes rare

Plant interactions: Larva feed on hard pine species. Adults feed on nectar from various flowers.

Interesting facts: The caterpillars will defoliate young pine needles.

JUNIPER HAIRSTREAK

Callophrys gryneus

CHRISTIAN NUNES

Size: 26–32 mm

Description: Upper side of forewings is reddish brown, darker near the base and at the margins. Females may be lighter in color. Beneath forewing is rusty red with white postmedian lines edged with reddish brown. Hindwings are distinctively green, with the same type of postmedian lines as above.

Habitat: Piñon-juniper woodlands and forest openings, disturbed areas, bluffs, barrens; where host plants are found

Range: Throughout the western United States

Active season: Mid-spring to late summer, depending on location

Conservation status: None

Plant interactions: Larval hosts are junipers, including California juniper (*Juniperus californica*), Utah juniper (*J. osteosperma*), and Rocky Mountain juniper (*J. scopulorum*), possibly others. Adults feed on flower nectar from dogbane (*Apocynum* spp.), milkweed and butterfly weed (*Asclepias* spp.), clover (*Trifolium* spp.), and many others; also mud. Single eggs are laid on host plants; larvae feed on foliage then drop to base of plant and pupate in litter and hibernate.

Interesting facts: Proximity to junipers is the best identifying characteristic for this butterfly.

DUSKY-BLUE GROUNDSTREAK

Calycopis isobeon

Size: 22–32 mm

Description: Dorsal side of wings is dusky blue; hindwing has two tails. Ventral wings are grayish brown; forewing with postmedian line edged in reddish orange; hindwing with same postmedian line, as well as large submarginal spots in orange and black.

Habitat: Forest edges, valleys in foothills; developed, disturbed sites/old fields, ditches/roadsides, gardens in urban/suburban areas

Range: Texas

Active season: Winter to fall

Conservation status: None

CHUCK SEXTON

Plant interactions: Larvae feed on plant debris at the base of plants, especially in the cashew family (Anacardiaceae), including cashew, pistachio, sumac, poison ivy, poison oak, and poison sumac. Adults feed on flower nectar.

Similar species: Similar to the red-banded hairstreak (*Calycopis cecrops*), but ventral red lines are thinner.

HOPS AZURE

Celastrina humulus

Size: 21–27 mm

Description: Variable; sexually dimorphic. Dorsal wings on males are powdery blue; female are blue near the base, with black on costal and outer portions of forewing and costal portions of hindwing. Ventral wings are white with small black marks ranging from almost absent to more heavily marked.

CHRISTIAN NUNES

Habitat: Canyon bottoms, rockslides, talus slopes in alpine areas; where host plants are found

Range: Colorado Front Range and possibly Montana; locally abundant

Active season: Midsummer

Conservation status: None

Plant interactions: Larvae feed on hops (*Humulus* sp.) and lupine (*Lupinus* sp.). Adults feed on flower nectar of both native and exotic plants, as well as mud, dung, and honeydew.

Interesting facts: A Colorado brewing company created an ale named after this hops-loving butterfly.

REAKIRT'S BLUE

Echinargus isola

Size: 16–23 mm

AMY YARGER

Description: Dorsal forewing is pale dusky blue with darker veins and border; hindwing similar with one or more black spots on margin at central back. Ventral forewing is silvery gray with five postmedian black spots bordered in white. Female is usually darker overall.

Habitat: Grasslands, desert, streambanks, disturbed and weedy areas

Range: Southern United States. Common in the southern part of its range, where it will hibernate. Unable to survive freezes and less common to the north. Specimens at the far north of its range are most likely migrants.

Active season: Mid-spring to early fall; year-round in warmer areas

Conservation status: None

Plant interactions: Larvae feed on flowers, seeds, and foliage of plants in the pea family (Fabaceae), including species of milkvetch (*Astragalus* spp.), indigo bush (*Dalea* spp.), mesquite (*Prosopis* spp.), and mimosa (*Albizia* spp.). Adults feed on flower nectar. Single eggs are laid on the flower buds.

Interesting facts: Monotypic, or the only species in its genus *Echinargus*. Ants, attracted to the caterpillars' "sugary secretions," appear to help caterpillars avoid parasitism.

COLORADO HAIRSTREAK

Hypaurotis crysalus

Size: 32–38 mm

JULIE ARINGTON

Description: A beautiful, exotic-looking butterfly. Dorsal surface is iridescent purple with wide dark margins containing orange spots; a small tail on the hindwing, which is common to hairstreaks. Ventral surface is light gray with black-centered orange spot near tail.

Habitat: Open areas and canyons in montane and foothill areas where oak trees, especially Gambel oaks (*Quercus gambelii*) grow

Range: Colorado, Utah, New Mexico, Arizona, eastern Nevada, southern Wyoming

Active season: Summer to early fall

Conservation status: None

Plant interactions: Larvae feed on leaves of trees in the beech family (Fagaceae), particularly those of the Gambel oak (*Q. gambelii*). Eggs are laid on leaves or bark; the larvae then feed on the foliage. Adults roost in the tree in late summer. Adults feed on tree sap, raindrops, and maybe insect honeydew.

Interesting facts: The Colorado Hairstreak was designated the official Colorado State Insect in 1996 thanks to the fourth graders from Wheeling Elementary in Aurora, Colorado, and their teacher, Melinda Terry. The teacher and students successfully persuaded the Colorado legislature to pass Colorado Senate Bill 96-122, making Colorado the thirty-seventh state with an official state insect. Remains active after sunset.

LORNA MCCALLISTER

SILVERY BLUE

Glaucopsyche lygdamus

Size: 22–32 mm

Description: Dorsal wings are iridescent blue with darker edges, fringe gray to white. Female is darker. Ventral wings are off-white to tannish gray, with gray to white fringe and row of postmedian round black spots circled in white. These spots are sometimes absent.

Habitat: Shrubland/savanna, conifer forest openings, deciduous forest openings in montane areas; open woods, coastal dunes, prairies, meadows, road edges, rocky moist woods, and brushy fields in the foothills

Range: Throughout the western United States

Active season: Mid-spring to late summer, depending on elevation

Conservation status: None

Plant interactions: Larvae feed on members of the pea family (Fabaceae), including but not limited to milkvetch (*Astragalus* spp.), lupine (*Lupinus* spp.), sweet clover (*Melilotus* spp.), and sweet pea (*Lathyrus* spp.). Adults feed on flower nectar, including the sunflower family (Asteraceae), as well as bird droppings, mammal dung, and mud. Single eggs laid on flower buds and young foliage on which caterpillars feed.

Interesting facts: Ants may protect caterpillars from parasitism as they feed on their honeydew.

CHRISTIAN NUNES

G. piasus (dorsal view)

ARROWHEAD BLUE

Glaucopsyche piasus

Size: 29–35 mm

Description: Male dorsal wings are purplish blue with a wide border and checkered fringe. Females are duller in color. Ventral side is gray with many small black spots. Hindwing has a postmedian band of white "arrowheads" pointing inward. Males look for females near host plants during daytime.

Habitat: Coastal dunes in California; mountains elsewhere, including scrub, woodland openings, roadsides, open areas, and streamsides

Range: Throughout the western United States except Texas

Active season: Spring through summer

Conservation status: None

Plant interactions: Larvae feed on lupines (*Lupinus* spp.) and milkvetch (*Astragalus* spp.) species, flowers and fruits. Adults feed on flower nectar. Eggs laid on host plant's flower buds.

Interesting facts: Uncommon in its range.

CHRISTIAN NUNES

JOHN SULLIVAN

LUSTROUS COPPER

Lycaena cupreus

Size: 29–31 mm

Description: Dorsal side of the male wings are coppery brown tinged with bright purple; female's wings are brown with cream and black spots. Dorsal side of the female hindwings are brown with a row of orange crescents next to a row of small black dots. Ventral side of the wings of both sexes is gray with black spots. Hindwing has a submarginal row of red-orange spots. Males perch and patrol for females. Half-grown caterpillars hibernate.

Habitat: Alpine species; found in meadows, sagebrush, rocky treeless areas

Range: Rocky Mountain range; also California's Sierra Nevada

Active season: One flight throughout the summer

Conservation status: None

Plant interactions: Larval hosts are in the buckwheat family (Polygonaceae). Females lay eggs on or near host plants for caterpillars to eat. Adults feed on flower nectar from a variety of plants.

Interesting facts: This is one of the only "true" species of the *Lycaena* genus because other subgenera are often separated into their own genera.

GORGON COPPER

Lycaena gorgon

Size: 32–38 mm

Description: Dorsal side of the male is coppery brown with a reddish tinge. Females are dark brown with cream and black spots. Dorsal side of female hindwings has a row of orange crescents next to row of small back spots. The ventral side of both sexes is gray with black spots. Hindwing has a submarginal row of red-orange spots. Hindwings have no tails.

Habitat: Chaparral, foothill canyons and woodland, rocky outcrops, sagebrush

Range: California and Oregon

Active season: Late spring through early summer

Conservation status: None

Plant interactions: Larvae feed on plants in the buckwheat family (Polygonaceae). Adults feed on flower nectar.

Interesting facts: Males are territorial and perch on the ground, patrolling for females.

DANIEL J FITZGERALD

L. gorgon, male

BRIAN WRIGHT

L. gorgon, female

JULIE ARINGTON

PURPLISH COPPER

Lycaena helloides

Size: 30–38 mm

Description: Dorsal side is brown with iridescent purple, a wide dark margin with scattered dark spots; hindwing with jagged orange band at outer margin. Female is more orange. Beneath forewing is peachy copper with black spots; hindwing light gray with lavender sheen, small black spots, and thin orange jagged marginal band.

Habitat: Montane shrubland/savanna riparian stream banks, shrubland, edges, wetlands and marshes; agricultural/croplands, disturbed sites, old fields, ditches, roadsides

Range: California, Colorado, Idaho, Montana, Nevada, New Mexico, Oregon, Utah, Washington, Wyoming; Alberta, British Columbia

Active season: Late spring to mid-fall, depending on geographic location

Conservation status: None

Plant interactions: Larval hosts are plants in the buckwheat family (Polygonaceae), including knotweeds (*Polygonum* spp.) and docks (*Rumex* spp.); also cinquefoils in the rose family (Rosaceae). Adults feed on flower nectar from a wide variety of plants, including yarrow (*Achillea* spp.), milkweed (*Asclepias* spp.), rabbitbrush (*Ericameria* spp.), thistle (*Cirsium* spp.), fleabane (*Erigeron* spp.), tansy aster (*Machaeranthera* spp.), sweet clover (*Melilotus* spp.), mint (*Mentha spp.*), goldenrod (*Solidago* spp.), and asters (*Symphyotrichum* spp.). Eggs are scattered at base of host plant. Caterpillars feed on leaves.

Similar species: Similar to dorcas copper (*L. dorcas*), whose range is more to the east but may overlap with *L. helloides* in the Rocky Mountains.

JULIE ARINGTON

BLUE COPPER

Lycaena heteronea

Size: 29–35 mm

Description: Small butterfly with a white body; some blue hairs on top of the abdomen. Underside of forewings is white with black spots; underside of hindwings is white with brown spots. Dorsal surface of the male is bright blue; females' is dark brown with spots. Fringes of wings are white.

Habitat: Mostly found at high elevations in meadows, sagebrush, open forests

Range: From the Rocky Mountains west to the Pacific coast and north into British Columbia

Active season: Adults fly one flight between late spring and late summer.

Conservation status: None

Plant interactions: Larvae feed on buckwheat species (*Eriogonum* spp.) in the buckwheat family (Polygonaceae). Adults feed on nectar from a variety of flowers but prefer wild buckwheat.

Interesting facts: Young caterpillars feed on the underside of the leaf; older caterpillars eat the whole leaf.

CHRISTIAN NUNES

AMERICAN COPPER

Lycaena phlaeas

Size: 32–35 mm

Description: Dorsal side of the forewings is an iridescent yellow-orange with dark gray margins and black spots. Underside of the forewings is a dull orange with light gray margins and black spots. Dorsal side of the hindwings is gray with orange margins with black spots; a small tail. Underside of the hindwings is light gray.

Habitat: Disturbed areas, including grasslands, prairies, woodland clearings, ditches

Range: The range for these butterflies is Holarctic, covering North America, Europe, Asia, and North Africa. Different subspecies will be found in different areas of the United States. *L. p. americana* is found from Kansas east to the Atlantic coastline; *L. p. arethusa* in the northwest United States.

Active season: Adults have one flight from midsummer through early fall.

Conservation status: None

Plant interactions: Larvae feed on herbs in the buckwheat family (Polygonaceae). Adults feed on flower nectar from a variety of plants, including buttercup (Ranunculaceae), white clover (Trifolium repens), butterfly weed (Asclepias tuberosa), and yarrow (*Achillea* spp.).

Interesting facts: Usually seen only singly or in twos. Eggs overwinter.

JULIE ARINGTON

RUDDY COPPER

Lycaena rubidus

Size: 29–41 mm

Description: Dorsal side is bright reddish orange with subtle black spots, subtle orange jagged margin inside of narrow black border, and unchecked white fringe. Female is duller in color; black spots much more distinct, orange marginal zigzag inside narrow black border, and unchecked white fringe. Underside of both sexes is grayish white, maybe with a yellow hue; forewing disk is orangey; hindwing with or without subtle black spots.

Habitat: Montane—herbaceous, conifer forest edge, conifer forest openings, deciduous forest edge; foothills—herbaceous meadows/grasslands, conifer forest edge, conifer forest openings, deciduous forest edge; desert—sagebrush. Dry areas where the soil is sandy or gravelly.

Range: Western United States and Canada

Active season: June to August, depending on elevation

Conservation status: None

Plant interactions: Larval hosts are dock (*Rumex* spp.) species in the buckwheat family (Polygonaceae). Adults feed on flower nectar from a wide range of plants, including but not limited to yarrow (*Achillea* spp.), pearly everlasting (*Anaphalis* spp.), *Cleome*, spurge (*Euphorbia* spp.), sunflowers (*Helianthus* spp.), black-eyed Susan (*Rudbeckia* spp.), and stonecrop (*Sedum* spp.); also mud. Single eggs are laid singly on or at base of the host plant.

Interesting facts: Larvae are tended by ants, possibly for sticky secretions.

RICHARD GREEN

GREAT COPPER

Lycaena xanthoides

Size: 33–44 mm

Description: Dorsal side of adults is brown-gray with orange margins on base of hindwings and orange tinges in some cells of the forewings. Hindwings have a small tail. Underside of adults is pale gray with some black spots.

Habitat: Open foothills and canyons

Range: Oregon and California

Active season: Late spring through midsummer

Conservation status: Some subspecies are losing range due to invasive European weeds.

Plant interactions: The host plant for caterpillars is curly dock and other *Rumex* species. Adults visit a variety of flowers, including gum plant (*Grindelia* spp.), horehound (*Marrubium* spp.), dogbane (*Apocynum cannabinum*), heliotrope (*Heliotropium* spp.), and many others.

Interesting facts: Males are territorial and patrol streambeds for females.

ACMON BLUE

Plebejus acmon

Size: 20–29 mm

Description: Dorsal side of males is blue with a dark border. Females are brown with occasional blue scales, a dark border, and orange submarginal cells on the hindwings. Underside is white with black spots. Hindwing above and below with red-orange submarginal band.

Habitat: Wide variety of habitats, including deserts, fields, prairies, weedy areas, and mountains

Range: Western United States, mostly in California

Active season: Many flights from early spring through mid-fall

Conservation status: None

Plant interactions: Larval host plants are in the pea (Fabaceae) and buckwheat (Polygonaceae) families. Adults feed on nectar.

Interesting facts: This species is one of the most common western blues. Caterpillars overwinter. Acmon blues will puddle in the mountains with other blues. Larvae are kept in the ant nest; in return, they provide honeydew to the ants (University of California, Davis).

Similar species: *P. lupini* is similar to *P. acmon*; however, *P. lupini* is found at higher elevations on rocky slopes.

JAMES BAILEY

Dorsal view of female

JAMES BAILEY

Dorsal view of male

JAMES BAILEY

Ventral view

ARCTIC BLUE

Plebejus glandon

Size: 22–26 mm

Description: This species will vary in terms of color and pattern depending on geographical location. Typically, the dorsal side of the wing on the male is a gray-blue; wings of the female are an orangish brown. Both sexes have dark cell spots on both wings. Underside of the wings has postmedian black spots lacking or enclosed by white patches. Forewings typically have more black spots; hindwings tend to lack the black spots, showing only white spots.

RICH READING

Habitat: Alpine meadows, bogs, gravelly hills

Range: Holarctic but found in North America from Alaska to northern Arizona and New Mexico. Their range typically follows the Rocky Mountains.

Active season: One flight from late spring through early fall, but most common in late summer

Conservation status: None

Plant interactions: Larvae feed on plants in the primrose family (Primulaceae). Adults feed on nectar from flowers.

Interesting facts: Most commonly observed puddling.

BOISDUVAL'S BLUE

Plebejus icarioides

Size: 29–35 mm

Description: Undersides of wings are white with black or white postmedian spots. Dorsal side of wings is blue with light blue veins and black margins for males; blue or brown for females.

LYLE ROSBOTHAM

Habitat: Variety of habitats, from forests to meadows and prairies, chaparral, coastal dunes

Range: Western North America from British Columbia south through California and east to the Great Plains

Active season: Mid-spring to late summer

Conservation status: None

Plant interactions: Larvae feed on *Lupine* species in the legume family (Fabaceae). Adults feed on nectar from flowers of composites.

Interesting facts: Caterpillars feed on leaves, then flowers. Caterpillars produce a sugary secretion that is eaten by ants for nutrition, with the ants protecting them.

LUPINE BLUE

Plebejus lupini

Size: 22–29 mm

Description: The underside of the wings is light gray with black spots outlined in light gray. The underside of the hindwings has an orange margin, which may be separated into separate chevrons. Dorsal side of the male is light blue with darker borders; females are dark brown.

Habitat: Mountain meadows, chaparral, rocky outcrops

Range: Western United States and southwestern Canada; mostly found in the mountainous regions and high plains

Active season: In California there is one flight through the summer. Elsewhere there are several flights from early spring through early summer.

Conservation status: A few highly localized populations are of conservation concern.

Plant interactions: Larvae feed on leaves, flowers, and fruits or plants in the buckwheat family (Polygonaceae).

JAMES BAILEY

P. lupini (dorsal view)

JAMES BAILEY

P. lupini (ventral view)

Interesting facts: Eggs laid on flowers, which are eaten by caterpillars. The butterfly is referred to as the "lupine blue" because of its blue color, which is similar to that of a lupine.

Similar species: *P. acmon*, but *P. lupini* is more likely to be found in the mountains.

MELISSA BLUE

Plebejus melissa

STEVE VANLOH

Size: 22–35 mm

Description: Female adults are brown with few blue scales. Males are blue with a narrow dark border. Continuous orange border on the hind- and forewings seen from both above and below.

Habitat: Prairies, dunes, weedy open areas, meadows

Range: Western population is found throughout the Intermountain West from Canada to California. Eastern population is in the New Hampshire and New York area.

Active season: April to October

Conservation status: None

Plant interactions: Larvae from the eastern population feeds on lupine; western population feeds on members of the pea family (Fabaceae). Adults feed on nectar mostly from members of the sunflower family (Asteraceae).

Interesting facts: Sparkly blue-green scales near the outer edge of the hindwing catch the light as the butterfly flies.

GREENISH BLUE

Plebejus saepiolus

JULIE ARINGTON

Size: 25–32 mm

Description: Gray underside with some orange borders on the hindwings (no tails) and some irregular dark spots. Dorsal side is bright iridescent green-blue, but with faded gray margins. Females have blue at the base of the wing and more of a brown on the outside. Dorsal forewings have a dark dash mid-wing.

Habitat: Wide range of habitats, from stream edges to meadows and open forests

Range: Alaska to California, mainly west of the Rocky Mountains; east across southern Canada to the Great Lakes

Active season: One flight from late spring to midsummer

Conservation status: None; however, the San Gabriel blue subspecies is extinct.

Plant interactions: Caterpillars feed on clover flowers (*Trifolium* spp.); adults feed on clover nectars.

Interesting facts: Half-grown caterpillars hibernate over the winter.

SHASTA BLUE

Plebejus shasta

DANIEL J. FITZGERALD

Size: 20–23 mm

Description: Adult underside is gray with dark gray cells on fore- and hindwings, with black postmedian spots. Hindwings have an outer margin with some iridescent green spots. Dorsal side of males is light blue; females are generally darker, with an orange band on the hindwing.

Habitat: Alpine fields, high-plains prairies, forest openings, sagebrush

Range: High elevations, from Alberta and Saskatchewan in the north to California, Nevada, Utah, and Colorado in the southernmost parts of the range

Active season: One flight during summer, between June and August

Conservation status: None

Plant interactions: Larvae feed on species in the pea family (Fabaceae), such as *Astragalus* spp., *Lupinus* spp., and *Trifolium* spp. Adults feed on flower nectar.

Interesting facts: In high elevations the butterflies take two years to mature.

CHRISTIAN NUNES

P. shasta (dorsal view)

CORAL HAIRSTREAK

Satyrium titus

CHRISTIAN NUNES

Size: 25–38 mm

Description: Underside of wings is gray with a bright orange row of submarginal cells on the hindwings and slightly on the forewings, which are ringed with black and white. Adults have no tail.

Habitat: Old fields and meadows; also shrubby areas and stream sides

Range: Widespread through North America except for the southernmost states. Range spills into southern Canada.

Active season: One flight from late spring through late summer

Conservation status: None

Plant interactions: Larvae feed on plants in the rose family (Rosaceae). Adults feed on nectar from a variety of flowers, especially butterfly weed (Asclepias tuberosa).

Interesting facts: Caterpillars feed on leaves and fruit at night.

Similar species: Similar to the Acadian hairstreak (*Satyrium acadica*), which has a tail on its hindwing and is associated with willows, its host plant.

GRAY HAIRSTREAK

Strymon melinus

HEIDE KEEBLE

Size: 22–35 mm

Description: Caterpillar is green or white with long hairs on its dorsal surface. Adults have one tail on the hindwing. Dorsal side of the wings is gray with a slight blue sheen and an orange spot near the tail of the hindwing. The underside of the wings changes color depending on the season, from a dark gray in spring and fall to a light gray in summer. There is usually an orange patch on the top of the head.

Habitat: Open prairies and meadows; also disturbed weedy areas

Range: Widespread throughout the United States, although rare in the Great Plains; also north through southern British Columbia, south through Venezuela

Active season: Two flights in the north from late spring through early fall. Three to four flights in the south from late winter to mid-fall

Conservation status: None

Plant interactions: Caterpillars feed on flowers and fruits from a variety of plants, including that of the pea (Fabaceae) and mallow (Malvaceae) families. Adults feed on a variety of flower nectars.

Interesting facts: Most widespread hairstreak in North America. Caterpillars are sometimes in a mutualistic relationship with ants, which protect them in exchange for the sugary solution the caterpillar secretes. Caterpillars can cause economic damage.

Family Nymphalidae

Brush-footed Butterflies

Nymphalids are the largest and most diverse family of butterflies. They are generally medium-sized butterflies. Wing coloration and shape of this group are highly varied, but they are often brightly colored. Underwings may be of duller colors, imitating bark or leaves. Nymphalids are identified by their reduced front legs; these are usually held close to their body and are not used for walking, giving the impression of the butterfly being four-legged. This group includes some of the most well-known butterflies, including monarchs, fritillaries, admirals, ladies, and tortoiseshells.

CALIFORNIA SISTER BUTTERFLY

Adelpha californica

RON WOLF

Size: 65–100 mm

Description: Medium to large butterfly with a distinct bright orange patch in the upper corner of each forewing. Dorsal surface of wings is dark brown to black; a creamy white band extends from the forewing below the orange patch to the hindwing, giving the appearance of connecting near the tip of the abdomen when wings are held open. Ventral wing surface is ornately and variably patterned with browns, blues, purples, oranges, and whites; distinct blue band runs along the wing edges of forewing and hindwing. Outer edge of the white band is partially fringed by a thin blue band.

Habitat: Oak woodlands

Range: Western California, Nevada, Oregon, and southwestern Washington in its northernmost range

Active season: Spring through autumn, rarely extending to winter

Conservation status: None

Plant interactions: Caterpillars feed on various oaks, especially canyon live oak (*Quercus chrysolepis*) and coast live oak (*Q. agrifolia*). Adults feed on nectar but rely on tree sap, fallen rotting fruit, and animal dung.

Interesting facts: Their oak diet makes them unpalatable to predators. They lay single green eggs. Males engage in mud-puddling behaviors.

Similar species: This species is part of a large mimicry complex of similar-looking species, but they generally do not overlap in range. May resemble Lorquin's admiral (*Limenitis lorquini*), which has orange tips instead of an orange patch in the upper dorsal forewing.

MICHAEL J. ANDERSEN

ARIZONA SISTER BUTTERFLY
Adelpha eulalia

Size: 75–125 mm

Description: Medium to large butterfly with a distinct bright orange patch in the upper corner of each forewing. Dorsal surface of wings is dark brown to black; a creamy white band extends from the forewing below the orange patch to the hindwing, giving the appearance of connecting near the tip of the abdomen when wings are held open. Ventral wing surface is ornately and variably patterned with browns, blues, purples, oranges, and whites; outer edge of the white band is fully fringed by a thin blue band.

Habitat: Oak woodlands, conifer woodlands, riparian canyons; most often near bodies of water

Range: Southern Rocky Mountain region, extending as far south as Mexico; inclusive of southern Nevada, Arizona, and New Mexico. May occasionally extend to southeastern California.

Active season: Spring through autumn, rarely extending to winter

Conservation status: None

Plant interactions: Caterpillars feed on various oaks (*Quercus* spp.). Adults feed on nectar rarely, but primarily rely on tree sap, fallen rotting fruit, and animal dung.

Interesting facts: Their oak diet makes them unpalatable to predators.

Similar species: This species is part of a large mimicry complex of similar-looking species, but they generally do not overlap in range. They are larger than the California sister (*A. californica*). May resemble Lorquin's admiral (*Limenitis lorquini*), which has orange tips instead of an orange patch in the upper dorsal forewing.

MILBERT'S TORTOISESHELL
Aglais milberti

DALE L. PATE

Size: 40–60 mm

Description: Small and colorful butterfly. Dorsal side is brown to black in center, with wide band that grades from yellowish cream to dark orange. Narrow dark brown to black band on the border of forewing and hindwing; band may contain light blue spots along its length.

Habitat: Primarily riparian habitats; also found in semi-disturbed areas like roadsides, trails, pastures, and gardens

Range: Western North America

Active season: Late spring to autumn

Conservation status: None

Plant interactions: Caterpillars feed on nettles (*Urtica* spp.). Adults feed on nectar of flowers like thistles (*Cirsium* spp.) and goldenrods (*Solidago* spp.).

Interesting facts: Females may lay egg clutches that include as many as 900 eggs. The early instar caterpillars feed communally in a web, which they leave to forage solitarily in later instars. They use their silk to build shelters with folded leaves. Species overwinters as adults, sometimes in groups.

GULF FRITILLARY
Dione vanillae

BRIONNA MCCUMBER

Size: 60–95 mm

Description: Medium orange butterfly with long forewings. Dorsal side brightly orange. Three white dots lined with black located on the top of the forewing, close to the abdomen. Ventral side is brownish and marked by iridescent silvery-white spots. A sexually dimorphic species; females noticeably larger than males and usually darker or more marked.

Habitat: Open sunny habitats like grasslands, fields, pastures, forest edges, gardens

Range: Southern United States, extending to South America

Active season: Varies across its range—late winter to late autumn

Conservation status: None

Plant interactions: Passion-vines (*Passiflora* spp.) are hosts for the caterpillars. As adults, they feed on nectar from flowers like lantanas (*Lantana* spp.) and asters (family Asteraceae).

Interesting facts: They possess defensive chemicals they store in special abdominal glands; when faced with danger, they may release these chemical compounds, which create an odor avoided by predators like birds.

TERRY IRELAND

UNCOMPAHGRE FRITILLARY

Boloria acrocnema

Size: 20–30 mm

Description: Small and rare fritillary. Dark brown center closest to the body creates a triangular shape when wings fully spread, extending to a pale orange or tan and a rusty brown toward wing edges; dark brown to black lines and dots. Ventral hindwing with a thick white bar dividing the crimson-brown inner half from the grayish coloring toward the outer wing. Body rusty brown to brownish black. Sexually dimorphic; females lighter in coloration than males.

Habitat: High-elevation mountain fields

Range: San Juan Mountains and southern Sawatch Mountains of Colorado

Active season: Midsummer

Conservation status: Added to the endangered species list in 1991 by US Fish and Wildlife Service

Plant interactions: Caterpillars are specialists and feed on their host, snow willow (*Salix reticulata* ssp. *nivalis*).

Interesting facts: One of the smallest known ranges of any North American butterfly.

Similar species: Can be difficult to differentiate from other fritillary species. This butterfly was only relatively recently recognized as its own species (1978).

RICH READING

ARCTIC FRITILLARY

Boloria chariclea

Size: 30–40 mm

Description: Fritillary of variable coloration. Wings are predominantly rusty, orange, orange-brown, or brown with brown-black markings. Dorsal side with black dots extending throughout median band. Hindwing underside has a margin of white spots lined with brown. Median band in hindwing sharply points in the center.

Habitat: Subalpine and alpine meadows, tundra, taiga, marshes, streams, acid bogs

Range: Circumboreal; Rocky Mountain region in the North American West

Active season: Late summer

Conservation status: None

Plant interactions: Hosts on violets (*Viola* spp.), scrub willows (*Salix* spp.), and possibly blueberries (*Vaccinium* spp.), but more research is needed. Nectars on a variety of plants including Joe-Pye weed (*Eupatorium maculatum*), common milkweed (*Asclepias syriaca*), black-eyed Susan (*Rudbeckia hirta*), and goldenrod (*Solidago* spp.).

Interesting facts: While fritillaries are difficult to distinguish in flight, the Arctic fritillary may move slower than other butterflies in the group, and often hovers and soars between wingbeats.

Similar species: Fritillaries can be challenging to tell apart. Hindwing view is necessary for proper identification. Flight is late summer and habitat is boggy, which distinguishes from other early-season fritillaries. The dorsal side of the silver-bordered fritillary (*Boloria selene*) looks similar, but the underside hindwing is marked with prominent silver spots, which *B. chariclea* lacks.

SONYA ANDERSON

PACIFIC FRITILLARY

Boloria epithore

Size: 35–45 mm

Description: Dorsal sides of adults are a bright orange with black markings on the basal half of the wing near the thorax. Undersides of adults are orange with brown markings; the hindwing has a postmedian row of dark circles. The forewing is rounded, not pointed.

Habitat: Mountainous areas in meadows or forest openings

Range: Western coast of the United States, north into British Columbia

Active season: Throughout the summer

Conservation status: Populations in California's Santa Cruz Mountains may be jeopardized by lack of habitat.

Plant interactions: Larvae feed on *Viola* species. Adults feed on nectar from a variety of flowers.

Similar species: *B. chariclea* has a submarginal row of chevron spots pointing inward toward the base of the wing, while *B. epithore* has chevrons pointing outward. *B. kriemhild* looks similar but has a range southeast of the Rockies.

CHRISTIAN NUNES

SILVER BORDERED FRITILLARY

Boloria selene

Size: 35–54 mm

Description: The dorsal side of adults is orange with black markings. Underside of wings is marbled light brown, dark brown, and reddish color. Underside of hindwing has a metallic silver border along the outer wing margin with small postmedian spots. Underside of the hindwing has a basal spot, which is white with a black center.

Habitat: Marshes, wetlands, wet meadows

Range: Central Alaska through Canada and in the United States from Washington to Maine. The farthest south they have been recorded is northern New Mexico.

Active season: One flight midsummer in the north; two to three flights from late spring to early fall in the east

Conservation status: Populations especially in the plains and east of the Cascades are starting to decline due to the species' inability to adapt to changing habitats.

Plant interactions: Caterpillars feed on violets (*Viola* spp.); adults feed on nectar from composite flowers such as goldenrod (*Solidago* spp.) and black-eyed Susan (*Rudbeckia* spp.).

CANDY JONES

SMALL WOOD-NYMPH

Cercyonis oetus

Size: 30–45 mm

Description: Small and common wood-nymph butterfly, brown to dark brown in coloration. Dorsal forewing with two black eyespots; upper eyespot is larger and closer to body than lower eyespot. In males, only upper eyespot may be present. Forewing underside with two eye spots, upper eyespot larger. Wing margin checkered.

Habitat: Variety of habitats, including chaparral, sagebrush, grasslands, scrub, open woodland, meadows

Range: North American West; rarely ventures into Texas

Active season: Summer; early fall in parts of its range

Conservation status: None

Plant interactions: Hosts on grasses, including fescue (*Festuca* spp.) and bluegrass (*Poa* spp.). Adults will feed on nectar, mud, dung, and carrion.

Interesting facts: Young caterpillars of the species will spend the winter in unfed diapause until spring arrives. They will feed and pupate in spring and fly in summer.

Similar species: Smaller than other wood-nymphs.

ANDY BIRKEY

COMMON WOOD-NYMPH

Cercyonis pegala

Size: 45–75 mm

Description: Abundant and large wood-nymph butterfly. Brown and variable. Dorsal side of forewing with two large eyespots surrounded by yellow; lower eyespot usually larger than upper eyespot. Ventral side is brown and striated; ventral forewing with eyespots on dorsal side. Ventral forewing eyespots may be surrounded by prominent yellow or pale patch in the southern or coastal parts of the range; reduced or absent in other parts of the range. Ventral hindwing with submarginal row of variable eyespots.

Habitat: Open and sun-exposed areas, including prairies, open meadows, bogs, old fields

Range: Present in the North American West, extending across most of the continental United States. Rarely extends to the southwestern United States; absent in southern Florida.

Active season: Late spring to early fall, with peak in summer

Conservation status: None

Plant interactions: Caterpillars will host on grasses like purpletop (*Tridens flavus*). Adults will nectar on a variety of flowers; may feed on rotten fruit as well.

Interesting facts: Young caterpillars will hatch in fall but hibernate without feeding until spring.

GERRY SNYDER

GORGONE CHECKERSPOT

Chlosyne gorgone

Size: 30–45 mm

Description: Medium orange and black checkerspot. Dorsal forewing is orange with patterned black markings; dorsal hindwing has a submarginal row of black dots along an orange band. Ventral hindwing with zigzag marbled brown and white bands; median band of pale white chevron markings.

Habitat: Open spaces where host plants are abundant, including open woodlands, forest edges, streams, prairies, savannas; tolerant of disturbed spaces like urban and roadside sites

Range: Alberta east to southwest Manitoba and southern Ontario; south through the Great Plains to central New Mexico, central Texas, Louisiana, and central Georgia. Isolated populations in the Appalachians and the east slope of the Rocky Mountains.

Active season: Late spring to summer

Conservation status: None

Plant interactions: Uses a variety of species in the sunflower family (Asteraceae) as host plants, including sunflowers (*Helianthus* spp.), black-eyed Susan (*Rudbeckia hirta*), and loosestrifes (*Lysimachia* spp.). Adults feed on nectar of a variety of flowers, favoring yellow flowers.

Interesting facts: Early instar caterpillars will feed communally.

RON WOLF

NORTHERN CHECKERSPOT

Chlosyne palla

Size: 35–48 mm

Description: Variable, smallish checkerspot. Dorsal wing margins are alternating black and white lines. Dorsal surface is extremely variable and location dependent; ranges from oranges to reds to blacks, always checkered, most often with a light orange-yellow median row and darker postmedian row. Ventral surface is checkered with a diagnostic median off-white band in hindwing and white wing base closest to body.

Habitat: Coastal chaparral, open woodland, sagebrush, meadows, streamsides

Range: Southern British Columbia and Alberta south to southern California; south through the Rocky Mountains to Utah and Colorado

Active season: Mid-spring to summer

Conservation status: None

Plant interactions: Host will vary across range and elevation; includes goldenrod (*Solidago* spp.), rabbitbrush (*Ericameria* spp.), and asters (family Asteraceae). Adults feed on flower nectar.

Interesting facts: Males will guard their chosen territory, often in rocks or paths.

Similar species: May be confused with the pearl crescent (*Phyciodes tharos*), which lacks the distinctly checkered dark and white fringe margin.

JAMES BAILEY

C. whitneyi (dorsal view)

ROCKSLIDE CHECKERSPOT

Chlosyne whitneyi

Size: 32–41 mm

Description: Dorsal side wings of the adults is orange or pale orange with glossy black. Females' may be much darker. Underside of hindwing has a light orange marginal band, then alternating orange and creamy white bands on remainder of wing. Underside of the forewing is mainly light orange, with some creamy patches on the submarginal band.

Habitat: Alpine areas such as rocky slopes above tree line

Range: Along the Rocky Mountains from Canada to Colorado and through the Sierra Nevada in California

Active season: One flight from mid- to late summer

Conservation status: None

Plant interactions: Caterpillars feed on alpine plants in the sunflower family (Asteraceae). Adults will feed on nectar from alpine plants.

CAT CHANG

C. whitneyi (ventral view)

ANDY BIRKEY

COMMON RINGLET
Coenonympha tullia

Size: 34–40 mm

Description: Extremely variable medium satyr butterfly. Coloration from pale cream to dark brown; can be bright and orange. Ventral forewing grayish with a wavy median white band that extends from forewing to hindwing, usually with small eyespot near apex. Ventral forewing usually with orange or yellow patch and gray outer patch; ventral hindwing grayish, usually darker closest to the body.

Habitat: Grassy, open areas in a wide variety of habitats, including fields, meadows, grasslands, tundra

Range: Holarctic; present across the North American West except Texas

Active season: Spring to early fall

Conservation status: None

Plant interactions: Caterpillars feed on grasses and rushes. Adults feed on nectar.

Interesting facts: Common ringlets will overwinter as caterpillars in mats of dead grasses.

Similar species: Lighter and brighter than most other satyrs.

GERRY SNYDER

QUEEN

Danaus gilippus

Size: 80–98 mm

Description: Large and brightly colored butterfly. Dorsal side is rusty or pale brown with white dots scattered; black margins with two rows of white spots; lacks black veins entirely. Ventral wings are mahogany with black veins outlined with white; black margin with two rows of white spots. Thorax underside is black with white dots; abdomen is rusty brown.

Habitat: Open, sunny areas, including fields, deserts, roadsides, pastures, dunes, washes, waterways

Range: Wide range, including temperate and tropical regions of the Americas, Asia, and Africa. In the American West, confined to the southern part of the range.

Active season: Summer, but may be year-round in the warmer parts of its range

Conservation status: None

Plant interactions: Will host on various milkweeds (*Asclepias* spp.). Adults will feed on nectar from a variety of flowers.

Interesting facts: Like monarchs and other milkweed-feeding butterflies, queen butterflies are unpalatable to predators, sequestering toxins from their diet as caterpillars. They are part of a Müllerian mimicry complex, in which all similar species in the group are unpalatable.

Similar species: Similar to the soldier butterfly (*D. eresimus*), which lacks white outlines along ventral black veins. Soldiers also have a postmedian white band. Distinguished from monarchs (*D. plexippus*) by the lack of black dorsal veins.

MONARCH

Danaus plexippus

BRIONNA MCCUMBER

Size: 89–102 mm

Description: Large orange butterfly with bold black veins and border with white spots. The ventral side of the wings is a lighter orange. Monarch larvae—almost as showy as the adult stage in their yellow, black, and white stripes—ingest cardiac glycosides found in milkweed leaves, using these compounds as their own defense against predators.

Habitat: Meadows, grasslands, wetlands, croplands and developed landscapes

Range: Throughout North America. Monarch butterflies are among the most well-known butterfly species in North America, but they are not numerous in the Rocky Mountains, which divide the eastern and western breeding populations. On the eastern side of the Continental Divide, monarch butterflies migrate south in late summer and early autumn, overwintering in large groups in the oyamel fir forests of the Sierra Madre. The western population overwinters along the Pacific coast, although there is evidence that significant numbers of western individuals also migrate to Mexico to genetically mix with the eastern population. As days grow longer, the overwintering adults mate and begin the northward journey, laying eggs on their milkweed hosts along the way. Successive generations then spread throughout most of the United States and Canada in the summer months.

Season: Breeding season late spring to late summer; migrate south August to October

Plant interactions: Adult monarchs nectar on asters and milkweeds; larvae eat milkweed (*Asclepias* spp.).

Conservation status: Candidate for endangered status under US Endangered Species Act

Interesting facts: The loss of milkweed and breeding habitat in central North America is one of the biggest threats to the North American monarch population, along with climate change, pesticide use, and the loss of their forested overwintering habitats. The western population has been the hardest hit, with fewer than 2,000 individuals remaining. Monarch butterflies are the Idaho state insect.

Similar species: Viceroy (*Limenitis archippus*) is similar, but monarch is larger; viceroy has continual black veins in a broad "U" shape across hindwings.

ANNE AND ROB BRUMBAUGH

COMMON ALPINE

Erebia epipsodea

Size: 40–50 mm

Description: Small satyr butterfly. Wings are a rich dark brown. Dorsal pair of wings with a series of eyespots near the margins, centered in orange patches. Ventral forewing like dorsal; ventral hindwing like dorsal, with well-developed eyespots, grayish-brown background.

Habitat: Various open and moist spaces, including grassy fields, meadows, prairies, open woodlands, alpine tundra, alpine wetlands

Range: Rocky Mountain region, extending as far north as Alaska

Active season: Summer

Conservation status: None

Plant interactions: Larvae host on various grasses. Adults feed on various flowers.

Interesting facts: Caterpillars will overwinter in the base of grasses.

RON WOLF

VARIABLE CHECKERSPOT

Euphydryas chalcedona

Size: 32–55 mm

Description: Highly polymorphic and colorful checkerspot. Forewing narrow and pointed; dorsal wing background is dark brown to black with yellow, orange, red, and white spots. Underside with yellow, white, and orange bands. May display bright reds in dorsal or ventral wings. Antennae bright and tipped with yellow. Face and legs may appear rusty orange.

Habitat: Generalist—coastal to alpine

Range: Western North America, as far south as Baja California and as far east as the Rocky Mountains

Active season: Late spring to summer

Conservation status: None

Plant interactions: Caterpillars feed on various plants including figworts (Scrophulariaceae family) and forget-me-nots (Boraginaceae family). Adults nectar from a variety of flowers.

Interesting facts: In the high-elevation areas within their range, caterpillars may hibernate for multiple years.

Similar species: Forewing more narrow and pointed than those of other checkerspot butterflies, including Edith's checkerspot (*E. editha*). Unfeasible to reliably and superficially differentiate from Anicia checkerspot (*E. anicia*) or Edith's checkerspot (*E. editha*) in the field.

RON WOLF

EDITH'S CHECKERSPOT

Euphydryas editha

Size: 32–52 mm

Description: Variable checkerspot. Forewing rounded at apex; dorsal wing background is dark brown to black with yellow, orange, red, or white bands. Pale yellow or white small submarginal band; reddish postmedian band stretches from hindwing to forewing. Underside with yellow, white, and orange bands. May display bright reds in dorsal or ventral wings. Antennae tipped with yellow.

Habitat: General—from coastal to alpine; inclusive of chaparral, meadows, open woodlands

Range: North American West, less common in the southwestern states

Active season: Late spring to summer

Conservation status: Two subspecies—the Bay checkerspot (*E. e. bayensis*) and the Quino checkerspot (*E. e. quino*)—are listed as endangered under the Endangered Species Act of 1973.

Plant interactions: Caterpillars will host on various plants, including species of paintbrush (*Castilleja*), beardtongues (*Penstemon* spp.), lousewort (*Pedicularis* spp.), owl's clover (*Orthocarpus* spp.), Chinese houses (*Collinsia* spp.), and plantain (*Plantago* spp.). Adults feed on nectar from various flowers.

Interesting facts: Young caterpillars live in loose silk webs.

Similar species: Checkerspots are polymorphic. It's difficult to reliably and superficially differentiate from variable checkerspot (*E. chalcedona*) or Edith's checkerspot (*E. editha*) in the field. Forewings more rounded than species above.

RICH READING

VARIEGATED FRITILLARY
Euptoieta claudia

Size: 45–80 mm

Description: This butterfly has tawny orange dorsal surface with black spots near the margin and dark thick veins and markings. Underside is light brown with a mottled pattern on the hindwing and no silver spots. Typically, smaller than other fritillaries.

Habitat: Prairies, meadows, open sunny areas

Range: Fairly widespread throughout the United States but absent from the Pacific Northwest. Tend to be found in higher elevations in South and Central America.

Active season: Three broods in the north from mid-spring through mid-fall. Four broods in the south from spring through fall.

Conservation status: None

Plant interactions: Larvae feed on leaves of violets and pansies (*Viola* spp.), flax (*Linum* spp.), passion vine (*Passiflora* spp.), moonseed (*Menispurmum* spp.), stonecrop (*Sedum* spp.), and other plants. Adults feed on nectar from flowers.

Interesting facts: Sometimes referred to as a pest of violets. This species is extremely difficult to approach; because of this, its genus name was taken from the Greek word *euptoietos*, meaning "easily scared."

COMMON BUCKEYE

Junonia coenia

BRIONNA MCCUMBER

Size: 40–70 mm

Description: Small and colorful butterfly. Brown dorsal side. Dorsal forewing with two distinct orange bars on top and two striking eyespots; dorsal hindwing with two eyespots, eyespots with a purple to pink crescent patch. Ventral side light or rusty brown; forewing with pale band ending in large eyespot and hindwing with variable number of small eyespots.

Habitat: Generalist among sunny open areas with low vegetation

Range: Resident in southern United States to southern Mexico and parts of the Caribbean. Migratory brood reaches as far north as southern Canada.

Active season: Spring through fall; year-round in the southern parts of its range

Conservation status: None

Plant interactions: Caterpillars will host on plants from the snapdragon family (Scrophylariaceae), including snapdragon (*Antirrhinum* spp.) and toadflax (*Linaria* spp.); the plantain family (Plantaginaceae), including plantains (*Plantago* spp.); and the acanthus family (Acantheceae), including ruellia (*Ruellia nudiflora* spp.). Adults feed on a variety of flowers.

Interesting facts: Migratory; adults will move north in late spring and early summer for temporary range expansion, reaching southern Canada. In late summer and fall, adults will move south. Ventral wing color varies depending on seasonality and environmental conditions. During the wet season, ventral hindwing may look light brown or tan. During the dry season, ventral hindwing may look pinkish or reddish.

SARAH TRIPLETT

AMERICAN SNOUT

Libytheana carinenta

Size: 35–50 mm

Description: Elongated labial palps give the distinctive appearance of a snout. Forewings with squared edges. Dorsal wings brown with orange patches near base of both wings. Ventral wings are mottled grays and purples.

Habitat: Forest edges and clearings, low vegetation fields; disturbed sites, including roadsides and suburban spaces

Range: Residents in southern United States and Mexico. Periodic range expansion northward to include northern United States and southern Canada.

Active season: Summer to early fall

Conservation status: None

Plant interactions: Caterpillars feed on several species of hackberry (*Celtis* spp.). Adults feed on nectar from a variety of flowers.

Interesting facts: Will perform seasonal migrations to the northern reaches of their range. Adults will overwinter in the southern parts of the range. Some years, conditions lead to population explosions where the butterflies will be seen in huge numbers along the southern portion of their range.

BRIONNA MCCUMBER

VICEROY
Limenitis archippus

Size: 60–85 mm

Description: Large and colorful butterfly. Dorsal wings dark orange with black veins. Black margin with a row of complete white dots. Notable black line across the hindwing in both dorsal and ventral sides.

Habitat: Moist open or shrubby areas, open riparian spaces, disturbed sites like roadsides

Range: In the West, east of the US Cascade and Sierra Nevada mountain ranges. Extends to southeast Canada in the north and central Mexico and Florida to the south.

Active season: Late spring to early fall; year-round in parts of its range

Conservation status: None

Plant interactions: Caterpillars feed on trees in the willow family (Salicaceae), including willows (*Salix* spp.) and poplars and cottonwoods (*Populus* spp.). Adults feed on a variety of flowers, favoring composites. May also feed on carrion, dung, or decaying matter if nectar sources are low.

Interesting facts: The viceroy butterfly is the Kentucky state butterfly. Belongs to a Müllerian mimicry complex along with the monarch (*Danaus plexippus*) and the queen (*D. gilippus*) butterflies.

Similar species: Distinguished from the monarch butterfly (*D. plexippus*) by black line that cuts through the middle of the hindwing.

CATHY FENNELLY

WEIDEMEYER'S ADMIRAL

Limenitis weidemeyerii

Size: 55–95 mm

Description: Large black and white butterfly. Dorsal wings are black with a white median band, giving the appearance of a continuous line across fore- and hindwings. Ventral side same as dorsal, with prominent white median band. Base of ventral hindwing is white with dark crossing lines.

Habitat: Deciduous and coniferous forests, aspen groves, riparian spaces; disturbed sites, including roadsides, towns, suburbs

Range: Western North America, generally exclusive of coastal range. Not usually present in British Columbia or Texas.

Active season: Summer to early fall

Conservation status: None

Plant interactions: Caterpillars will host on aspen and cottonwood (*Populus* spp.), willows (*Salix* spp.), ocean spray (*Holodiscus* spp.), and shadbush (*Amelanchier* spp.). Adults feed on flower nectar, tree sap, and carrion.

Interesting facts: Caterpillars hibernate in shelters built with leaves.

KYLE BURTON

MOURNING CLOAK

Nymphalis antiopa

Size: 55–100 mm

Description: Large distinctive butterfly. Dorsal surfaces brown with a bright cream-yellow band across the margins, a series of bright blue spots on the inner side of the margin. Ventral surface ashy brown, wood-like in pattern, with a pale band across the margins.

Habitat: Habitat generalist, but found especially in riparian sites

Range: Northern Hemisphere, including the entire western North America

Active season: Spring to fall

Conservation status: None

Plant interactions: Hosts on willows, including black willow (*Salix nigra*), weeping willow (*S. babylonica*), and silky willow (*S. sericea*); also American elm (*Ulmus americana*), cottonwood (*Populus deltoides*), aspen (*P. tremuloides*), paper birch (*Betula papyrifera*), and hackberry (*Celtis occidentalis*). Adults feed only occasionally on nectar, preferring tree sap, especially of oaks, and rotten fruit.

Interesting facts: This butterfly overwinters as an adult in crevices and logs. Also the Montana state butterfly.

ANNE AND ROB BRUMBAUGH

CALIFORNIA TORTOISESHELL
Nymphalis californica

Size: 30–70 mm

Description: Dorsal side orange-brown with dark margins on all wings and noticeable black spots on both wings; darker toward wing bases. Ventral side mottled brown and wood-like with dark wing base.

Habitat: Chaparral and brushy areas, woodlands, forest openings

Range: Western United States, occasionally farther north; absent in Texas

Active season: Spring to fall

Conservation status: None

Plant interactions: Hosts on various species of wild lilac (*Ceanothus* spp.). Adults feed on nectar.

Interesting facts: This butterfly overwinters as an adult. May undertake large migrations, where thousands of individuals gather in the West.

Similar species: Distinguished from comma butterflies (*Polygonia faunus* and *P. gracilis*) by absence of silver sickle-shaped spot in the center of the hindwing.

RICH READING

NORTHERN CRESCENT

Phyciodes cocyta

Size: 30–45 mm

Description: Dorsal side is orange and brown with dark borders on all wings. The central orange patches are mostly open and uninterrupted, with some dark markings. Ventral side is orange and tan.

Habitat: Moist open spaces, including near streams and marshes

Range: Across western North America, except California and Texas. Range expands to eastern North America in the Appalachians region.

Active season: Summer

Conservation status: None

Plant interactions: Hosts on asters in the sunflower family (Asteraceae). Adults feed on flower nectar, especially of dogbane (*Apocynum* spp.), fleabane (*Erigeron* spp.), and white clover (trifolium repens).

Interesting facts: Overwinters as third-stage caterpillar.

Similar species: May be similar to other crescent butterflies. Antennae tips usually orange and black.

LISA HILL

MYLITTA CRESCENT

Phyciodes mylitta

Size: 30–38 mm

Description: Adults have a bright orange dorsal side of their wings with dark markings. The upper submarginal orange crescents are variable in width. Ventral side of wings are yellow-orange with some black spots on the hindwings, but mostly just a marbled look.

Habitat: Meadows, prairies, roadsides, parks; found up to 8,000 feet in the mountains

Range: Recorded in the western United States from the Rocky Mountains west to the Pacific coast, from southern British Columbia south to Mexico

Active season: Two broods fly in the north from mid-spring to early fall. In the south there are several broods that fly from late winter through mid-fall.

Conservation status: None

Plant interactions: Larvae feed on thistles (*Cirsium* spp. and *Silybum* spp.). Adults feed on nectar from a variety of flowers.

Interesting facts: Caterpillars hibernate when they are halfway grown.

LYLE ROSBOTHAM

FIELD CRESCENT

Phyciodes pulchella

Size: 25–45 mm

Description: Adults' dorsal sides are orange with thick black marks/bands; some cells are creamy white. Overall, they are very dark for most crescents. Ventral side of the forewing is yellow-orange with a black mark on the inner margin. Ventral side of the hindwing is yellow with some rusty-orange markings.

Habitat: Meadows, open areas from the plains to the mountains

Range: From the Rocky Mountain range west to the Pacific Ocean; from Alaska, south through British Columbia to Mexico

Active season: In the mountains there is one flight during the summer. In the plains there are typically two flights from late spring through early fall. In lowland California there are three to four flights from mid-spring through mid-fall.

Conservation status: None

Plant interactions: Larvae feed on leaves on plants from the sunflower family (Asteraceae). Adults feed on nectar from a variety of flowers.

Interesting facts: Partially grown caterpillars hibernate over winter.

ANDREA CARPIO

PEARL CRESCENT
Phyciodes tharos

Size: 32–45 mm

Description: Dorsal side is orange with thick black marginal borders on hindwings and forewings, sometimes with a slight silver border. Postmedian and submarginal areas have thin black marks. Ventral side of the wings is a light brown-yellow, with the forewings having some black marks. One light-colored crescent encircled by black on the submarginal area of the hindwing. Males typically have black antennal knobs.

Habitat: Open areas such as prairies, meadows, forest openings, roadsides

Range: Primarily in the eastern United States from the Rocky Mountains to the Atlantic Ocean and north into southern Canada

Active season: Flies most of the year in the southern United States and Mexico. Several broods occur from mid-spring through mid-fall in the north.

Conservation status: None

Plant interactions: Caterpillars feed on leaves from the sunflower family (Asteraceae). Adults feed on nectar.

Interesting facts: The coloration of these butterflies varies considerably.

CHRISTIAN NUNES

P. arachne (ventral view)

ARACHNE CHECKERSPOT
Poladryas arachne

Size: 32–45 mm

Description: Dorsal side of wings is a light orange with many cells outlined in black; margins are black with silver scales. Dorsal hindwing has two false eyespots submedially. Abdomen is black with orange stripes and white spots. Ventral side of wings is orange with a mixture of orange and bright white on the hindwing.

Habitat: Desert grasslands, meadows, prairies

Range: Southwestern United States, as far north as Wyoming and as far south as northern Mexico

Active season: Multiple flights from late spring through early fall

Conservation status: None

CHRISTIAN NUNES

P. arachne (dorsal view)

Plant interactions: Larvae host on species of beardtongue (*Penstemon* spp.). Adults feed on nectar.

GREEN COMMA

Polygonia faunus

ARNOLD SKEI

Size: 45–64 mm

Description: Jagged scalloped wing edges. Dorsal side of the wings is rusty orange with wide dark borders. Dorsal side of hindwing has a border of yellow spots. Ventral side mimics a leaf and is mottled brown with greenish submarginal spots. Ventral side of hindwing has a white C-shaped spot in the center.

Habitat: Forests, canyons, and near streams

Range: Found from the Rocky Mountains to the Pacific Ocean and north into central Alaska. Not found in the central United States, but found in the Midwest and New England, north through Newfoundland, and throughout the Great Smoky Mountains.

Active season: One brood from late spring to late summer

Conservation status: None

Plant interactions: Larvae feed on a variety of hosts such as willows (*Salix* spp.), gooseberries (*Ribes* spp.), nettles (*Urtica* spp.), birch (*Betula* spp.), and elm (*Ulmus* spp.). Adults feed on nectar, dung, and carrion.

Interesting facts: Adults hibernate over the winter and mate in the spring.

HOARY COMMA

Polygonia gracilis

KYLE BURTON

Size: 40–55 mm

Description: Dorsal wings are dark orange-red with dark margins; hindwing with a series of yellow spots near margin, sometimes running together. Ventral side is gray-brown with a lighter outer half and darker toward the wing base; silver hooked spot in the middle of the hindwing.

Habitat: Varied; generalist

Range: North American West, except Texas

Active season: Spring to fall

Conservation status: None

Plant interactions: Larvae feed on currants and gooseberries (*Ribes* spp.), western azalea (*Rhododendron occidentale*), and mock azalea (*Rhododendron menziesii glabellum* spp.). Adults feed on flower nectar and sap.

Interesting facts: Overwinters as adults.

Similar species: May be confused with other Polygonia species. *P. gracilis* can be differentiated by its two-toned ventral side, with the outer half being paler than wing bases.

CHRISTIAN NUNES

QUESTION MARK

Polygonia interrogationis

Size: 57–76 mm

Description: Wing shape is scalloped with tails on the hindwings and the front wings. Dorsal side of wings is bright orange with a rusty brown submarginal band and a fine gray-violet border. Dorsal side also has some black spots on the hind- and forewings. Ventral side of the butterfly is mottled brown (leaflike), with a white question mark shape in the center of the hindwing.

Habitat: Forests, parks, gardens; can be found in urban areas

Range: Mostly in the eastern United States, from southern Canada to Florida, east to the Rocky Mountains, and south to Mexico

Active season: Overwintered adults fly in early spring. Summer form will fly from late spring to early fall; winter form will mate and overwinter.

Conservation status: None

Plant interactions: Larvae feed on elm (*Ulmus* spp.), hackberry (*Celtis* spp.), and nettles (*Urtica* spp.). Adults feed on rotting fruit, dung, and carrion; will also feed on flowers when preferred foods are scarce.

Interesting facts: Named for the white "question mark" spot on its hindwing.

RON WOLF

SATYR COMMA

Polygonia satyrus

Size: 45–64 mm

Description: Wings are scalloped with short tails on the hindwings. Dorsal side is yellow-orange, with a brighter yellow closer to the margins. Forewing has two black spots on the bottom edge in the center of the wing. Hindwings do not have a black border. Ventral side is red-brown to light orange with a silver comma in the center of the hindwing.

Habitat: Valleys, near streams, in open meadows, riparian areas, wooded areas

Range: Western United States from the Rocky Mountains to the Pacific Ocean; in southern Canada and northern British Columbia

Active season: Two to three flights along the Pacific Coast from midwinter to mid-fall. Two flights in the southwest from early summer through early fall.

Conservation status: None

Plant interactions: Larvae feed on a variety of nettles (Urticaceae). Adults feed on tree sap, rotting fruit, and flower nectar.

Interesting facts: Swift flier that rarely goes long distances.

Similar species: Very similar to *P. comma*, but *P. satyrus* is lighter above with larger submarginal pale spots from above. Also, *P. satyrus* has a larger comma mark on the ventral side of the hindwing.

APHRODITE FRITILLARY

Speyeria aphrodite

LYLE ROSBOTHAM

Size: 63–83 mm

Description: Geographically variable. In general, dorsal side is a light orange with black crescent spots near margins. Wings are darker and browner closer to the thorax. Ventral side of the hindwings is reddish brown, with white spots outlined in black and a pale submarginal band. Sub-margins have white triangles. Ventral side of forewing has black markings closer to the body, white markings closer to the wing margin. Males lack black scales along veins. For both males and females, there is a black spot on the front wings near the discal cell.

Habitat: Prairies, mountain meadows, woodland openings, bogs

Range: From British Columbia south through the Rocky Mountains and east through the northern United States; north through the East Coast (Tennessee to Maine)

Active season: One flight from early summer through early fall

Conservation status: None

Plant interactions: Caterpillars feed on violet species (*Viola* spp.). Adults feed on nectar from flowers such as milkweed (*Asclepias* spp.) and viper's bugloss (*Echium* volgare).

Similar species: Similar to *S. cybele*, *S. atlantis*, *S. hesperis*, *S. nokomis*, and *S. idalia* in the west. These species tend to have gray eyes and black scaling along the veins, which is not true for *S. aphrodite*, especially males. East of the Great Plains, the great spangled fritillary and Atlantis fritillary are similar, but males have black scaling on the veins in contrast to *S. aphrodite* males. Also, *S. aphrodite* has a black spot on the front wings next to the discal cell, while other fritillaries do not.

CALLIPPE FRITILLARY

Speyeria callippe

KYLE BURTON

Size: 50–64 mm

Description: Dorsal sides are tawny brown with black scales on the veins. Both forewings and hindwings have lighter submarginal cells outlined in black. Ventral sides of wings are a light yellow with silver spots outlined in black. Hindwings have silver submarginal cells. Eyes are gray.

Habitat: Prairies, chaparral, sagebrush

Range: Western United States from the Rocky Mountains west to the coast, north through southern British Columbia, and south to Mexico; absent from Arizona and New Mexico

Active season: One flight from late spring through late summer

Conservation status: The subspecies *callippe* is ranked T1: critically imperiled due to extreme rarity.

Plant interactions: Larvae feed on violet species (*Viola* spp.). Adults feed on nectar.

Interesting facts: Unfed first-year caterpillars hibernate until spring.

CORONIS FRITILLARY

Speyeria coronis

BRIONNA MCCUMBER

Size: 50–86 mm

Description: Dorsal side is light orange with black marking; submarginal cells are light-colored ovals. Ventral side of the hindwing is orange with silver spots and silver triangles outlined in black in a submarginal row. Forewing is orange with basal black markings and silver triangles in a submarginal row. Eyes are gray.

Habitat: A variety of habitats, from mountains to valleys, meadows, sagebrush, forest openings

Range: From southern Washington east to the Great Basin and south through Colorado; found as far south as southern California

Active season: One flight from early summer through early fall

Conservation status: None

Plant interactions: Larvae feed on violets. Adults feed on flower nectar.

Interesting facts: First-stage caterpillars overwinter before feeding.

EDWARD'S FRITILLARY

Speyeria edwardsii

RON WOLF

Size: 63–86 mm

Description: Dorsal side is a tawny orange with black markings and submarginal cells that are light orange ovals. Fringe of wings' dorsal and ventral sides is silver scales. Dorsal side of hindwing is gray-green with large silver spots, elongated closer to the body but more triangular in submarginal area. Dorsal side of forewing has more black markings closer to the body but still has the silver submarginal spots.

Habitat: Shortgrass prairies, meadows, road edges

Range: Along the Rocky Mountain range from Alberta south through northeastern New Mexico

Active season: One flight from early summer through early fall

Conservation status: None

Plant interactions: Caterpillars feed on violet (*Viola* spp.) plants. Adults feed on flower nectar.

Interesting facts: Caterpillars overwinter unfed.

TOM PETERSON

GREAT BASIN FRITILLARY

Speyeria egleis

Size: 45–60 mm

Description: Dorsal side is orange-brown with delicate dark markings that are evenly spaced. Ventral side is pale orange with silver markings and submarginal markings on the hindwing and dark markings on the forewing with silver submarginal triangles; margins of ventral sides of the wings have bright orange ovals. Eyes are gray; wings are typically short and broad.

Habitat: Inhabits mountainous meadows, rocky ridges, sunny forest openings

Range: West of the Rocky Mountains, north to Washington and south to California; absent from Arizona and New Mexico

Active season: One flight over the summer

Conservation status: None

Plant interactions: Caterpillars feed on violets (*Viola* spp.). Adults feed on nectar.

Interesting facts: *Speyeria egleis* is rarer than other species of *Speyeria*.

Similar species: Similar in looks to many other species of *Speyeria*, *S. egleis* generally has shorter and broader wings than other species, with the dorsal dark pattern being delicate and less fused.

NORTHWESTERN FRITILLARY

Speyeria hesperis

Size: 50–70 mm

RICH READING

Description: These butterflies are variable in pattern. Typically, the dorsal wing is orange-brown with a darker brown near the body. Outer margins of forewings are typically black, sometimes orange. Ventral side of the forewing is lighter than that of the hindwing. Hindwing has silver spots and a light brown submarginal band.

Habitat: Forest opening, hillsides, meadows

Range: In North America from Alaska south to Arizona and New Mexico, as far east as the Rocky Mountains in the United States. Found in Canada as far east as Manitoba.

Active season: One flight from early summer through mid-fall.

Conservation status: Subspecies *elko* and *hanseni* are of conservation concern due to their small ranges.

Plant interactions: Larvae feed on violet plants (*Viola* spp.). Adults feed on nectar from a variety of plants, including species of *Gaillardia*, rabbitbrush (*Ericameria* spp.), shrub cinquefoil (Dasiphora fruticosa), and plants in the mint family (Lamicaceae).

Interesting facts: Overwinters as young caterpillar and matures in the spring.

MORMON FRITILLARY

Speyeria mormonia

Size: 38–61 mm

KYLE BURTON

Description: A small fritillary with large antennal clubs. Dorsal side of wings is a tawny orange, similar to most fritillaries. Margins are black with light orange ovals and a thin band of orange outside of black margins. Ventral sides are light brown with white ovals on the hindwing.

Habitat: Mountain meadows, prairies, subarctic forest openings

Range: Western United States from the Rocky Mountains to the Pacific coast; populations as far north as Alaska and through British Columbia

Active season: One flight from early summer to early fall

Conservation status: None

Plant interactions: Larvae feed on violet species (*Viola* spp.). Adults feed on nectar from a variety of flowers.

Interesting facts: Male adults emerge before female adults.

ROBERT G. BROWN

S. *zerene* (dorsal view)

ZERENE FRITILLARY

Speyeria zerene

Size: 54–70 mm

Description: Similar to other fritillaries, the dorsal side of the wings is a tawny orange with black markings; may have black margins with light orange submarginal ovals; others may not have black margins on dorsal side of wings. Ventral side of wings is light orange with silver ovals on hindwing and triangular marginal spots.

CHRISTIAN NUNES

S. zerene (ventral view)

Habitat: Coastal meadows, mountain meadows, riparian areas

Range: Northwestern United State as far north as southern British Columbia and as far west as the Rocky Mountains

Active season: One flight from early summer through early fall

Conservation status: A few subspecies (*hippolyta*, *myrtleae*, and *behrensii*) are critically imperiled.

Plant interactions: Larvae feed on leaves of violets.

Interesting facts: Females delay egg laying until late summer. First-stage caterpillars overwinter (on a silk mat) unfed, then feed on violet leaves.

Similar species: Coronis fritillary is similar; however, Zerene has more triangular silver margins.

WEST COAST LADY

Vanessa annabella

RON WOLF

Size: 38–57 mm

Description: Dorsal side is orange-brown with an orange second bar (subapical) on the forewing. Dorsal side of hindwing has three or four blue eyespots submarginally. Ventral side of the wings has a complex pattern with obscured eyespots.

Habitat: Open areas such as meadows and prairies, roadsides, gardens, disturbed areas

Range: United States from Canada south through Guatemala and east through the Rocky Mountains and south Texas

Active season: Many flights throughout the year in the lowlands; two flights, summer and fall, in the Rocky Mountains

Conservation status: None

Plant interactions: Caterpillars feed on many plants in the mallow family (Malvaceae). Adults feed on nectar from a variety of flowers.

Interesting facts: Adults hibernate.

RED ADMIRAL

Vanessa atalanta

BRIONNA MCCUMBER

Size: 45–76 mm

Description: Dorsal side is black with white spots near the tips of the forewings and a red medial band. Hindwings are blackish brown with wide red-orange marginal band. Winter form is small; summer form is larger and brighter. Ventral side of hindwings is complex; ventral side of forewings is similar to dorsal side.

Habitat: Riparian areas, marshes, gardens, moist woods

Range: Widespread throughout North America, from Alaska to Guatemala and California to Maine

Active season: Two flights from early spring through mid-fall in the north; overwinters in south Texas.

Conservation status: None

Plant interactions: Caterpillars feed on plants from the nettle family (Urticaceae). Adults feed on sap from trees, fermenting flowers, and bird droppings; they only feed on nectar from flowers when other food sources are not available.

Interesting facts: Adults hibernate.

PAINTED LADY

Vanessa cardui

BRIONNA MCCUMBER

Size: 51–73 mm

Description: An orange butterfly from the dorsal side, with black-tipped forewings with white markings. Hindwings are also orange with five submarginal spots, occasionally scaled in blue. Ventral side of hindwing is a mottled, complex pattern with four submarginal eyespots.

Habitat: Open areas such as meadows and fields, but can be found in other areas

Range: These butterflies are found worldwide, especially in Eurasia and North America. Migrates south in Europe during the fall.

Active season: One to three flights from late spring to mid-fall; three to four flights in south Texas from mid-fall to early spring

Conservation status: None

Plant interactions: Larvae feed on a wide variety of plants (one hundred-plus) but prefer species in the sunflower (Asteraceae) and mallow (Malvaceae) families. Adults feed on nectar from composites that are usually taller (3–6 feet).

Interesting facts: Adults overwinter only in areas without severe freezing. Adults fly year-round in the south/near the equator, where temperatures are mild.

Similar species: Similar to the American lady (*V. virginiensis*) and West Coast lady (*V. annabella*), except American lady and West Coast lady have an orange bar submedially on the leading edge of the forewing and blue eyespots on the upper hindwings. The painted lady does not have such markings.

AMERICAN LADY

Vanessa virginiensis

Size: 45–67 mm

ANNE AND ROB BRUMBAUGH

Description: Adult is larger in size than other "lady" species. Dorsal side of the wings is orange, with the forewing showing a black apical patch with small white spots and a whitish-orange bar on the leading edge of the forewing subapically. Ventral side of hindwing is complex, with brown markings and two large eyespots.

Habitat: Open habitats such as meadows and fields, urban gardens, old fields, forest edges, deserts. This species tend to be found at higher elevations.

Range: Widespread throughout North America and south to Columbia and Venezuela. This species overwinters in the south and migrates north to breed.

Active season: Adults fly year-round in the south; there are three to four broods from late spring through mid-fall in areas where there are mild, not freezing, winters.

Conservation status: None

Plant interactions: Larvae feed on plants in the Asteraceae family, such as pussytoes (*Antennaria* spp.), everlastings (*Anaphalis* spp.), and cudweeds (*Pseudognaphalium* spp.). Adults exclusively eat nectar from flowers.

Interesting facts: Caterpillars are solitary; adults hibernate.

Similar species: Like the painted lady (*V. cardui*) and West Coast lady (*V. Annabella*), but the American lady has only two eyespots on the ventral side of the hindwings.

Family Papilionidae

Swallowtails and Parnassians

Swallowtails are large and charismatic butterflies, named for a well-developed taillike extension projecting from the bottom of their hindwings, characteristic of most butterflies in this group. Unlike in brush-footed butterflies, all six legs are visible and used for walking or perching. Parnassians are alpine swallowtails that lack a tail but will have bright red or orange spots in their generally white hindwings. These butterflies are often brightly colored and include the largest butterflies in the world.

BRIONNA MCCUMBER

CHRISTIAN NUNES

B. philenor (ventral view)

PIPEVINE SWALLOWTAIL
Battus philenor

Size: 70–130 mm

Description: Caterpillars are black with red dots. Chrysalis is light blue. Adults are an iridescent blue or blue-green with a submarginal row of five white ovals. Ventral side of the hindwing is an iridescent blue with a submarginal row of seven round orange spots. The body is black with white spots.

Habitat: A wide variety of open habitats, including open woodland and woodland edges

Range: California into Mexico and up to New England; not found in the Great Plains, Pacific Northwest, Idaho, Utah, or Wyoming

Active season: Late spring through summer. Adults also fly from late summer and fall in the South and Southwest.

Conservation status: None

Plant interactions: Caterpillars feed on pipevines (*Aristolochia* spp.), both native and cultivated. Adults feed on nectar from a wide variety of flowers.

Interesting facts: Caterpillars feed in small groups when young but become solitary when older. This butterfly overwinters in the pupal stage.

CANADIAN TIGER SWALLOWTAIL

Papilio canadensis

JASON COOPER

Size: 67–80 mm

Description: Adults are yellow; dorsal forewings have broad black stripes. Ventral side of the forewing has yellow spots on the margin that are merged into a band. Hindwings have orange spots within marginal yellow cells. Extremely rare black female form.

Habitat: Northern deciduous and evergreen-deciduous woods and forest edges

Range: North America from Alaska southeast across Canada to New England; also found in Wyoming and the Great Lakes

Active season: Late spring through midsummer

Conservation status: None

Plant interactions: Caterpillars feed on leaves of birch (*Betula* spp.), aspen (*Populus* spp.), and black cherry (*Prunus* spp.). Adults feed on nectar from flowers.

Interesting facts: The Canadian tiger swallowtail can survive colder winters and experiences higher mortality in hot weather.

Similar species: Like the eastern tiger swallowtail (*P. glaucus*) and western tiger swallowtail (*P. rutulus*), but the Canadian tiger swallowtail is smaller.

PALE SWALLOWTAIL

Papilio eurymedon

RON WOLF

Size: 64–90 mm

Description: Adults are creamy white with black stripes. Forewing is narrow and pointed; hindwing has a long, twisted tail.

Habitat: Foothills, open woodlands, chaparral, streams

Range: British Colombia to northern Mexico; from the Rocky Mountains west to the coast

Active season: One flight mid-spring through midsummer; many flights in southern California early spring through late summer

Conservation status: None

Plant interactions: Caterpillars feed on leaves from trees and shrubs in the rose (Rosaceae), buckthorn (Rhamnaceae) and birch (Betulaceae) families. Adults feed on nectar from California buckeye (*Aesculus californica*), yerba santa (*Eriodictyon californicum*), and wallflower (*Erysimum* spp.).

Interesting facts: Originally identified and described in 1805 by Edward Donovan as *P. antinous*. It was later described by Hippolyte Lucas as *P. eurymedon* in 1852. Normally the older name would be the official one, but that name had been overlooked, so Lucas's name was accepted.

Similar species: Similar to the eastern tiger swallowtail (*P. glaucus*) and the western tiger swallowtail (*P. rutulus*), but the pale swallowtail is paler than those species.

INDRA SWALLOWTAIL
Papilio indra

CHRISTIAN NUNES

Size: 62–72 mm

Description: Caterpillar is black and pink striped (later stages), black and spiky in early stages. Adult abdomen is all black, with a yellow dash on the sides near the head. Wings are mostly black with yellow markings; hindwings have some red and blue markings and short tails.

Habitat: Mountains, desert mountains, canyons

Range: Rocky Mountains west to the coast; from southern British Columbia into northern Mexico

Active season: One flight from early spring through late summer, with additional late-flying individuals in desert populations

Conservation status: Several subspecies occur only on federal lands.

Plant interactions: Caterpillars feed on aromatic herbs of carrot (Apiaceae) family. Adults feed on nectar from a variety of flowering plants.

Interesting facts: *P. indra* is of interest to evolutionary biologists due to the subspecies having a desert habitat, isolating the various populations and resulting in a sort of island biogeography.

OLD WORLD SWALLOWTAIL
Papilio machaon

CHRISTIAN NUNES

Size: 65–75 mm

Description: Yellow butterfly with black markings on the fore- and hindwings. Hindwings have red-orange eyespots with some blue and black border touching the inner edge of the hindwing. Other blue markings can be seen on the hindwing above the tail of the wing. Fifth instars are green with thin black stripes and stripes of yellow and black dots.

Habitat: Open hilltops, mountain meadows, tundra

Range: Holarctic, with a wide distribution in Eurasia and western North America

Active season: One flight in the north during the summer; two flights in the south

Conservation status: None

Plant interactions: Caterpillar feed on sagebrushes (*Artemisia* spp.); southern populations feed on *A. dracunculoides*. Boreal subspecies are recorded feeding off plants in the carrot family (Apiaceae).

Interesting facts: The plants the caterpillars feed on have key chemical similarities to members of the citrus family (Rutaceae), which is probably an ancestral host family.

Similar species: Similar to other tiger swallowtails. "Shoulders" on body are usually bright yellow.

LYLE ROSBOTHAM

TWO-TAILED SWALLOWTAIL
Papilio multicaudata

Size: 90–127 mm

Description: Yellow butterfly with black stripes on forewing (male has narrow black stripes). Hindwing has two tails; margins at base are blue and red. Body is yellow with a black stripe down the center. Late-instar caterpillars are light brown-orange with a one black and yellow stripe around body.

Habitat: Foothill slopes and canyons, moist valleys, streams, woodlands, parks, roadsides, suburbs, cities

Range: North America from the Rocky Mountains west to the coast, down into West Texas and Mexico, and north into British Columbia and Alberta

Active season: One flight from late spring to late summer in the north; year-round in the south

Conservation status: None

Plant interactions: Caterpillar hosts are ash (*Fraxinus* sp.), hoptree (*Ptelea* sp.), and chokecherry (*Prunus virginiana*). Adults feed on nectar of flowers from thistles (*Cirsium* sp.), milkweed (*Asclepias* sp.), California buckeye (*Aesculus californica*), lilac (*Syringa* sp.), and others.

Interesting facts: Thought to be one of the largest butterflies in North America.

Similar species: Similar to eastern and western swallowtails, but black stripes are narrower and *P. multicaudata* has two tails on each hindwing.

BLACK SWALLOWTAIL
Papilio polyxenes

BRIONNA MCCUMBER

Size: 80–110 mm

Description: From the dorsal view, forewings and hindwings are black with yellow spots along the margins. Hindwings from the top have two orange eyespots with black pupils, along with the typical blue cells and yellow discal spots. Similar to all swallowtails, hindwing has a tail. Ventral side of the wings is like the dorsal side. Body is black with yellow spots on the sides.

Habitat: Open areas, including fields, suburbs, marshes, deserts, roadsides

Range: From central Colorado east to the coast.

Active season: One to two flights from mid-spring to mid-fall in northern regions of range; three flights in southern regions

Conservation status: None

Plant interactions: Caterpillars feed on leaves on plants of the carrot family (Apiaceae), including Queen Anne's lace (*Daucus carota*), celery (*Apium graveolens*), and dill (*Anethum graveolens*). Occasionally feeding on plants in the citrus family (Rutaceae). Adults drink nectar from flowers of red clover (*Trifolium pratense*), milkweed (*Asclepias* spp.), and thistles (*Cirsium* spp.).

Interesting facts: The black swallowtail butterfly is the official state butterfly of New Jersey. Overwinters as a chrysalis.

Similar species: Similar to the spicebush swallowtail (*P. troilus*), but the black swallowtail has a continual series of orange dots on the hindwing, not interrupted by a blue stripe.

WESTERN TIGER SWALLOWTAIL
Papilio rutulus

ANNE AND ROB BRUMBAUGH

Size: 70–100 mm

Description: Large tiger swallowtail with yellow and black pattern. Dorsal surface is yellow with broad black border and tiger stripes.

Habitat: Varied; includes riparian woodlands, wooded suburbs, canyons, parks, roadsides, oases

Range: Western North America

Active season: Summer

Conservation status: None

Plant interactions: Feeds on cottonwood and aspen (*Populus* spp.), willows (*Salix* spp.), wild cherry (*Prunus* spp.), and ash (*Fraxinus* spp.). Adults feed on flower nectar from a variety of plants.

Interesting facts: Overwinters as a chrysalis.

Similar species: Like the two-tailed swallowtail (*P. multicaudata*), but this species has only one pair of projections and the stripes are thicker.

ANISE SWALLOWTAIL
Papilio zelicaon

LAURA MORALES

Size: 70–90 mm

Description: Adults have yellow wings with black bars and markings. Hindwings are also yellow with orange eyespots near the tail (not connected to hindwing margin). Anal cell of hindwing is yellow. Fifth-instar caterpillars are green with blue stripes, orange and black dotted rings around the body.

Habitat: Bare hills, mountains, gardens, fields, vacant lots, roadsides

Range: North America from British Columbia to southern California and east to the Rocky Mountains

Active season: One flight from mid-spring through midsummer

Conservation status: None

Plant interactions: Caterpillars eat plants in the carrot family (Apiaceae) or the citrus family (Rutaceae).

Interesting facts: Young caterpillars eat leaves; older ones eat flowers. Adults feed on flower nectar.

SIERRA NEVADA PARNASSIAN

Parnassius behrii

GRIGORY HEATON

Size: 49–53 mm

Description: Mainly white-winged butterfly. Hindwings have two prominent orange eyespots in the center of the wing with a black outline. Abdomen is gray with light yellow hairs. Dorsal side of the forewing has two black spots, with one to three small yellow orange spots on the leading edge.

Habitat: Rocky outcrops, alpine tundra, stream edges

Range: Serra Nevada range in California

Active season: One flight from midsummer to early fall

Conservation status: While this species is not currently listed as endangered, its small range and high-elevation habitats makes it susceptible to climate change.

Plant interactions: Caterpillars feed on stonecrop (*Sedum* sp.) and other members of the Crassulaceae family. Adults feed on nectar from stonecrop flowers, as well as from plants in the sunflower family (Asteraceae).

Interesting facts: Caterpillars feed on leaves, sometimes flowers and fruits, and hibernate as eggs.

CLODIUS PARNASSIAN

Parnassius clodius

RON WOLF

Size: 50–62 mm

Description: Adult butterflies have black thoraxes (with yellow hairs) and black abdomens. Head is yellow with black eyes. Forewings are a light white color, with loss of scales on edges of front wings. Dorsal surfaces of the forewing cell have three gray bars. Each hindwing has two red spots outlined in black. Females have a red anal bar. Mated females have a white pouch at the end of their abdomens.

Habitat: Open woods, alpine areas, meadows, rocky outcrops

Range: Mostly along the West Coast of the United States into British Columbia; populations also found in Idaho, Montana, Wyoming, and Utah

Active season: One flight from early to midsummer

Conservation status: Subspecies *strohbeeni*, from the Santa Cruz Mountains, is extinct.

Plant interactions: Caterpillars feed on the poppy family (Papaveraceae). Adults feed on flower nectar.

Interesting facts: Overwinters as a caterpillar in decaying leaf litter; pupates in the spring.

Similar species: Similar to the Sierra Nevada (*P. behrii*) and Rocky Mountain (*P. smintheus*) parnassians. However, *P. clodius* does not have red markings on the forewings.

RICH READING

ROCKY MOUNTAIN PARNASSIAN
Parnassius smintheus

Size: 45–64 mm

Description: Antennae have black and white rings. Wings are white, with forewings having two red spots close to the leading edge. Hindwings also have two red spots. Two to three black bars along the leading edge of the forewings.

Habitat: Open forests, meadows, grasslands

Range: Along the Rocky Mountains up into Alaksa, with occurrences in Washington, Idaho, Montana, and California

Active season: One flight during the summer

Conservation status: None

Plant interactions: Caterpillars feed on *Sedum* spp. in the stonecrop (Crassulaceae) family. Adults feed on nectar from flowers in the Sedum genus and the Asteraceae family.

Interesting facts: During mating, parnassian males insert a hard waxy secretion called a sphragis, which prevents other males from mating with the female.

Similar species: *P. clodius* is similar but larger and has black antennae compared to the black and white antennae of *P. smintheus*.

Family Pieridae

Sulphurs and Whites

The white and sulphur butterflies are small to medium-sized butterflies. They come in shades of whites, yellows, and oranges, often with dark markings like black spots, margins, or veins on the wings. Unlike in brush-footed butterflies, all six legs are visible and used for walking or perching. The caterpillars of some butterflies in this group, like the abundant cabbage white (*Pieris rapae*), can be considered agricultural pests.

BRIAN WRIGHT

SLEEPY ORANGE

Abaeis nicippe

Size: 35–57 mm

Description: Dorsal side of forewing is orange with black outer and costal margins and a single dark mark referred to as the "sleepy dash," which mimics a closed eye. Female margins are much less distinct. Ventral side is pale orange in summer, darker to brick red later in the season. Caterpillars are green with a white stripe.

Habitat: Found at lower elevations in open areas, including pine forest openings, desert scrub, old fields, gardens, roadsides

Range: Southwestern United States into Mexico

Active season: Mid- to late summer in the north; year-round farther south. Multiple flights to the south.

Conservation status: None

Plant interactions: Larvae feed on cassia (*Senna* spp.) and clover (*Trifolium* spp.), partridge pea (*Chamaecrista fasciculata*), and wild sensitive plant (*C. nictitans*) from the pea family (Fabaceae). Adults feed on nectar from many flowers. Males frequently visit mud puddles for salts and minerals.

Interesting facts: Common name may derive from its "sleepy dash" or its tendency to hibernate in the South on cooler winter days.

Similar species: Orange sulphur (*Colias eurytheme*) is similar, but its black outer margins are more regular.

ANDREA CARPIO

SARA ORANGETIP

Anthocharis sara

Size: 27–40 mm

Description: Dorsal side of male forewing is white with a showy reddish-orange spot bordered in black. Females are often cream in color and spots are smaller, paler, with a dark and white border. Ventral side of hindwing has dark green to yellow marbling.

Habitat: Canyons, open woodlands, orchards, meadows, streams

Range: Oregon to Baja California, mainly west of the Cascade and Sierra Nevada ranges

Active season: Early spring to summer, with one to two flights

Conservation status: None

Plant interactions: Larval host plants include mustards (Brassicaceae), both native and introduced. Adults drink nectar from the flower of host mustards, thistles (*Cirsium* spp.), fiddlenecks (*Amsinckia* spp.), and *Brodiaea* spp.

Interesting facts: Increased moisture and late-flowering mustards (*Brassica* spp.) can extend the breeding season for these butterflies.

Similar species: While as an adult it's almost indistinguishable from *A. julia*, *A. sara* is a coastal species.

ADRIAN CARPER

JULIA ORANGETIP

Anthocharis julia

Size: 25–32 mm

Description: Also called the southern Rocky Mountain orangetip. Dorsal side of the male forewing is white with bright orange wingtips. Female is more pale yellow than white. Ventral side of the hindwing has yellow veins and is marbled green. There is usually a white ray in the middle of the hindwing.

Habitat: Foothill and mountain canyons, meadows, streamsides

Range: Southeastern Wyoming south through the Colorado Rockies into New Mexico

Active season: Early spring to midsummer

Conservation status: None

Plant interactions: Larval host plants are rockcress (*Arabis* sp.), violets (*Viola* sp.), and other plants in the mustard family (Brassicaceae). Adults are nectar feeders.

Interesting facts: One of the earliest butterflies to emerge in its region.

Similar species: While as an adult it's almost indistinguishable from *A. sara*, *A. julia* is found in the Rocky Mountain region; *A. sara* is a coastal species.

LYLE ROSBOTHAM

QUEEN ALEXANDRA'S SULPHUR
Colias alexandra

Size: 42–57 mm

Description: Dorsal side of male forewing is bright yellow with black border and small black cell spot, which is also visible from below. Females are yellow to white with a black border that is less distinct or entirely absent. Dorsal hindwings are similar, with greenish to yellowish-white fringe. Ventral side of hindwing is greenish with white cell spot that may be softly ringed in pale pink. Caterpillars are green; eggs are red.

Habitat: Montane and foothill open areas, including roadsides, fields, forest openings, sagebrush flats

Range: Throughout the western United States except Texas

Active season: Spring to late summer, depending on location

Conservation status: None

Plant interactions: Larval host plants include plants in the pea family (Fabaceae), including *Astragalus* spp., lupines (*Lupinus* spp.), golden banner (*Thermopsis* spp.), and clover (*Trifolium* spp.). Adults feed on nectar from a wide range of flowers.

Interesting facts: Extremely variable depending on gender, elevation, and more.

ORANGE SULPHUR

Colias eurytheme

Size: 35–70 mm

RON WOLF

Description: Dorsal side of male forewing and hindwing is bright orange with black borders and yellow veins. Forewing has black cell spot, while spot on hindwing is orange. Ventral side of wings is similar in color but with black spots on the margin instead of a solid black border. Ventral forewing has white dot ringed in black; hindwing has two silver-white dots, one larger and one smaller, both ringed in brownish pink. Females' overall color is pale orange to white, and black border is irregular. The butterfly is quite variable in coloration. Eggs are red.

Habitat: Open spaces at varying elevations, including alfalfa fields, pastures, vacant lots, roadsides

Range: Southern Canada to Mexico, coast to coast

Active season: Spring to late fall, depending on location

Conservation status: None

Plant interactions: Larval host plants include alfalfa (*Medicago sativa*), clover (*Trifolium* spp.), and other members of the pea family. Adults feed on nectar from a variety of flowers.

Interesting facts: One of the most common butterflies in North America and the world. Caterpillars in large numbers can seriously damage alfalfa crops.

Similar species: *C. philodoce* is similar but smaller, more yellow than orange, and with narrower dark margins.

MEAD'S SULPHUR

Colias meadii

Size: 38–51 mm

CHRISTIAN NUNES

Description: Dorsal side of forewing and hindwing are orange to yellow with purple iridescence, black border, and pink fringe. Black-orange spot on forewing. Females are pale yellow or white; black border is not solid. Ventral side of forewing and hindwing are pale orange-yellow with light green border and pink fringe. White spot on hindwing ringed in pink.

Habitat: High mountains at or above tree line

Range: Rocky Mountains from Alberta to New Mexico

Active season: Mid- to late summer

Conservation status: None

Plant interactions: Larvae feed on members of the legume family, such as clover (*Trifolium* sp.) and *Astragalus* sp. Adults feed on nectar from a wide range of flowers, usually members of the sunflower family (Asteraceae).

KYLE BURTON

CLOUDED SULPHUR

Colias philodice

Size: 38–51 mm

Description: Dorsal side of forewing is yellow with black margins, yellow veins, and oval black cell spot, also visible from underneath. Hindwing is yellow with partial black margin and orange spot. Females are pale yellow with uneven black margin. Ventral side of forewing is yellow with dark submarginal dots. Hindwing is yellow with pink submarginal dots and central silver-white spot ringed twice in reddish pink with smaller pink spot adjacent. Eggs are cream colored when laid and turn crimson within a few days.

Habitat: Open areas including alfalfa and clover fields, roadsides

Range: Throughout the western United States, more concentrated near the Rocky Mountains; very common in the eastern United States

Active season: Spring to fall, but most active in midsummer

Conservation status: None

Plant interactions: Larval food is varied but mostly in the legume family (Fabaceae). Adults feed on nectar from plants such as alfalfa (*Medicago sativa*), clovers (*Trifolium* spp.), milkweed (*Asclepias* spp.), and teasel (*Dipsacus* spp.).

Interesting facts: Clouded sulphurs can hybridize with orange sulphurs. Clouded sulphurs have erratic flying behavior and are known for mud-puddling.

Similar species: *C. eurytheme* is similar but larger in size; more orange than yellow, with a wider black margin.

LARGE MARBLE

Euchloe ausonides

Size: 30–51 mm

Description: Dorsal side of forewing off-white with black markings at tip of wing and black discal spot touching costa. Dark pattern at apex of wing. Below white with green marbling at tip. Ventral side of hindwing has green marbling and yellow veins. Larvae are dark bluish gray with black dots. Adults fly in a zigzag way.

LYLE ROSBOTHAM

Habitat: Montane and foothills areas where open and more moist, including forest openings, meadows, trails, other open sunny areas

Range: Alaska south to California and northern New Mexico, east to the Rocky Mountains

Active season: Late winter to late summer, depending on altitude and latitude

Conservation status: None. The related island marble (*E. a. insulanus*), thought to be extinct, was found on San Juan Island in Washington. Conservation efforts focus on restoring its ecosystem, the Puget Sound lowland prairie.

Plant interactions: Larvae feed on buds, flowers, and sometimes seeds of mustard plants (Brassicaceae). Adults feed on nectar from the Brassicaceae family, including fiddlenecks (*Amsinckia* spp.) and *Brodiaea.*

Interesting facts: Flies erratically and seldom rests.

Similar species: *E. olympia* has sparser marbling on hindwing and is white with a pinkish hue.

CHRISTIAN NUNES

E. olympia (dorsal view)

OLYMPIA MARBLE
Euchloe olympia

Size: 30–51 mm

Description: Adults are white with a gray spot at the end of the cell in the dorsal forewing. Ventral side of hindwings has greenish-yellow marbling forming three distinct bands with white in between. Larvae are green with gray and white stripes.

Habitat: Various open areas, including prairies, foothills, lakeshore dunes, shale barrens, meadows, open woodlands

Range: In the United States, from the Rocky Mountains east to the Smoky Mountains

CHRISTIAN NUNES

E. olympia (ventral view)

Active season: One flight from spring to midsummer; early in Texas, later in the north

Conservation status: None

Plant interactions: Larvae eat rockcress (*Arabis* spp.) and hedge mustard (*Sisymbrium officinale*). Adults feed on nectar from chickweed (*Stellaria media*) and rockcress.

Similar species: The differences between *E. olympia* and the similar *E. ausonides* can only really be seen in the larval fifth-instar phase. *E. ausonides* larvae grow lighter, whereas *E. olympia* larvae grow darker, making the differences quite noticeable.

LYLE ROSBOTHAM

PINE WHITE

Neophasia menapia

Size: 45–58 mm

Description: White butterfly. Forewings are black at tips, with a black margin on the leading edge that ends in a black ball tip. Forewings have the same pattern from the ventral side and dorsal side. Ventral side of the hindwings is white with black venation. Dorsal side of hindwings is white. Caterpillars are dark green with white side stripes. Eggs are laid stuck together in a row on a conifer needle. Eggs hibernate.

Habitat: Western coniferous forests

Range: From the Rocky Mountains west to the coast; also found through British Columbia and Alberta

Active season: Summer to mid-fall

Conservation status: None

Plant interactions: Caterpillars eat needles of pines, including ponderosa pine (*Pinus ponderosa*) and Douglas fir (*Pseudotsuga menziesii*). Adult feeds on nectar, especially from bee balm (*Monarda* sp.) and rabbitbrush (*Ericameria* spp.).

Interesting facts: Caterpillars feed in groups when they are young and move apart when they are older. Caterpillars pupate at the base of the host tree after descending from the tree on a silken thread. Some people view it as a pest because the caterpillars defoliate conifer trees. Adults are thought to have one of the most graceful flights.

CLOUDLESS SULPHUR

Phoebis sennae

ANDREA CARPIO

Size: 48–80 mm

Description: Lemon-yellow butterfly. Female has a dark spot on the forewing. Ventral side of the hindwings in both sexes has two silver, black-rimmed spots. Larvae are green with a yellow lateral stripe and blue markings. Pupae can be either green or pink, in the shape of a folded leaf.

Habitat: Disturbed open areas, including parks, yards, gardens, beaches, road edges, abandoned fields, scrub

Range: Permanent resident from Argentina north to southern Texas and the Deep South; also in California and the US Southwest and East

Active season: Late summer to fall

Conservation status: None

Plant interactions: Caterpillars feed on cassia (*Senna* spp.) and other woody herbaceous plants in the pea family (Fabaceae). Adults feed on nectar from flowers with long tubes, such as *Bougainvillea*, cardinal flower (*Lobelia cardinalis*), *Hibiscus*, *Lantana*, and wild morning glory (*Calystegia sepium*).

Interesting facts: Named for Phoebe, sister of Apollo.

MARGINED WHITE

Pieris marginalis

CHRISTIAN NUNES

Size: 38–57 mm

Description: The butterfly has two forms, a spring and a summer. Adult summer form is pure white above and below. Adult spring form is white; ventral side of hindwing with yellow-green/gray-green veins. Larvae are green with hairs.

Habitat: Forests, meadows, deciduous woods, streams

Range: In the United States from the Rocky Mountains west to the coast and up through southern British Columbia and Alberta

Active season: Two flights from late winter to summer in the West

Conservation status: None

Plant interactions: Larval hosts are plants in the mustard family (Brassicaceae). Adults feed on nectar from mustard flowers.

Interesting facts: This species utilizes both disturbed and intact habitat, demonstrating the ability to adapt to changes in its environment.

ERIC CASEBOLT

CABBAGE WHITE

Pieris rapae

Size: 45–65 mm

Description: Adults have white wings, forewings dipped in black. Females have two black dots in the middle of their forewing. Males have one black dot on the dorsal side of each forewing. Cabbage worms (larvae) are 35 mm in length, green and velvety. The final four instars have yellow stripes running through their green body.

Habitat: Almost any type of open space, including weedy areas, gardens, roadsides, cities, suburbs

Range: Introduced species from Europe; widespread throughout the United States and up to central Canada

Active season: Spring to fall

Conservation status: None

Plant interactions: Larvae prefer cabbage plants but will eat anything in the mustard family (Brassicaceae) and occasionally some plants in the caper family (Capparaceae). Adults feed on nectar from flowers in the Brassicaceae family as well as dandelions (*Taraxacum officinale*), red clover (*Trifolium pratense*), asters (*Symphyotrichum* spp.), and members of the mint family (Lamiaceae).

Interesting facts: This very common species has two to three generations a year in the northern parts of its range. Typically live three to six weeks.

RICH READING

BECKER'S WHITE

Pontia beckerii

Size: 40–50 mm

Description: Adults are white. Dorsal forewings have subapical black marks forming a "Z" shape. Ventral side is strongly patterned with green/yellow scales. Two distinct square black bars with a curved white center are in center of forewing (seen from above and below).

Habitat: Arid brushlands, desert foothills, canyons, fields

Range: Rocky Mountains across to the West Coast and north to British Columbia and Alberta

Active season: Spring through mid-fall (usually two to three flights)

Conservation status: None

Plant interactions: Larval host plants are weedy plants in the mustard family (Brassicaceae) and some plants from the caper family (Capparaceae). Larvae tend to feed on the green fruits. Adults feed on flower nectar from a variety of plants, including hedge mustard (*Sisymbrium officinale*) and alfalfa (*Medicago sativa*).

Interesting facts: Males patrol ravines in search of females. Females lay eggs singly on host stems, buds, leaves, flowers, and fruits.

CHRISTIAN NUNES

WESTERN WHITE

Pontia occidentalis

Size: 38–53 mm

Description: Adults are white butterflies with black markings. Dorsal side of the forewing has black marginal cells that are lighter than the submarginal wing stripe. Hindwing veins from the ventral side are outlined in a gray-green.

Habitat: Mountain peaks, slopes, hilltops, railroad yards, open plains, and roadsides

Range: In the United States and Canada from Alaska south to central California; mostly west of the Rocky Mountains but up to Canada as far east as Ontario

Active season: One flight in the north in the summer; two flights in the south from late spring through summer

Conservation status: None

Plant interactions: Caterpillars feed on flowers and fruits of plants in the mustard family (Brassicaceae). Adults feed on nectar from a variety of plants.

Interesting facts: Caterpillars prefer flowers, buds, and fruit to leaves. Chrysalids hibernate over winter.

Similar species: The checkered white (*P. protodice*) may be mistaken for a male western white. If there are five to six spots on the forewing and these spots are much darker than the outer spots, it's most likely a western white; the checkered white has only two to three of these spots. Also, *P. occidentalis* typically replaces *P. protodice* at higher elevations.

KYLE BURTON

CHECKERED WHITE

Pontia protodice

Size: 38–63 mm

Description: Adults are sexually dimorphic. Males are mostly white with some dark markings on the dorsal side of the forewing. Females have more markings on the dorsal side of the forewing. Larvae are gray with yellow stripes at higher instars. Pupa is bluish gray.

Habitat: Wide variety of sites, including dry weedy areas, vacant lots, fields, pastures, sandy areas, railroad beds, roads

Range: Widespread across the United States; permanent resident in the southern United States and Mexico. Does not occur in most of the New England states.

Active season: Three flights from spring through fall

Conservation status: None

Plant interactions: Larvae feed on mustard family (Brassicaceae) and caper family (Capparaceae), including bee plant (*Cleome serrulata*). Adults feed on nectar from Brassicaceae family plants and alfalfa (Medirago sativa).

Interesting facts: Caterpillars prefer flowers, buds, and fruits more than leaves.

Similar species: The checkered white may be mistaken for a male western white (*P. occidentalis*). If there are five to six spots on the forewing and these spots are much darker than the outer spots, it's most likely a western white; the checkered white has only two to three of these spots. Also, *P. occidentalis* typically replaces *P. protodice* at higher elevations.

SPRING WHITE

Pontia sisymbrii

LUANN WRIGHT

Size: 30–45 mm

Description: Dorsal sides of adults' wings are white with dark veins. Forewing has a narrow black cell bar. Ventral side of hindwings has yellowish-olive veins with a black outline. Larvae are yellow, black, and white striped.

Habitat: Desert hills and other dry slopes, rocky canyons and outcrops, roadsides, open coniferous forests

Range: British Columbia down to southern California; Rocky Mountains to the west coast of North America

Active season: One flight from midwinter through midsummer

Conservation status: None

Plant interactions: Larvae feed on plants in the mustard family (Brassicaceae).

Interesting facts: Young caterpillars feed on leaves, older ones on flowers.

CALIFORNIA DOGFACE

Zerene eurydice

CINDY PENCEK

Size: 51–63 mm

Description: Adults are sexually dimorphic. Males are pinkish orange with black/purple border with a dark eyespot almost touching the border; male hindwings are yellow-orange. Females are typically yellow without markings. Very fast flier.

Habitat: Foothills, chaparral, oak or coniferous woodlands

Range: North-central California south to Baja California, west of the central mountains and deserts

Active season: Two flights—one in spring, one in summer

Conservation status: None

Plant interactions: Larvae feed on false indigo (*Amorpha californica*), in the pea family (Fabaceae). Adults feed on nectar.

Interesting facts: California state butterfly. Called "dogface" for the "poodle silhouette" on the male.

Family Riodinidae

Metalmarks

Metalmarks are small to medium-sized butterflies. They are named for the metallic-colored spots found on wings of most metalmarks. Their shapes, colors, and habits are highly variable, and they may resemble butterflies from other families. They often display bright structural colors. Their antennae are generally not hooked, like in skippers, and generally not striped, like in blues and hairstreaks. Most species in this group are found in the tropics of Central and South America. A small number of species are distributed across North America.

MICHAEL J. ANDERSEN

MORMON METALMARK
Apodemia mormo

Size: 22–33 mm

Description: Body is grayish brown and lacking markings. Dorsal side of wings is brown with orange patch toward base, white and black markings, and checkered fringe. Ventral side of wings is similar.

Habitat: Arid lands

Range: West of the Rocky Mountains into southern Canada and northern Mexico

Active season: Midsummer to fall in the north, spring to late fall in the south; varies depending on time of host plant bloom

Conservation status: None

Plant interactions: Larval host plants include various wild buckwheats (*Eriogonum* spp.). Adults also feed on nectar from buckwheat flowers; will feed on other yellow-flowered plants as well.

Interesting facts: There are approximately 1,000 species of metalmarks worldwide, with about 90 percent in the New World; about 24 species in North America (Pyle, 1981).

MICHAEL J. ANDERSEN

NAIS METALMARK

Apodemia nais

Size: 32–35 mm

Description: Body is black with orange stripes on the abdomen. Dorsal side of forewings is orange and black with checkered fringe and a white spot near the tip. Hindwings are similar. Ventral side of forewing is orange with black markings. Hindwing is gray with black markings and orange submarginal band. Eyes are green. Mature caterpillars hibernate in leaf litter.

Habitat: Open woodland, brushy chaparral, foothills, mountain canyons, streams

Range: Rocky Mountains from Colorado south to New Mexico and Arizona

Active season: One brood from late spring to summer

Conservation status: None

Plant interactions: Larval host plant is Fendler's snowbrush (*Ceanothus fendleri*). Adults feed on flower nectar from a wide range of plants, including dogbane (*Apocynum* spp.), black-eyed Susan (*Rudbeckia* spp.), spearleaf stonecrop (*Sedum lanceolatum*), rockspray (*Holodiscus dumosus*), and butterfly weed (*Asclepias tuberosa*).

Interesting facts: Males of this species are often found drinking at mud puddles to obtain the salts they need for reproduction.

KYLE BURTON

FATAL METALMARK
Calephelis nemesis

Size: 20–25 mm

Description: Overall color is brown with darker and lighter markings. Male's forewing is pointed. Dorsal side of forewings is light brown with somewhat darker median band and checkered fringe. Hindwings are similar. Ventral side is orange with dark spots on the margins. Metallic markings very subtle.

Habitat: Brushy riparian areas, including chaparral canyons, ditches, grasslands, agricultural fields

Range: Southwestern United States, including California, Nevada, Utah, Arizona, New Mexico, and Texas, extending into Mexico; locally common near larval host plants

Active season: Spring to fall; up to year-round where suitable

Conservation status: None

Plant interactions: Larval host plants include seepwillow (*Baccharis glutinosa*), bush sunflower (*Encelia* spp.), and possibly *Clematis* species. Adults feed on flower nectar from a variety of plants.

Interesting facts: The intimidating species name of this unassuming butterfly likely came from the darker morphs of the species, which evoke Nemesis, the winged Greek goddess of retribution.

Flowers are valuable resources in many plant communities, and other animals may visit flowers for food, shelter, or reproduction without necessarily consistently pollinating them. Some insects may successfully carry pollen for certain plants and not others, so the definition is both flexible and situation specific. Other arthropods use flowers as a hunting ground and are found on flowers because they eat pollinators. All these animals have important roles in our ecosystem. Here are a few other groups of invertebrates often observed on flowers.

AMY YARGER

Species of jumping spider

SALTICIDAE: JUMPING SPIDERS

Size: 1–25 mm

Description: Robust, hairy body with front legs slightly larger and used for grasping; sometimes with brightly colored patterns on their body or pedipalps. Eight eyes on a flat "face," with the front row of four eyes being particularly large and mobile.

Habitat: Found in many different habitats, from forests to grasslands to urban areas

Range: Throughout western North America

Active season: Spring to fall

Conservation status: None

Plant interactions: Jumping spiders are ambush predators that wait on flowers for their next live meal. However, as they travel, they may carry pollen from one flower to another, which can assist with pollination of some plants. Their predaceous habits also assist with pest control.

Interesting facts: The eyesight of jumping spiders is adapted to detailed, three-dimensional vision, which allows them to precisely leap on prey.

Similar species: Crab spiders and lynx spiders have much smaller eyes.

AMY YARGER

Crab spider on *Asclepias speciosa*

THOMISIDAE: CRAB SPIDERS

Size: 2–11 mm

Description: Delicate flat-bodied spiders with long legs extended to the sides like a crab; often pale white, yellow, or pink; four front legs are bigger than back legs.

Habitat: Grasslands, forest openings and margins, developed gardens

Range: Throughout western North America

Active season: Spring to fall

Conservation status: Least concern

Plant interactions: Crab spiders are ambush predators that will perch on flowers, often blending into the background, to wait for an unwary pollinator.

Interesting facts: Crab spiders can change colors over a period of days to camouflage themselves on flowers. Because of the placement of their legs, they can move sideways and backward as well as forward. Females will guard their offspring until their second molt.

Ambush bug

REDUVIIDAE: AMBUSH BUGS

Size: 7–12 mm

Description: Small, diamond-shaped true bug with a jagged outline, small wings, and wide abdomen. This insect also has short antennae tipped with small knobs, as well as a piercing, sucking mouth used to kill and eat other arthropods. Green, yellow, and brown coloration often blends into the flowers it perches on.

Habitat: Grasslands, riparian areas, forest edges, farms, developed areas wherever there are flowering plants, especially native species

Range: Throughout western North America

Active season: June to October

Conservation status: None

Plant interactions: Members of the sunflower family, such as sunflowers (*Helianthus* spp.) and goldenrod (*Solidago* spp.) are favorite hunting grounds for these insects. Ambush bugs seem to prefer yellow or blue flowers over red or white flowers.

Interesting facts: These small predators can kill and eat insects much larger than themselves. They also can change their own coloration to a slight degree if needed for camouflage.

Similar species: Other true bugs (members of the Heteroptera order)—look for the grasping "muscular" arms and much shorter body on ambush bugs.

Short-horned grasshopper

ACRIDIDAE: SHORT-HORNED GRASSHOPPERS

Size: 9–80 mm

Description: Oblong insects with stubby antennae; long, strong legs adapted for jumping; and a hearing organ (tympanum) on the first segment of the abdomen.

Habitat: Warm grasslands, farms, developed areas, including parks, gardens, disturbed sites

Range: Throughout western North America

Active season: March to November

Conservation status: None

Plant interactions: These insects are generalist herbivores, chewing a wide variety of flowers, leaves, and stems, although some species are more picky than others.

Interesting facts: Short-horned grasshoppers are expert thermoregulators—when they need to warm up, they will position themselves to maximize exposure to the sun and sit close to the ground. Warmer temperatures cause them to "stilt," or lift their bodies away from the ground to promote air circulation.

Similar species: Katydids and leafhoppers also jump, but short-horned grasshoppers have shorter antennae than the former and much larger bodies than the latter.

Seed bug on milkweed pod

LYGAEIDAE: SEED BUGS

Size: 3–20 mm

Description: Elongated oval–shaped bugs, often with bold coloration and large eyes. These insects have piercing-sucking mouthparts like other true bugs, but eat only seeds.

Habitat: Meadows, farms, gardens; other open, sunny places with flowering plants

Range: Throughout western North America

Active season: July–October, although some species are observed overwintering.

Conservation status: None

Plant interactions: These insects eat a variety of seeds, often dependent on species.

Interesting facts: These insects inject their saliva into the seed with their beaks, then drink the liquified seed contents.

Similar species: Plant bugs, but seed bugs do not have a cuneus on their backs.

GLOSSARY

Abdomen—Rearmost main body region in insects; contains digestive, respiratory, excretory, and reproductive organs.

Adaptation—Heritable change, either physical or behavioral, in an organism or its components that improves its chance of reproductive fitness or survival.

Alpine—Habitats occurring above tree line in high-altitude regions, often with harsh conditions and sparse vegetation.

Antenna (plural antennae)—Segmented and paired sensory organs on the insect's head; variable in shape and size according to type of insect.

Aquatic—Living in watery habitats.

Basking—Behavior in which the insect rests in a sunny location with wings outstretched; used to warm up for flight.

Bioindicators—Sensitive species that reliably signal significant changes in the ecosystem by the increase or decrease of their population or via morphological, physiological, or behavioral changes.

Biological Control/Biocontrol—Beneficial insect species used by humans to control unwanted plants, insects, or other pests.

Bipectinate—Branched like a feather with projections radiating from a central shaft, as in some moth antennae.

Boreal—High-latitude ecosystems found in the Northern Hemisphere below the Arctic Circle; usually typified by coniferous forests and long, cold winters.

Brood cell—Structures containing eggs, larvae, and pupae found in insect nests.

Chitin—Complex polysaccharide found in the exoskeletons of insects and other arthropods; a tough, semitransparent material.

Circumboreal—Describes species found in far northern regions of North America and Eurasia.

Class—Taxonomic rank below phylum and above order, composed of organisms that share a common attribute.

Clypeus—Broad exoskeleton plate at the front of an insect's face above the mandibles.

Coevolution—Reciprocal evolutionary changes among closely associated species via interactions among species.

Coleoptera—Insect order including beetles, distinguished by hardened forewings called elytra.

Colony—Two or more individuals of the same species living with or closely connected to each other.

Compound eyes—Visual organs made up of a large number of identical yet independent photoreception units (ommatidia), each containing a single lens.

Cuneus—The triangular-shaped portion of the forewing, at the distal end of the body, found in some Heteropteran species.

Detritus—Accumulation of organic matter, including fallen leaves and other plant parts, animal remains, waste, and other debris, that falls onto soil or into water from surrounding habitats; the primary energy source for decomposers.

Developed—A landscape defined by purposeful modification by people, often dominated by impervious surfaces such as roads and buildings and managed vegetation, such as lawns, farms and gardens.

Dimorphic—The presence of two distinct forms of an organism in a population, as in differences in color or size between males and females.

Diptera—Insect order including flies; distinguished by reduced or absent hindwings.

Distal—Segment on an appendage farthest from the point of attachment to the body.

Distribution—General pattern of how individuals in a population are spread out in their range at a given time; usually uniformly, random, or clumped.

Disturbance—Temporary force or process that causes a pronounced change in the ecosystem and biodiversity.

Dorsal—Upper surface of an animal, as viewed from above.

Elytra—Hardened forewings of beetles; protective first pair of wings used to protect the delicate hindwings for flight.

Endoparasite—Parasite that lives inside another animal, feeding on internal organs or tissues, without killing it.

Entomologist—Scientist who studies insects.

Entomology—Branch of zoology that deals with insects.

Exoskeleton—Rigid, often articulated, outer covering on many invertebrates; used to support and protect the soft tissues.

Facial plate—Segment of exoskeleton above the mouthparts.

Family—Taxonomic rank below order and above genus composed of organisms that share a common attribute; a group of one or more genera sharing a common attribute.

Filiform—Describing a structure, such as an antenna, that is long, slender, and not tapering; threadlike.

Forage—To search for, gather, and utilize energy and nutrient resources.

Forager—Organism that forages.

Forewing(s)—Anterior pair of wings; pair of wings closest to the head of an insect having four wings. Forewings typically have more powerful muscles and generate most of the power for flight.

Fusiform—Describing a structure, such as an antenna, that is rounded but wider in the middle then tapers toward each end.

Generalist—Species that can live in different environments and eat many kinds of food; for pollinators, the word describes species that can pollinate a wide variety of plants.

Genus—Taxonomic rank between family and species; one or more species that have similar structures or characteristics or are related via a common ancestor.

Grub—Wormlike larval form of a beetle or other insect; usually short, plump, and soft-bodied.

Habitat—Preferred environment for an organism, providing the conditions and resources (i.e., food and shelter) where the organism can survive and reproduce.

Halteres—Modified hindwings, often reduced and knob-like, used for balance by flies.

Herbivore—Organism that feeds on plants.

Herbivory—Having a diet dominated by plant matter.

Hindwing—Posterior pair of wings; the pair of wings closest to the tail of an insect having four wings; hindwings help with lift and balance.

Honeydew—Waste fluid, watery but sticky due to the sugar content, excreted by aphids and other sucking insects

Host—Living organism that harbors another organism, for which it provides food or other resources in a symbiotic relationship. This relationship may be mutualistic, parasitic, or commensal.

Host plant—Plant on which an organism lives and often feeds during part of its life cycle.

Hymenoptera—Insect order including bees, wasps, ants, sawflies, and horntails; insects with a modified ovipositor on the rear of the abdomen that can inject venom.

Instar—Developmental stages of arthropods, including insects, between molts of their exoskeleton.

Invertebrate—An animal lacking a backbone or internal skeleton.

Kleptoparasitic—Method of resource acquisition in which an animal steals resources, such as food or shelter, from other animals.

Larva(e)—Juvenile form of an invertebrate; the stage between hatching and adulthood, usually physically different from the adult form.

Lepidoptera—Insect order composed of butterflies and moths, distinguished by scaly wings.

Longitudinal—Lengthwise along the long axis of a body.

Margin—Along the edge of a wing.

Medial—Toward the middle of a structure or body part.

Membranous—Consisting of or resembling a very thin, flexible layer of tissue.

Mimic—The state of one species looking like another, often for protection or defense.

Monolectic—Relating to a pollinator that collects pollen from a single species of flowering plant.

Monotrysia—An unranked group of moths characterized by the females having one, instead of two, genital openings.

Montane—Ecosystems found on the slopes of mountains below timberline, usually stratified according to altitude.

Nearctic—Biogeographic region composed of North America; region extending from the Mexican Plateau to Greenland, northern Canada, and Alaska.

Nectar—Sugar-rich liquid produced by flowering plants as an attractant for pollinators and other animal mutualists.

Obligate—Able to survive and/or reproduce only under one set of conditions or via a specific behavior.

Ocelli—Simple light receptors consisting of a single lens, used to detect movement.

Oligolectic—Pollinators specialized in collecting pollen from only a few related genera or species of flowering plants.

Order—Taxonomic rank below class, composed of families sharing similar characteristics.

Ovipositor—Tubular organ used to lay eggs, consisting of a pair of specialized appendages, found at rear of female insect abdomen.

Palp—Segmented, mobile appendage of an arthropod located near the mouth, usually involved with senses of taste and touch.

Parasite—An organism that lives on and gets its nutrients at the expense of another living organism.

Parasitic—Living on another organism as a parasite.

Parasitoid—Organism that spends its larval stage in or on another organism, feeding on and eventually killing it.

Pectinate—Having projections like the teeth of a comb.

Plumose—Describing a structure, such as an antenna, that is feather-like.

Pollen—Microscopic grain-like structures that deliver sperm to the egg within the female parts of a flowering plant as part of sexual reproduction.

Pollination—Act of transferring pollen grains from the male reproductive parts of a flowering plant to the female parts of a flowering plant of the same species.

Postmedial—Located behind the midpoint.

Prairie—Grassland with moderate temperatures and few trees.

Predaceous/Predatory—Living by preying on other animals.

Predator—Organism that primarily gets nutrition through killing and consuming other animals.

Proboscis—Elongated feeding tube on the head of an insect or other animal.

Pronotum—Platelike structure covering the thorax of some insects.

Proximal—Area of wing between the discal and marginal area, closer to the body.

Punctate—Spotted with pits or small depressions.

Pupa(e)—Third life stage in insects with complete metamorphosis that occurs between the larval and adult stages; during this stage, the larval structures break down and adult structures form.

Queen—In a colony of social insects, the only female capable of reproduction.

Range—Geographic area where a species can be found during its lifetime.

Riparian—Transitional ecosystem between an aquatic (usually freshwater) ecosystem and a terrestrial ecosystem (i.e., a wetland), typified by vegetation that can thrive in standing water.

Rostrum— Snoutlike projection on the head of some insects, most notably weevils.

Saprophagous—Having a diet based on dead or dying plant tissues.

Savanna—Ecosystem characterized by dry conditions and a scattered tree canopy above an understory dominated by grasses.

Scale—Microscopic platelike structures, often pigmented or structured to provide color on butterfly and moth wings and bodies.

Scopa—Pollen-carrying apparatus on bees; usually a dense mass of elongated hairs on the leg or belly.

Scutellum—Hard plate on the thorax of an insect.

Secrete—Process of producing and releasing a substance from specialized glands.

Segment—One of a series of repeated structures in an arthropod that form a larger body part, such as a thorax or antenna.

Social/Eusocial—Describes insects that share a common nest site and cooperate in caring for the young, showing reproductive division of labor and an overlap of generations.

Solitary—Insects that build and care for their own nests independently.

Sonication/Buzz pollination—Method of releasing pollen from closed anthers by applying vibrations.

Syndrome (Pollinator)—Floral characteristics used to predict the type of pollinator that will visit and assist in successful reproduction for the plant. These traits have evolved in response to natural selection influenced by the method and vector of pollination.

Specialist—Pollinator that has evolved a relationship with one or a few plant species.

Species—Taxonomic rank describing the largest group of living organisms capable of interbreeding and producing fertile offspring in nature. Species is the fundamental unit of biological classification and unit of measurement for biodiversity.

Subantennal—Located under the antenna of an insect.

Subgenera—Taxonomic rank directly below genus and above species; used to name groups of closely related species.

Submarginal—Under or next to the margin of an insect wing.

Subspecies—Taxonomic rank directly below species indicating further categorization based on minor but consistent differences in morphology or genetics. Individuals of different subspecies can still interbreed and produce fertile offspring.

Subtropical—Ecosystems between temperate and tropical zones with hot summers and mild winters with infrequent freezes.

Suture—Narrow junction between two rigid plates of an exoskeleton, often consisting of flexible membrane.

Tarsi—The most distal parts of the insect leg (i.e., the foot), which are not true segments but may be divided into two to five parts.

Temperate—Ecosystems located between the tropics and polar regions, described by distinct seasonality.

Tergum—Dorsal plate on the abdomen or thorax in an insect.

Thermoregulation—Ability of animals to maintain a temperature that supports activities for survival. Because they are ectothermic, insects regulate their temperature via behavior such as basking.

Thorax—Middle body segment where wings and legs are attached.

Tribe—Taxonomic rank above genus but below family.

Tropical—Ecosystems located between the Tropics of Cancer and Capricorn, centered on the equator. Weather in tropical ecosystems is consistently warm.

Venation—Arrangement, including number and position, of veins supporting the membrane in an insect's wing.

Ventral—Lower surface of the body.

Wing cell—Membranous area enclosed by veins in an insect's wing.

Worker—Individuals withing a social insect colony not able to reproduce but performing key activities for survival, such as larval care, foraging, and defense.

REFERENCES

"10,000 Things of the Pacific Northwest," n.d. http://10000thingsofthepnw.com.

Ackerman, James D. "Pollination Biology of *Calypso bulbosa* var. *occidentalis* (Orchidaceae): A Food-Deception System." *Madroño* 28, no. 3, 1981, 101–10. JSTOR, www.jstor.org/stable/41424311.

"Aerial Yellowjacket," January 28, 2014. https://www.northeastipm.org/schools/pests/aerial-yellowjacket/.

Alabama Butterfly Atlas. USF Water Institute, University of South Florida. alabama.butterflyatlas.usf.edu.

Alcock, John. "Blister Beetle Love and Defense." ASU—Ask A Biologist, May, 19, 2017. https://askabiologist.asu.edu/blister-beetle-defense.

"*Androloma Maccullochii*—Insects of the Greater Yellowstone Ecosystem," n.d. Montana State University. https://www.montana.edu/yellowstoneinsects/lepidoptera/noctuidae/androloma_maccullochii.html. Accessed April 3, 2024.

"The Amateur Anthecologist," n.d. https://amateuranthecologist.blogspot.com.

"Art Shapiro's Butterfly Site," June 18, 2022. https://butterfly.ucdavis.edu.

"Bees: Genus Halictus (Sweat Bees)." *The Great Sunflower Project*. www.greatsunflower.org/halictus.

"Bees of Canada, a Royal Saskatchewan Museum Initiative," n.d. https://www.beesofcanada.com.

Beverley, Claire. "Polistes dominula (European paper wasp)." *CABI Compendium* (2022).

Biota of North America Program, The, n.d. http://www.bonap.org.

Björklund, Neil Henning. *Butterflies of Oregon*. www.butterfliesoforegon.com.

Bryant, Peter J. *Natural History of Orange County, California*, n.d. https://nathistoc.bio.uci.edu.

"Bug of the Week." https://bugoftheweek.com.

Bug of the Week—Field Station. https://uwm.edu/field-station/category/bug-of-the-week/.

Bumble Bee Watch. www.bumblebeewatch.org.

"Bumble Bees of Washington State." *A Field Guide to the Bumble Bees of Washington State*, October 1, 2020. https://washingtonbumblebees.org.

"Buprestidae of Texas with Notes on Texas Types," n.d. https://www.texasento.net/TXBuprestidae.htm.

"Busy Bees: An Up-Close Look at One Bee Species' Scramble to Mate." *Entomology Today*, September 13, 2018. entomologytoday.org/2018/09/13/busy-bees-up-close-look-one-bee-species-scramble-mate-diadasia-rinconis/.

"Butterflies and Moths of North America | Collecting and Sharing Data About Lepidoptera," n.d. https://www.butterfliesandmoths.org.

Butterflies of America. Butterflies of America Foundation. www.butterfliesofamerica.com.

"Ceratina." Bee Pollinators of Oregon. odabeeguide.weebly.com/ceratina.html.

"Coleopera Family Descriptions," n.d. https://www.zoology.ubc.ca/bcbeetles/Text%20files/family%20descriptions.htm.

"Colorado Front Range Butterflies | a General Guide to the Butterflies of the Northern Colorado Front Range," n.d. https://coloradofrontrangebutterflies.com.

"Colorado Insects of Interest—Yellow Jackets." Colorado State University of Agricultural Sciences. webdoc.agsci.colostate.edu/bspm/arthropodsofcolorado/Yellowjackets.pdf.

"Cotton Home Page (ACIS)," n.d. https://ag.arizona.edu/crops/cotton/.

Cranshaw, Whitney. "*Epicauta Fabricii*." Bugwoodwiki. Center for Invasive Species and Ecosystem Health at the University of Georgia. wiki.bugwood.org/HPIPM:Epicauta_fabricii.

Dallas County Lepidopterists' Society, The. www.dallasbutterflies.com.

"Different Types of Honey Bees, The." NC State Extension Publications. content.ces.ncsu.edu/the-different-types-of-honey-bees.

Discover Life. www.discoverlife.org.

Doyle, Toby, et al. "Pollination by Hoverflies in the Anthropocene." *Proceedings of the Royal Society B: Biological Sciences* 287, no. 1927, May 2020, 20200508. PubMed Central. doi.org/10.1098/rspb.2020.0508.

Dyer, Judith G., and Alvin F. Shinn. "Pollen Collected by *Calliopsis Andreniformis Smith* in North America (Hymenoptera: Andrenidae)." *Journal of the Kansas Entomological Society* 51, no. 4 (January 1, 1978): 787. https://digitalcommons.usu.edu/bee_lab_du/18/.

Eaton, Eric R., "Hybotid Dance Flies." *Bug Eric*, blogger, 1 May 2015. bugeric.blogspot.com/2015/05/hybotid-dance-flies.html.

Eby, C., et al. "Phenylacetaldehyde attracts male and female apple clearwing moths, *Synanthedon myopaeformis*, to inflorescences of showy milkweed, *Asclepias speciosa*." *Entomology Experimental and Applied* 147, 2013, 82–92. doi:10.1111/eea.12045.

"The Echinacea Project," n.d. https://echinaceaproject.org.

Egstad, Emma. "Bee Spotlight: Pugnacious Leafcutter Bee." *Bee & Bloom*, November 10, 2020. https://www.beeandbloom.com/blog/bee-spotlight-pugnacious-leafcutter-bee.

"Encyclopedia of Life," n.d. https://eol.org.

"Endangered Resources." Wisconsin Department of Natural Resources. dnr.wisconsin .gov/topic/EndangeredResources.

"Exotic Bee ID," n.d. https://idtools.org/tools/1078/index.cfm.

"Factsheet—*Anthophora* Bees." BioNET-EAFRINET Keys and Fact Sheets. keys.lucid central.org/keys/v3/eafrinet/bee_genera/key/african_bee_genera/Media/html.

"Featured Creatures," n.d. https://entnemdept.ufl.edu/creatures/.

"First Importation of Honeybees into North America." *Beesource Beekeeping Forums*, July 9, 2015. beesource.com/threads/first-importation-of-honeybees-into-north -america.313539/.

Fretwell, Kelly, and Brian Starzomski. *"Melanostoma mellinum." Biodiversity of the Central Coast*, 2015. centralcoastbiodiversity.org/melanostoma-mellinum.html.

"Funereal Duskywing." *Learn About Butterflies*. https://learnbutterflies.com/funereal -duskywing/

Glassberg, Jeffrey. *Butterflies Through Binoculars: The East*. Oxford University Press, 1999.

Global Biodiversity Information Facility. 2019. gbif.org. https://www.gbif.org.

Goyret, Joaquín, et al. "Why Do Manduca Sexta Feed from White Flowers? Innate and Learnt Colour Preferences in a Hawkmoth." *The Science of Nature* 95, no. 6 (February 21, 2008): 569–76. https://doi.org/10.1007/s00114-008-0350-7.

Hippa, H., T. R. Nielsen, and F. Christian Thompson. "*Eristalis Obscura* (Loew) (Diptera, Syrphidae): Synonyms and Morphological Variation in the Holarctic Region." *ResearchGate*, January 1, 2009. https://www.researchgate.net/publication/316505700_Eristalis_obscura_Loew_Diptera_Syrphidae_Synonyms_and_morphological_variation_in_the_Holarctic_region.

Hoffmann, Michael P., and A Frodsham. *Natural Enemies of Vegetable Insect Pests*. Cornell University, 1993.

Holm, Heather. *Pollinators of Native Plants: Attract, Observe and Identify Pollinators and Beneficial Insects with Native Plants*. First ed., Pollination Press LLC, 2014.

Idaho Species. Idaho official Government Website. idfg.idaho.gov/species/.

Iftner, David C. *Butterflies and Skippers of Ohio*, 1992.

"iNaturalist," n.d. https://www.inaturalist.org.

"Insect, Bugs and Spider Identification—North America," n.d. https://www.insectidentification.org.

Integrated Pest Management. "Invasives," n.d. https://www.canr.msu.edu/ipm/Invasive_species/.

"Integrated Taxonomic Information System," n.d. https://www.itis.gov.

"Integrated Weed Control Project," n.d. https://invasives.wsu.edu/index.htm.

"IUCN Red List of Threatened Species, The," n.d. https://www.iucnredlist.org.

Jacobs, Steve. "Baldfaced Hornet." *PennState Extension*, February 2010; Revised February 2015. extension.psu.edu/baldfaced-hornet.

Jankauski, Mark, et al. "Carpenter Bee Thorax Vibration and Force Generation Inform Pollen Release Mechanisms during Floral Buzzing." *Scientific Reports* 12, no. 1, Aug. 2022, 12654. doi.org (Crossref), doi.org/10.1038/s41598-022-16859-z.

"Jason Gibbs," n.d. https://sites.google.com/site/dialictus/home.

Johnson, Michael D. "The Pollen Preferences of *Andrena (Melandrena) dunningi Cockerell* (Hymenoptera: Andrenidae)." *Journal of the Kansas Entomological Society* 57, no. 1, 1984, 34–43. JSTOR. http://www.jstor.org/stable/25084478.

Knisley, C. Barry, and Tom D Schultz. *The Biology of Tiger Beetles and a Guide to the Species of the South Atlantic States*. Virginia Museum of Natural History, 1997.

Langellotto, Gail. Garden Ecology Lab, October 28, 2016. https://blogs.oregonstate.edu/gardenecologylab/.

Layberry, Ross A., Peter W. Hall, and J. Donald Lafontaine. *The Butterflies of Canada*. University of Toronto Press, 1998.

LeBuhn, Gretchen. *Field Guide to the Common Bees of California: Including Bees of the Western United States*. University of California Press, 2013.

Linsley, E. G., and J. W. Macswain. "Observations on the Life History of *Trichodes ornatus* (Coleoptera Cleridae) a Larval Predator in the Nests of Bees and Wasps." *Annals of the Entomological Society of America* 1943, 589–601. https://doi.org/10.1093/aesa/36.4.589.

Marino, Paul C., et al. "Conserving Parasitoid Assemblages of North American Pest Lepidoptera: Does Biological Control by Native Parasitoids Depend on Landscape Complexity?" *Biological Control* 2006, 173–85. https://doi.org/10.1016/j.biocontrol.2005.12.017.

Mead, C. E. "Collops bipunctatus as an Enemy of the Colorado Potato Beetle." *The American Naturalist*, 1899. archive.org/details/jstor-2453976.

"Michigan Natural Features Inventory," n.d. https://mnfi.anr.msu.edu.

Miller, Jeffrey C., and Paul C. Hammond. *Lepidoptera of the Pacific Northwest : Caterpillars and Adults*, 2003. https://doi.org/10.5962/bhl.title.150497.

Minckley, R. L., S. L. Buchmann, and W. T. Wcislo. "Bioassay Evidence for a Sex Attractant Pheromone in the Large Carpenter Bee, Xylocopa varipuncta (Anthophoridae: Hymenoptera)." *Journal of Zoology* 224, 1991, 285–91. doi: 10.1111/j.1469-7998.1991.tb04805.x.

Monroe, Lynn, and Gene Monroe. *Insects & Kin of the Colorado Front Range: Plains, Foothills, Montane, Subalpine, Alpine: A Natural History & Photographic Survey: Includes Rocky Mountain National Park, East Slope*, 2021.

Montana Natural Heritage Program. Montana Field Guide. FieldGuide.mt.gov.

Myers, P., et al., 2019. "ADW: Home." Animaldiversity.org. https://animaldiversity.org.

National Wildlife Federation. nwf.org.

"NatureServe Explorer," n.d. https://explorer.natureserve.org.

North American Insects & Spiders. www.cirrusimage.com.

Opler, Paul A. *A Field Guide to Western Butterflies*. Houghton Mifflin, 1998.

OSU Extension Service. Oregon State University. extension.oregonstate.edu.

Otterstatter, Michael C., et al. "Contrasting Frequencies of Parasitism and Host Mortality among Phorid and Conopid Parasitoids of Bumble-bees." *Ecological Entomology*, 27, no. 2, Apr. 2002, 229–37. DOI.org (Crossref), doi.org/10.1046/j.1365-2311.2002.00403.x.

Packer, Laurence. "Species Profile: *Halictus harmonius*." Edited by M. D. Shepherd, et al. *Red List of Pollinator Insects of North America*, CD-ROM Version 1, May 2005. The Xerces Society for Invertebrate Conservation, Portland, Oregon.

Pickett, C. H., S. E. Schoenig, and M. P. Hoffmann, 1996. "Establishment of the squash bug parasitoid, Trichopoda pennipes Fabr. (Diptera: Tachnidae), in northern California." *Pan-Pacific Entomologist*, 72: 220–26.

"PNW Bumble Bee Atlas," n.d. https://www.pnwbumblebeeatlas.org.

"PNW Moths | Homepage," n.d. http://pnwmoths.biol.wwu.edu.

"Pollinator of the Month," n.d. https://www.fs.usda.gov/wildflowers/pollinators/pollinator-of-the-month/.

Project Noah. www.projectnoah.org.

Pyle, Robert Michael, and National Audubon Society. *National Audubon Society Field Guide to Butterflies: North America*. Knopf, 1981.

"Raising Butterflies—How to Find and Care for Butterfly Eggs and Caterpillars," n.d. http://www.raisingbutterflies.org.

Rifkind, Jacques, "*Enoclerus gahan*: predators of chemically protected ladybird beetles (Coleoptera: Cleridae and Coccinellidae)," 2016. Insecta Mundi, 1019. digitalcommons .unl.edu/insectamundi/1019.

Russell, Avery L., et al. "Brawls Bring Buzz: Male Size Influences Competition and Courtship in *Diadasia rinconis* (Hymenoptera: Apidae)." *Journal of Insect Science* (online), 2018. doi.org/10.1093/jisesa/iey083.

Schmidt, B. Christian. "*Hemaris thetis* (Boisduval, 1855) (Sphingidae) Is a Distinct Species." *Journal of the Lepidopterists' Society* 63, no. 2, 2009, 100–109.

Scott, James A. *The Butterflies of North America: A Natural History and Field Guide*. Stanford University Press, 1992.

Shapiro, Arthur M., 1978. "Phenotypic and Behavioral Convergence of 'Silver-Spotted Skippers' (Lepidoptera: Hesperiidae)" *Biotropica* 10, no. 2, 159–60. doi:10.2307?2388021. JSTOR 2388021.

Sommaggio, Daniele. "Syrphidae: Can They Be Used as Environmental Bioindicators?" *Elsevier eBooks*, 1999, 343–56. https://doi.org/10.1016/b978-0-444-50019-9.50019-4.

"Sphingidae of the United States of America." n.d. https://www.sphingidae.us/. Accessed April 3, 2024.

"Synopsis of the Adult and Larval Plant Associations for New World Acmaeoderini, A (Coleoptera: Buprestidae)." *Cerambycid Research*, APHIS/PPQ's National Identification Services (NIS). cerambycids.com/buprestidae/Hosts/acmaeodera.html.

"Syrphid Flies of the North Coast & Cascades." US National Park Service. www.nps.gov/articles/syrphid-flies-of-the-north-coast-and-cascades.htm.

"Uncompahgre Fritillary Butterfly." US Fish and Wildlife Service. www.fws.gov/species/uncompahgre-fritillary-butterfly-boloria-acrocnema.

Urban Garden Ecology. gardenecology.pdx.edu.

Ureña, Onanchi, and Paul Hanson. "A fly larva (Syrphidae: Ocyptamus) that preys on adult flies." *Revista de Biologia Tropical* 58, no. 4, 2010, 1157–63. doi:10.15517/rbt .v58i4.5401.

US Department of Agriculture, Beatriz Moisset, PhD, and Stephen Buchmann, PhD. *Bee Basics*. Lulu.com, 2016.

Utah State University Extension. Utah State University. extension.usu.edu.

Vermont Atlas of Life. Vermont Center for Ecostudies. val.vtecostudies.org/projects/vtbees/nomada/.

Wasbauer, Marius S., and Lynn Siri Kimsey. *California Spider Wasps of the Subfamily Pompilinae (Hymenoptera Pompilidae)*. University of California Press, 1985.

"Wasps, Surprisingly Cool Pollinators. " *Maryland Agronomy News*, August 31, 2020. https://blog.umd.edu/agronomynews/2020/08/31/wasps-surprisingly-cool-pollinators/.

"Welcome to BugGuide.Net!" n.d. 2003-2024, Iowa State University. https://bugguide.net/node/view/15740.

"Welcome to the Digital Atlas of Idaho," n.d. https://digitalatlas.cose.isu.edu.

Westcott, Richard, and Delbert La Rue. "New Anthophilous Host Associations for Adult Acmaeodera eschscholtz, 1829 (Coleoptera: Buprestidae) Species from the Western United States and Texas." *Insecta Mundi*, July 2017. digitalcommons.unl.edu/insecta mundi/1072.

"Wild Bees Texas." Sharp-Eatman Nature Photography. www.wildbeestexas.com.

Williams, Paul, et al. *Bumble Bees of North America: An Identification Guide*. Princeton University Press, 2014.

Wisconsin Horticulture. "Wisconsin Horticulture," n.d. https://hort.extension.wisc.edu.

"World Wasps, Bees, Ants." WaspWeb, n.d. http://waspweb.org/World_wasps/index.htm.

INDEX

ABOUT THE AUTHORS

Sonya Anderson, an assistant curator in the Horticulture Department at Denver Botanic Gardens, takes care of the educational Birds and Bees Walk, a lively pollinator and wildlife garden, the Steppe Garden, and the Darlene Radichel Plant Select Garden.

Sonya's exploration into the realm of pollinating insects and their plant companions began with her hands-on pollinator observations in these gardens. Moving beyond pollinator syndromes, she sought to personally witness the interactions between pollinators and plants to inform her plantings and garden design. This journey has led her deeper into the captivating and intricate world of pollination.

Shiran Hershcovich is an entomologist from Panama City, Panama. She earned her degree in molecular biology from the University of California, Berkeley,in 2019. In 2021, she joined Butterfly Pavilion, where she curates the conservatory's living collections of butterflies. She's worked on research and conservation initiatives such as field assessments on vulnerable butterfly populations in Mongolia and the construction of a sustainable butterfly farm in Indonesia. Shiran leads the Colorado Butterfly Monitoring Network, a regional community science program. Before her time at Butterfly Pavilion, she worked in invertebrate research at the Essig Museum of Entomology and the Smithsonian Tropical Research Institute.

Lorna McCallister completed a BS in wildlife ecology and conservation and a minor in entomology from the University of Florida in 2015. Since 2015 Lorna has worked on various wildlife research projects in the United States and abroad for state, federal, and nonprofit organizations, working with a wide variety of species and ecosystems. In 2020 she received a MSc in interdisciplinary ecology from the University of Florida. For her thesis she studied how changes to savanna vegetation affect insect and avian pollinators in the Kingdom of Eswatini. This project initiated her interest in pollinator research and native bee conservation. Lorna is also a hobbyist beekeeper who manages honey bee hives for multiple organizations, teaches beginner beekeeping classes, and is active in local beekeeping associations.

Amy Yarger has worked in the public horticulture field since 1996. She received a bachelor's degree in ecology and evolutionary biology at the University of California, Irvine, and then studied plant-animal interactions at the University of Michigan. Amy currently leads Butterfly Pavilion's local pollinator habitat initiatives, such as Pollinator Districts and the Urban Prairies Project, which restores habitat in urban and suburban natural areas. Her work at the Butterfly Pavilion, where she has worked since 2000, touches on many of her passions: plants, insects, habitat conservation, and science education.